CultureShock!
A Survival Guide to Customs and Etiquette

South Africa

Dee Rissik

 **Marshall Cavendish**
Editions

This 5th edition published in 2011 by:
Marshall Cavendish Corporation
99 White Plains Road
Tarrytown, NY 10591-9001
www.marshallcavendish.us

Copyright © 2008 Marshall Cavendish International (Asia) Private Limited
Copyright © 2000 Times Media Private Limited
Copyright © 1994 Times Editions Private Limited
All rights reserved

First published in 1994 by Times Editions Pte Ltd; 2nd edition published in 2000
by Times Media Pte Ltd; 3rd edition published in 2001. 4th edition by Marshall
Cavendish International (Asia) Private Limited in 2008, reprinted 2009
Copyright © 2008, 2011 Marshall Cavendish International (Asia) Private Limited
All rights reserved

Other Marshall Cavendish Offices:
Marshall Cavendish International (Asia) Private Limited. 1 New Industrial Road,
Singapore 536196 ■ Marshall Cavendish International. PO Box 65829, London
EC1P 1NY, UK ■ Marshall Cavendish International (Thailand) Co Ltd. 253 Asoke,
12th Flr, Sukhumvit 21 Road, Klongtoey Nua, Wattana, Bangkok 10110, Thailand
■ Marshall Cavendish (Malaysia) Sdn Bhd, Times Subang, Lot 46, Subang Hi-Tech
Industrial Park, Batu Tiga, 40000 Shah Alam, Selangor Darul Ehsan, Malaysia

Marshall Cavendish is a trademark of Times Publishing Limited

ISBN 13: 978-0-7614-6059-6

Please contact the publisher for the Library of Congress catalogue number

Printed in Singapore by Times Printers Pte Ltd

Photo Credits:
All black and white photos by the author. All colour photos from Photolibrary.
■ Cover photo: Getty Images

All illustrations by TRIGG

ABOUT THE SERIES

Culture shock is a state of disorientation that can come over anyone who has been thrust into unknown surroundings, away from one's comfort zone. *CultureShock!* is a series of trusted and reputed guides which has, for decades, been helping expatriates and long-term visitors to cushion the impact of culture shock whenever they move to a new country.

Written by people who have lived in the country and experienced culture shock themselves, the authors share all the information necessary for anyone to cope with these feelings of disorientation more effectively. The guides are written in a style that is easy to read and cover a range of topics that will arm readers with enough advice, hints and tips to make their lives as normal as possible again.

Each book is structured in the same manner. It begins with the first impressions that visitors will have of that city or country. To understand a culture, one must first understand the people—where they came from, who they are, the values and traditions they live by, as well as their customs and etiquette. This is covered in the first half of the book.

Then on to the practical aspects—how to settle in with the greatest of ease. Authors walk readers through topics such as how to find accommodation, get the utilities and telecommunications up and running, enrol the children in school and keep in the pink of health. But that's not all. Once the essentials are out of the way, venture out and try the food, enjoy more of the culture and travel to other areas. Then be immersed in the language of the country before discovering more about the business side of things.

To round off, snippets of basic information are offered before readers are 'tested' on customs and etiquette of the country. Useful words and phrases, a comprehensive resource guide and list of books for further research are also included for easy reference.

CONTENTS

DEDICATION

For my partner, David, who shares my love of lands strange and wonderful, my love of Africa and of life. And who, although an Australian, understands the magnetism, the lifelong ties that draw me back to South Africa time and again.

In parts of South Africa where rainfall is sparse, like in the Great Karroo, windmills are often a common sight on farms, steadily pumping underground water into reservoirs.

White Rhinos are said to be far more docile than their Black Rhino cousins, but caution when in their presence is always wise as they can run remarkably fast for such a prehistoric-looking animal! The leviathan of the bushveld strides towards the rest of the elephant herd in Welgevonden Game Reserve in Limpopo province.

PREFACE

Moving from the cosy confines of wherever you call home to the strange and wonderful (or initially sometimes far from wonderful) ways of a new land, a new people and a new culture, is certainly no easy task. In fact, it rates very high on the ladder of the most stressful thing we do in our lives.

But one of the best ways to minimise the hassles, inconveniences and insecurities we all feel when surrounded by things strange and new, is to be as well-informed as possible about each aspect of the life we are about to begin.

Being a born and bred South African who has had the privilege of living and working in a wide variety of foreign countries and cultures, I am only too aware of how the initial difficulties seem insurmountable: the smallest setback can seem like a major calamity in those early days. But once you are an old hand, you can rest assured you will look back at those tetchy moments in stunned amazement and with a large dose of merriment.

I hope reading this book will give you a little insight into who we South Africans really are, how we live and how we have changed. I hope it will be enough of a taste of the Rainbow Nation to make your stay, however long or short it may be, a positively memorable one.

Writing this book was no easy task, but for the first edition I had the assistance of my mother, Jan Rissik, whom I thank for all the hours of research she did for me, for reading some of my copy and bouncing ever more ideas off me. Now, more than a decade later, I hope this fully updated, new edition again captures the spirit of a very different country. My great appreciation and thanks is extended to everybody who has helped me put this book together—wittingly, deliberately, or quite unintentionally by simply being South African.

MAP OF SOUTH AFRICA

ZIMBABWE

BOTSWANA

MOZAMBIQUE

NAMIBIA

● PRETORIA

SWAZILAND

SOUTH AFRICA

LESOTHO

ATLANTIC OCEAN

INDIAN OCEAN

FIRST IMPRESSIONS: SHIFTING SANDS

CHAPTER 1

'I heard the drum beat behind your footsteps
And the children of the south began to sing.'
—Mazisi Kunene, South African poet

IT MAY SEEM STRANGE FOR ME to be writing about my 'first impression' given that I was born and raised here. But the explanation is simple. I have lived away from South Africa on so many occasions in my adult life—sometimes for a number of years at a time, sometimes only for a year or two, or even just a few months—that each time I return home, I find myself almost as an outsider looking in on my countrymen, my kith and kin and our volatile nation. It is always with renewed amazement, with sheer delight that I re-experience the changes, reconnect with who we are becoming.

This is probably because in many ways we really are a new nation. From 26–28 April 1994, when we all stood together in queues that were hours, if not days, long, we really were voting not just for a democratic government, but for a totally new existence. The changes in South Africa since then have been monumental, and, some say with justification, miraculous. Of course they have not all been easy, but I think it is that very grittiness that gives South Africa an edge, a dynamism that gets under your skin. It's that sense of really being alive. And I sorely miss it when I am away. I regret at times the fact I have not always experienced each change as it happens, that I have missed out, at least first-hand, on some of the political imbroglios that have been blown wide open by our ever-watchful press, the growth of vast new business empires by people who were once disbarred from leading a real life, the transformation of our culture from racially segregated pastiches into a rich and constantly changing whole.

But then I step off a plane at OR Tambo International Airport (and even the airport has changed its name twice in the last decade or so!) in Johannesburg and within seconds the transformation from an outsider to being 'at home' begins. At first I notice all the little details that could otherwise become background noise in our busy heads. I notice how so many

Naming of Airports

In 1994, the post-apartheid government decided on a policy of not naming airports after politicians. Hence Jan Smuts International Airport (named after a former prime minister) was changed to Johannesburg International Airport, as were the Cape Town and Durban airports. In 2006, it was decided that Johannesburg International Airport would be renamed, again, as OR Tambo International Airport, in honour of the late anti-apartheid statesman.

people smile and are warm and friendly. I notice how pleasant and helpful ordinary people can be. How they greet each other, and me, even if they don't know me, and even if they may never see me again. I notice how brightly the sun shines and the utterly blue sky. I notice the *pizzazz* with which our youth wear their clothes, their attitudes, their iPods, their hope! I see them all as if for the first time, again. And I marvel at how much has changed. I marvel at our fortune at having been given a second chance, a chance to start our country all over again, and I marvel at the new and exciting way we are going about it.

Sometimes, from afar, I wish I had a closer understanding of who our new young South Africans really are and where they plan to take our country, our future. But when I get back and meet them again, face to face, I realise there is no knowing where we are going, but I do know I have every confidence they will make exciting, new choices.

Just recently I had the most wonderful experience of enjoying my country through the eyes of a very dear friend from New York (a French Canadian, born and raised in Montreal) who had never before set foot on the African continent. I have been lucky to be able to include Lise Curry's insightful and generous first-timer's impressions. You enjoy!

My South African Journal (12–26 February 2007)

A dream come true—embracing the land of Africa. Right off the plane at the Johannesburg airport, I feel a sense of ease—

The author, left, with Lise Curry, a friend from New York, on an excursion in the bush near Nedile Game Lodge in the Welgevonden Game Reserve. It was Lise's first ever visit to South Africa.

not only because Dee and David are there to greet me, but because I sense all around me an atmosphere of welcome.

As we drive into town, Johannesburg strikes me as a world-class city with beautiful neighbourhoods—all hills, glorious trees and well-tended homes—though I cannot help noticing that every house is strung with wire (electric fencing), surrounded with steel gates and posted with prominent security signs warning of an 'Armed Guard Response'. I am not taken aback. I do not relate this especially to South Africa; after all, you see such features in many European spots.

It is the following day that I really feel I have landed in Africa. As we head out of the city for a 4-day visit to the Nedile Game Lodge, the landscape outside the city of scrub brush is exactly what I had imagined the 'African terrain' to be. And as we drive north I observe some scenes that first brought to me the dichotomy of feelings that have stayed with me ever since.

While we were travelling on a modern highway I saw people walking, mostly alone, on either side of the road. And I couldn't but help realise that they were walking long distances in the full African sun because I too was travelling those same forlorn distances from one remote crossroad to another—but by car. I couldn't help thinking: Walking to where? To seek work, to seek shelter, to seek aid? The question stays though we move on, soon to arrive at the land of total enchantment.

As we arrive at the game lodge entrance we are received by our guide Walter, and I know the very minute I board the Land Rover that this is why I've travelled so far. The air is magical, my first sighting of wild life completely stuns me and the drive up and down valleys and mountains, through the mix of stony terrain, unusual trees, bushes and grasses, makes me feel I have entered another world.

The lodge is magnificent—a 5-star establishment. The accommodation is superb, the surrounding landscape awe-inspiring and the service first-class. The key element is of course our guide. As Walter takes us on twice-daily excursions into the bush, we quickly realise that we totally lucked up. Walter is extremely knowledgeable and totally sensitive to the land, the flora, the animals, the birds. He projects such a feeling of security and belonging that I'm overtaken by an intense sense of wonder and harmony. He stops the Land Rover frequently to point out plants and he tells us of the traditional use black people make of them. He points out birds (that we surely would have missed), gives comments on the land and the various animals we encounter. I am transfixed by his passion.

He led us to observe almost all the major animal species and birds of the region, including a lioness and her two daughters right after a kill, an owl on a kill, rhinos right near us, zebras, giraffes, warthogs, wildebeest, kudus, jackals and a magnificent male lion making his way down the road all alone at sundown.

The Ranger and The Bull Elephant

One adventure will forever stay with me and I've recounted it dozens of times already: on one of our outings we came across a herd of elephants. A young bull started walking towards the Land Rover. As the elephant approached Walter told us to remain quiet, that he would deal with the situation. The elephant came to within a couple of feet of us on the passenger side. Walter started speaking, "Hey, boy, you've come over to say hello? OK, now, go back." The elephant took two steps back and then flauntingly another step forward. Walter spoke more loudly and banged the vehicle with his hand upon which the elephant somewhat sheepishly stepped back and rejoined his group. To Walter's immense credit I never had an ounce of fear—all as a result of the total confidence we had in him. From the very start he gave us to feel his total respect for and communion with the animals.

I was so totally immersed in our experience at Nedile that I had not a thought of any life before or after. The staff at the lodge was a big factor in our contentment. All the service people, except the guides, were Tswana or Venda, including the chef who prepared great buffets and sit-down dinners. All the food was superb. The produce was incredible: I had the best peaches and pineapple ever at their table.

Still floating on a cloud, we headed back to Johannesburg.

There I was warmly and hospitably received at the homes of Dee's friends. Bronwen, an artist and teacher, owns a house in a 'mixed' neighbourhood and is committed to stay in the area as she loves the multicultural atmosphere. Clive, an international artist and curator, and his partner, Rocco, a well-known musician, are settled in a beautifully redesigned house and grounds. I felt welcomed everywhere and also privileged to be on the inside. The feelings I retain from my social exposure in Johannesburg, inside and out, remind me of the societal atmosphere in Montreal that prevailed in the 1960s during my college years when the English, though a small minority, still held dominion over the French Canadian population. Though major changes would soon come, as they have now in South Africa, both populations in Quebec took time to adapt. So too are the South Africans. Real change takes time. I was struck by many beautiful street scenes, but also troubled by the incredible crowdedness of the city's black neighbourhoods and the living conditions in the townships. Although some areas had some nice houses, these were crowded onto minuscule properties, as were the shanties a few streets further..

When I took a tour of the townships I felt so intrusive, yet I know how important it is that the living conditions be seen first hand in order to precipitate change. But to see women doing laundry at a sort of water hole some few miles from a cosmopolitan centre, to see people fetch water at communal water taps, seemed so retrograde. It truly shocked me. If I had observed the same scenes in far-off areas

I would not have been so disturbed. But not so near to a modern and rich city. At the same time I found it incredibly moving to see people living such an archaic way of life yet keeping on day after day. The striking sight of the mini-bus taxis making the round trips from city centre to townships crowded to overcapacity with people who have no other option to get to work filled me with admiration and compassion. All that in plain sight of others going to work comfortably in their private cars.

From Johannesburg, I went on to Cape Town with great anticipation. All I'd heard of Cape Town was how beautiful it is. And it is so. My lovely hotel, right on the waterfront, with full view of Table Mountain, started my stay on the right note. Somehow, everything seemed to me sotto voce—the perfect weather, the perfect views. The next day, on an excursion to Cape Point, I met a fellow visitor from Edmonton, in Canada, a member of the Royal Canadian Mounted Police on assignment for the United Nations in Sierra Leone. After we talked a bit, he asked me if I had noticed what he had. He was totally astounded to observe that here he was in Africa and everybody around was white. And right he was. The fact is the only black people I came across in Cape Town—at the hotel, in the shops and on the various excursions and outings I took—were a few front-desk staff, some restaurant help and some public service workers. Most everyone I saw was white. It surprised me.

However, those observations could not take away the incredible experience of travelling to Cape Point, climbing up to the lighthouse and feeling truly at the tip of Africa. Looking out at this magnificent view, I felt such a sense of communion with the earth, the ocean and the sky, it brought me to a spiritual plane I can never forget. And again, the land in these parts: I found such wonderment in the trees, the wine lands, the penguin retreats, the seals sunning on their rocks.

My heart is filled with emotion as I write these lines. I am so grateful for the opportunity to have lived this experience. I do know that it has changed me. It opened new vistas outward and inward. All I can call for is more rapid progress to bring greater parity in living conditions. I wish for this with all my heart for this most beautiful country—South Africa.

—Lise Curry, Brooklyn New York

THE LAND AND ITS HISTORY

CHAPTER 2

'Never, never and never again shall it be that this beautiful
land will again experience the oppression of one by another
and suffer the indignity of being the skunk of the world.'
—Inaugural address of Nelson Mandela, first democratically
elected president of South Africa, 10 May 1994

As ONE OF, OR PERHAPS EVEN the first cradle of mankind, South Africa has as long and convoluted a history as it has a diverse and dramatic geography and wide range of climate zones. Entwine all these and there is a life time's worth of things to explore, observe, immerse yourself in, or just chill out and enjoy.

THE LOOK

Two oceans, a warmer one down the east side of the country and a chilly one on the western seaboard, wash the 2,800 km (1,740 miles) coastline and its long, sandy and sometimes, rocky beaches. Dramatic mountains errupt from the ancient land and areas of vastly differing rainfall give rise to scrubby deserts, rolling plains, delicate indigenous forests and lush, semi-tropical vegetation. But it's not all beauty and environmental paradise. A fast-growing population means the need for ever more industrial and infrastructure development, as well as the exploitation of natural and mineral resources. Although the conservation lobby is strong, the country wages a constant battle to keep a balance between pristine natural beauty which drives a large part of the local and foreign tourist trade, and the upliftment of poorer population groups.

WHERE IS IT?

South Africa's land area is 1,184,825 sq km (457,463.50 sq miles), as compared to the continent of Africa which measures some

30 million sq km (11,583,065 sq miles). From west to east, it stretches from longitude 16°E of Greenwich to 33°E. The northernmost tip of South Africa is at latitude 22°S, just north of the Tropic of Capricorn, while the southernmost point, Cape Agulhas is at latitude 35°S.

Being the southernmost country of the African continent means it is a very long way, even by air, from Europe, Asia, North America and even North Africa.

As part of one of the three major land masses in the southern hemisphere, South Africa does not stretch quite as far south as either Australia or Tierra del Fuego in South America, but it still has gloriously warm, sunny summers from about October to March, which does mean no white Christmases. Late summer and autumn merge quickly into one another in April and May and winter generally sets in from June till late August. Spring is usually short with changeable weather.

A WORLD IN ONE COUNTRY

It is not a difficult task for the tourism industry to promote South Africa as a travel destination as its geographic and cultural diversity lends itself well to the well-worn slogan "a world in one country". In the east of the country there are rolling grasslands and lowveld bush, then forests and sugarcane plantations in the sub-tropical coastal belt. However in the west, the earth is baked-dry by furnace-like skies, fanned by desert winds, and sometimes threaded with rivers that are frequently dried by the droughts.

The Central Plateau

Perched atop a dramatic mountain range, the Drakensberg, the central plateau was mostly a treeless savannah at the time of the African mass migrations in the early- to mid-1800s, and the arrival of the first foreign settlers in the early 1800s. Today the geography is only altered by the massive urbanisation and extensive industrialisation. Major cities like Johannesburg, Pretoria and Bloemfontein rise high into the radiant blue African sky where once only grass swayed in the wind and thousands of antelope grazed peacefully.

Outdoor fun—diving into a crystal-clear mountain pool in the Magaliesberg, only an hour or two's drive from the harsh hustle of Johannesburg.

The Eastern Seaboard

From Kosi Bay in the north to Cape Agulhas in the south, the eastern seaboard is washed by the warm, balmy Indian Ocean. The KwaZulu-Natal coast being near the equator, has mild weather and warm seas, so holiday makers can 'do Durban' in mid-winter and still enjoy the surf. The eastern Cape coastal

South Africa's eastern seaboard is a top summer holiday destination because the beaches are long and golden and the weather is usually perfect for seaside fun.

Taking in the solitude and beauty of the semi-desert areas in the northern Cape Province. Colours are delicate and subtle, and temperatures are extremely high in the day.

areas are much drier than Durban, but still pleasantly hot and mostly sunny in the long summer months. Thus the region has developed some of the plumb holiday areas. Because of the long sandy beaches, interspersed with rocky outcrops, inlanders flock there over the Christmas/New Year summer holiday period. Winters are chilly and sometimes wet and grey, but usually only for a day or two at a time.

The Western Seaboard

Washed by the icy Atlantic Ocean, there are long, deserted, wind swept beaches along this coast, which until recently saw nary a soul bar a few local fishermen. Today the region is becoming very popular—ironically because of its isolation and semi-desert beauty. Just inland from this coast, if there is enough rain in the early spring, the desert bursts into a magical carpet of brightly coloured flowers for a few weeks. It is called Namaqualand and the most populous flower is the Namaqualand daisy.

In the centre of the southern Cape is the Karroo, a sparse and scrubby landscape, quite beautiful in its vastness under a dome sky. And right as far south as you can go is the Cape Point Nature Reserve, a natural World Heritage Site, where you can observe the colour change in the ocean at the exact point where the cold Benguela current on the west coast and the warm Agulhus current on the east coast merge.

LANDOWNERSHIP

Although landownership is one of the great South African dreams, it has also been one of the most controversial issues around, at least since the arrival of the white settlers. And it is going to remain so for many years to come. The Land Act of 1913, which basically stripped Africans of the right to own land where they chose, and then the later enforcement of apartheid, led to a great discrepancy in landownership between the different racial groups. Access limited by race is now a thing of the past, but redistribution of land and land ownership claims are some of the most thorny issues with which South Africa is now grappling.

Almost everyone aspires to own land in some shape or form. Some may want a home in the city, some prefer the rural areas. Others may wish to be part of a tribal community with communal landownership rights, and a growing number now want a holiday home—a seaside cottage, for example. Some like to have a city home and also remain part of their rural, tribal community.

One of the biggest purchases most South Africans are ever likely to make is a home. So a good grasp of the nitty-gritty of property buying—and if you are not a South African citizen, the government's changing views on landownership by foreigners—is a valuable starting point in the long search for a place to call your own. However, anyone can rent a home.

Who Farms Where

Agriculture in South Africa means food production for the nation and for export too. There are two major arms: a well-developed commercial sector which is still strongly, but not solely, in the hands of white farmers, and a predominantly subsistence-oriented sector in the rural areas. Both factors point to its importance to political stability as well as to the overall economy.

About 13 per cent of the country's surface area can be used for crop production, but less than a quarter of that is high-potential arable land and unpredictable weather conditions, including, on occasion, severe droughts, can have a large and often negative impact on the economy. Fortunately the country is expanding the diversity of its economy now, reducing the level of reliance on agriculture, but it will always be a very important sector.

People Of The Soil

Never underestimate the powerful symbolic importance of the soil to all rural South Africans, and many urban ones too. They feel very strongly about the land they live on, work on and love. For many, farming is certainly not an easy way of life. Many farmers barely scrape together a living, but for most of them the alternative of finding work in the towns and cities seems almost unthinkable. Of course there have been times in the country's history when severe droughts or economic recessions, or a combination of both, have forced many rural people to seek work in the cities. Some have stayed and become urbanites, or, using their city salaries, try to keep both lifestyles alive.

The love of the land stretches to many a city slicker too. Those who can afford it have bought smaller farms or small holdings where they can play at farming over weekends and holidays, returning to their city jobs during the week. Although this may have increased property prices, the negative side is that much of this land is not being used to its full agricultural potential.

Big City Life

As farmers love their farms, so city dwellers love their urban homes, spending a lot of time and money on them. It is one of the things on which people stretch their finances to breaking point. The reason is perhaps that they tend to spend a lot of time at home and in their gardens. A lot of entertaining is done at home and children tend to spend a lot of time playing with friends at each other's homes, rather than playing in the few parks or shopping centres and streets.

The variety of homes is extensive, especially in the cities, ranging from huge mansions on a hectare of land with a swimming pool and tennis court, to more modest but still good homes with three or four bedrooms and a garden, or the more humble tiny township home, built by the apartheid government for black people in designated areas on the outskirts of the towns. Most are modest and even poor in structure and design, but often the community spirit in the townships is very good.

As the urban population swells—along with the belief and to some extent reality too—that cities are where the most work is to be found, so the sprawl of informal housing grows. Frequently they are made of impermanent and found items such as plastic sheeting, sheets of tin and poles. The government has a hard time keeping the balance of not denying the poor in the community a right to a home however simple, and trying to retain some level of more formal urban planning.

Apartment living is not a top favourite among South Africans, probably because so much emphasis is placed on outdoor life, but there certainly is a number of apartments for rent and sale, especially in the suburbs closer to the city centres. And this trend is growing faster as the younger generations find it easier to adapt to apartment life, or at least choose to start their climb up the property ladder in a 'flat' as they are called in South Africa.

Homes in smaller towns are usually more modest than in the cities, but can have larger grounds as costs are much lower and space is at less of a premium. However homes, or often holiday homes, in some quaint old towns that are relatively close to the big urban metropolises such as Johannesburg or Cape Town, have seen dramatic escalation in house prices over the last few years as more affluent city dwellers seek some respite from stressful urban living.

Rural Lifestyle

Rural farmhouses tend to be larger and more rambling than urban homes—probably because they tend to be built by the owners, and have bits added on as and when the need arises. There tends to be the main house and outbuildings called the farmstead or *werf* (pronounced 'verff') with the labourers' homes built some distance away. Labourers' homes are often made by the employees themselves. They can be very simple mud-brick buildings, plastered with mud and roofed with thatching grass or corrugated iron sheeting.

Floors can be made with a mixture of cowdung and earth—a much warmer and less expensive option to concrete. Some rural labourers build more traditional tribal homes.

The national electricity supply organisation, Eskom, has a policy to supply electricity to the rural areas as quickly as possible, but still a good majority of rural Africans do not have electrified homes, nor do some of the farmers. Fuel-driven electricity generators are sometimes used but the most common light sources for the poor are candles and paraffin-burning lamps.

Township Style

The townships, mostly situated on the outskirts of cities, are a far cry from the middle class, leafy suburbs. Most houses in these areas were built by the apartheid government with as little imagination as possible. Homes are as square and as small as matchboxes and some may still not even have indoor sanitation. They are plastered to the land in straight rows with not much more than a hair's breadth of space between them. There are very few open spaces or parks in the townships and not many streets are even tarred. Fortunately, since independence there has been a drive to improve the quality of township homes and the upgrades are certainly visible in many areas. But what is lacking in infrastructure is made up in community spirit and innovation.

Of course, there are affluent black South Africans who, until the demise of apartheid, were forced to live in the townships and thus built large and beautiful homes there. When the Group Areas Act that segregated living areas by race was scrapped, some of the wealthier township dwellers moved into what were once exclusively white suburbs, but a number have chosen to stay in the townships among their friends and families.

Some of the townships, like Soweto for example, have become vibrant and fun places as crime and poverty have been alleviated somewhat. Sometimes, a lot more social life in shebeens (township pubs), small restaurants and clubs can be found in these areas than you would in the more staid and boring middle class neighbourhoods.

MORE PROVINCES, BIGGER CITIES

After the end of apartheid the four provinces that had made up South Africa were divided into a total of nine new ones, which the government of the time in 1994 felt would enable a more hands-on approach to bringing basic services to the many rural people who had in the past been somewhat neglected. To some degree this has been a success, although service delivery in many poor rural areas is still way off the mark expected in any developed country.

Most cities and even towns, on the other hand, have grown quickly, partly because of good economic growth, but also because more and more rural people flock to the urban areas to seek a better life—though not always to their benefit—and scarcity of low-cost housing has led to a number of shanty towns springing up.

Gauteng: Industrial Heart

Situated in the middle of the country, it is the engine of the country's economy. Gauteng is predominantly an urban area and the main cities are Johannesburg, Pretoria and Vereeniging in the south. All three, and their adjacent townships, almost merge into one huge urban and suburban mass with a population of close to 9 million people.

Gauteng is the most densely populated province and generates by far the most wealth for the country. All the major banks' headquarters, including the country's central bank, The Reserve Bank, are in Gauteng as are the head offices of most major business and manufacturing conglomerates, mining houses, financial institutions and the country's stock exchange.

Established on the back of the gold rush in the late 19th century, Johannesburg is the biggest city in the country, while Pretoria is the administrative capital centred around the Union Buildings, the main site of government administration.

The greater metropolitan area of Tshwane, which Pretoria is part of, was named for the son of an African chief who settled in the area hundreds of years ago. Gauteng is a Sotho (the predominant indigenous language of the region) word for "Place of Gold".

Western Cape: Beauty Spot

One of the areas best known to tourists because its capital is Cape Town and its natural beauty is stunning, the Western Cape is also a fairly large player in the country's economy. Most famous for its tourism—Table Mountain and the 24,310-hectare (60,071 acres) Table Mountain National Park, beautiful beaches and beach life, the winelands with their centuries old traditional Cape Dutch homesteads—this province also intertwines its agricultural sector of deciduous fruit, wheat and sheep farming and its fishing industry into its geographic beauty.

Cape Town, or the mother city as it is called, is the legislative capital of the country, but also a business centre. Much of the city is built around the harbour, one of the busier ones in the land and all of which centres around Table Mountain which is right up close—a dramatic setting.

The province has a second harbour, Saldanha Bay, up the west coast, which is a bulk port used mostly for exporting iron ore. It also has a larger per capita skilled workforce than most other provinces as a large portion of its population is urbanised and hence better educated and better trained.

Cape Town International Airport, to which almost all the major world carriers fly, albeit less frequently than to Johannesburg, is the second busiest in the country, with much of its trade being from tourism.

KwaZulu-Natal: Tropical Dream

This province, although the most populous with nearly 10 million people, is somewhat of a tourism Cinderella as far fewer foreigners are aware of its natural assets which include wonderful warm oceans lapping many hundreds of miles of beach; the major part of the country's most prominent mountain range, the Drakensberg; as well as a number of diverse and fascinating game parks. Nevertheless tourism is the province's biggest money spinner, although the paper, sugar, forestry and steel industries also play a large role.

Durban is its biggest city, built around the country's biggest and busiest port, which, with tourism, drives the KwaZulu-Natal economy. It also has an international airport. Other important cities are Pietermaritzburg, the provincial capital,

Richards Bay which grew up around its bulk port and Ulundi which is the heart of the Zulu nation's cultural heritage.

Eastern Cape: Big Open Spaces

Eastern Cape is a great livestock farming province which means that if you like uncluttered countryside and wide open spaces, it's your bundle—and a pleasure to drive through too. Its coastal cities are also great holiday venues and less crowded than the better known areas of the country. Sometimes the beaches are fairly windy, great for windsurfing!

Port Elizabeth, the province's major city, is predominantly industrial, and with nearby East London, both service a large sector of the province's automotive industry. Both are also port cities, although Port Elizabeth (or PE as it is more often called) has by far the larger harbour. A new major deep-water port and an adjacent industrial development zone are being constructed in the region to help stimulate economic growth in this less industrially developed part of South Africa.

PE, East London and Umtata all have airports, while Bisho is the provincial capital.

Mpumalanga: Outdoor Fun

Most of Mpumalanga has a mild and mellow climate which lends itself to tourism and outdoor life. It is the gateway to the country's most famous game reserve, the Kruger National Park, but it also has a number of exclusive (and expensive) game lodges that offer 5-star holidays and excellent game viewing.

Its economy is also driven by mining, especially coal mining, and it grows a lot of the country's export quality semi-tropical fruit. Thanks to Mpumalanga's large coal deposits, a high percentage of the power used in the industrial regions of Gauteng, in fact, for much of the country, is generated by the coal-fired power stations in the west of the province.

Nelspruit is both the capital and the largerst city in this province and its economy has boomed in the last decade or so due, in quite a large way, to it also being a major supply centre and gateway for neighbouring Mozambique's capital city, Maputo. The Maputo Development Corridor, a commercially driven transport corridor which links Gauteng to Mozambique both by rail and road runs through the province aiding its economic growth.

Free State: Mineral Wealth

The Free State may be land-locked—it borders six of the nine provinces in South Africa—but it has some of the richest natural resources in the country, most notably a large number of the nation's gold mines. Bloemfontein, its capital is also the country's judicial capital as it is the seat of the highest court in the land, the Appeal Court.

Two of the country's biggest rivers, the Vaal River and the Orange River, flow through this province, which is great for watersports! And also for irrigated agriculture.

Northern Cape: Space to Breathe

The Northern Cape is fairly sparsely populated, one of the geographically larger and also newly created provinces and as such had reason to build a new provincial parliament building in its capital, Kimberly. It is well worth a visit as it a great example of new local civic architecture, quirky decorative art and indigenous gardens, all a model of low maintenance.

Its driving force is the mining industry as it has some of the richest diamond deposits in the world. An added attraction is the Big Hole which was the first and major open pit diamond mine in the area and one of the largest in the world. Long since defunct, it it is now filled with water and has a very interesting museum adjacent to it. By the time mining was suspended at this site in 1914 it had yielded 2,722 kg (6,001 lb) of diamonds!

The vast majority of the province is rural farmland or nature reserves, much of it a semi-desert such as the Karoo where the vast open spaces and the huge vistas with enormous domed blue skies are a panacea for any city-dweller feeling the stress of the rat-race.

Limpopo:Ranching Territory

Limpopo, recently so named for the great river of the same name, that is the boundary between the province (and South Africa) and northern neighbour, Zimbabwe. It also has

The Big Hole, on the outskirts of Kimberley, the capital of Northern Cape province, once a small hill and the site of the diamond rush in the 1870s, was mined so avidly that it became a deep hole. Now, filled with water, it is a tourist attraction and has a great diamond mining museum too.

borders with Mozambique and Botswana. It is a good farming region, especially cattle ranching, but it also has good game farms and some excellent game reserves. As Mpumalanga is in the south, so Limpopo is the gateway to the northern regions of the vast Kruger National Park which runs down the entire eastern side of the country.

The province, with its capital city, Polokwane (previously Pietersburg), is also mineral rich especially in copper, chrome vanadium and coal.

North West: Platinum and Plastic

Blessed with vast platinum resources, much of which is mined not far from its capital city, Mafikeng, North West is also a good farming region.

But the coins also ring big into its coffers from the world famous Sun City—that mad mixture of pleasure resort, man-made 'sea' with man-made waves washing man-made sandy beaches, a gamblers haven, top end hotels and world class golf courses.

RECORD OF A LONG ROAD TRAVELLED

Whatever the reason for spending time in South Africa—as an immigrant, expat or long-term traveller—it's well worth understanding the high and low points of this land's troubled history. Understanding the realities of racial discrimination as it was legally applied in the 'old' South Africa is a good start to unravelling the sensitivities peculiar to the various segments of a once forcefully divided society.

Of course since 1994, when the first ever fully democratic elections brought Nelson Mandela and the African National Congress (ANC) to power, great strides have been made in the process of forming what Archbishop Desmond Tutu so aptly called the rainbow nation: a vibrant, new, multi-cultural country burying old hatchets and growing new friends at all levels. Most people have responded to the challenge admirably and in most parts of the country naked racism is rarely apparent.

But knowing what went on before will help you come to grips with the nation's hopes for its future society—a society in which the norms and values of different groups are interwoven and interlocked, but at the same time celebrating and acknowledging the very differences in various ways, such as respecting the days special to each culture or creed— Christmas, Eid-al-Fitr, Diwali.

Southern Africa, along with east Africa, boasts some of the oldest human remains found, leading archaeologists to believe human ancestry is probably traced to both regions.

THE LAND OF MILK AND HONEY

Human history is thought to have probably begun right here in South Africa with the earliest hominids hailing from some 4 million years ago, while an almost perfectly intact skull, now called Mrs Ples and estimated to be about 2.8 million years old, was found not far from Johannesburg.

Ever since the Stone Age (approximately 15,000 to 20,000 years before the present) the earliest contemporary South African people lived off the bounty of the land as hunter-gatherers. The San or Bushmen, lived in harmony with nature, wandering far and wide across the land. They abided by fixed customs refined over thousands of years of nomadic life. A number of their historically explicit rock paintings, more than 3,000 years old, depict scenes as diversely fascinating as their mythical rituals. Paintings showing the wild animals they hunted and the manner in which they conducted the hunt can still be found in sheltered caves across the country.

In the Kalahari desert, in neighbouring Namibia and Botswana, one can still find a few San living their traditional lifestyle, but it is now rare and they are becoming ever fewer. Most, however, have settled on farms or reserves created for them which means that much of their tradition has given way to a Western existence.

So Who Disturbed the Peace?
First the Khoikhoi…

The San's sublime existence was first disturbed some 2,000 years ago by the Khoikhoi who were pastoralists and herders keeping sheep and goats. They settled in the south and south-western part of the country and were thus the first indigenous people the European explorers encountered. At this time the

Bantu-speaking people from the central regions of Africa had already migrated southwards and settled in the north and north-east of present-day South Africa.

The Bantu-speaking people, distinguished from the San and the Khoikhoi by the fact they were metal workers (Iron Age people) and kept cattle, started moving into South Africa around AD 200–500, and by about AD 1100–1200 had constructed massive cities—much on a par with the Middle Ages in Europe—in places like Mapungubwe and Tulamela in north-eastern South Africa.

Then the European Explorers

In 1488, Portuguese sailor Bartholomeu Dias was the first recorded European to traverse the South African coast—there seems to be strong evidence the Chinese did this some 60 years earlier but left little or no trace—in his desperate search for a sea-route from Europe to the riches of the East. A permanent settlement was soon established on the southern tip of the continent by the Dutch while many hundreds of ships, Dutch, French, British and Portuguese called on this coastline for fresh supplies of water, wood and food en route to the East.

In 1652, Jan van Riebeeck (a member of the Dutch East India Company who had sailed to Japan, the west coast of India and even to the Arctic circle) arrived in the Cape with over 100 men to establish a permanent base, a fort and a foothold on the southern tip of Africa. They came into contact with the Khoikhoi (who they dubbed the Hottentots) and a few San which led to some clashes. Who was to know that these first conflicts between European and African were to continue in varying forms for centuries—in fact, right up till 1994 when the country finally became a fully-fledged democracy?

Mass Migrations from all Directions

The general population increase of the different groups in southern Africa during the late 18th and early 19th centuries led to pressures that eventually gave rise to the joining of the Zulu tribes into a major fighting force under their great warrior-leader, Shaka. Warlike, he buffeted the southern

African people, causing mass migrations, the Mfecane, on a far larger scale than the Great Trek of the Voortrekkers. Violence and tremendous hardship followed.

The colonists at the Cape added to this bubbling cauldron. From the settlement now known as Cape Town, Boer frontier farmers and the French Huguenot immigrants had moved inland—the French Huguenots had earlier left Europe to escape religious persecution at the hand of King Louis XIV.

> The early Dutch settlers were known as Boers, which is Dutch for farmers. As they settled the land, those who had no intention of returning to Europe came to call themselves 'Afrikaners', meaning in essence 'from this place'. The term has now come to encompass descendants of the Dutch, as well as other people who speak Afrikaans as a first language.

In a quest for even more land some of the settlers moved up the coast towards current day Port Elizabeth, but they soon clashed with various groups of Bantu tribes who were moving from what is now the KwaZulu-Natal coast towards the southern Cape. Skirmishes became bitter wars when both sides tried to capture larger pastures and precious water holes for their livestock.

That English Touch

Following the French capture of Holland during the Napoleonic Wars, Britain agreed to take over the administration of the troubled Cape Colony in 1795. This generous gesture was made to keep open the strategic sea-route to Britain's vast, valuable Indian territories. It was returned to the Dutch government in 1803, but Britain recaptured it in 1806 and administered it in various geographic shapes and political forms until 'union' in 1910.

The 1820 Settlers

In 1820, nearly 5,000 British immigrants landed at the Cape Colony where Port Elizabeth is today, having been promised portions of land to farm. However they had not been told how harsh and very different the farming conditions were to those at home, or that their farms were on the frontier and they would effectively be the buffer between the Colony and the Xhosa tribes. The battle for land between the two groups led to a number of wars and skirmishes, and large doses of ill will.

Despite years of poverty and hardship, the 1820 Settlers as they were called, made their mark as farmers, traders and craftsmen. Their cultural contributions soon became firmly embedded in the nature of South Africa. They also played a major role in the administration of the Cape as the British style of governing changed from despotic colonial power to an ever more representative system in the 1850s. British influence was strong not only in government, law and administration, but also in the broader social and cultural sense. Towns and villages commonly had a higher concentration of English speaking people. The Boers, although overall greater in number, were mostly rural people.

End Of Slavery

The straw that broke the back of those early Boers was the move introduced by the British which finally led to the official abolition of slavery in the Cape in December 1834. They had been expecting it for years—they heard rumour of the liberal winds of change blowing in Europe—but this forewarning did nothing to reduce their ire and although they received monetary compensation and slaves were 'apprenticed' for four years after their freedom, it was the final impetus for their departure from the colony.

The Great Trek

The Great Trek, the first mass migration of European immigrant South Africans, the Boers, began in 1835 and only ended in 1848. These frontier farmers were fiercely independent people and found life under what they perceived as British misrule quite intolerable.

The Voortrekkers, as they were called, loaded their precious possessions onto ox-wagons, their only means of transport, and headed into what was largely unknown territory to them. They faced enormous hardships: they coaxed their wagons across huge mountain ranges; confronted many dangerous wild animals; and were blighted with diseases, some of which wiped out their livestock and some, like malaria, killed almost entire groups of Boers in several regions.

Because the routes taken by the Voortrekkers into the interior of the country crossed those of the Bantu tribes at the time of their great upheaval, the Mfecane, the two groups were involved in a number of battles and bloody massacres, the most poignant being the Battle of Blood River, still commemorated by the die-hard Afrikaner conservatives annually on 16 December.

The Voortrekkers had no intention of ever returning south again. They vehemently opposed British encroachment on their rights and freedom with a deep and Calvinistic sense of indignation. Staunch Christians, they considered the ancestor-worshipping African tribes in the area to be heathens, inferiors—a mentality that was to dog the Afrikaner and finally lead to the implementation of apartheid in the late 1940s and onward. The official British policy of equality in church and state was anathema to them.

Boers Trying To Break Free

At first Britain left the Boers to their own devices, but not for long. When the Boers in KwaZulu-Natal wanted to establish the independent Republic of Natal in the 1840s, Britain objected but took no steps to govern them. The Boers in the Orange Free State, however, signed the Bloemfontein Convention in 1854 with the British (which granted them the right to self-government) and then drew up a republican constitution in the area they called Transorangia. Although all the Boers disliked the British, the Voortrekkers were not unified enough to lead the other Boers in their fight for independence. In fact, the Voortrekkers split up once they moved north. This disunity among the Boers continued until the Boer War united them a little—but even today this right wing group is not really unified.

THE RISE OF APARTHEID
Greed—The Root of All Evil

Before the discovery of diamonds in 1867 and the big gold deposits in 1886 the country's economy was based almost entirely on agriculture. The Boers, or Afrikaners, were all farmers as were a fair number of the English. Although quite a few whites had moved into the towns, almost the entire African population lived off the land under various tribal chiefdoms. Only a few Africans worked for the white farmers.

With the discovery of some of the world's extremely valuable diamond and gold deposits, exciting and cavalier times followed; but it also led to dramatic changes in the nature of South Africa—and South Africans.

1913 Land Act

Following the discovery of minerals, especially gold and diamonds, pressure was applied to try and prevent Africans from making a living on their own land. This exploitative drive culminated in the 1913 Land Act which made it illegal for Africans to purchase or lease land from Europeans anywhere in South Africa, except the designated African reserves. This law was the precursor to apartheid's policy of *bantustans* or homelands which came about many decades later.

This Act was a major tragedy for all indigenous South Africans. One of the country's most famous writers and politicians, Sol Plaatje, wrote, "South Africa has by law ceased to be the home of any of her native children whose skins are dyed with a pigment that does not conform with the regulation hue." Protests by the African National Congress (ANC) were to no avail.

During World War II, new energetic members like Nelson Mandela, Walter and Albertina Sizulu, and Oliver Tambo joined the ANC. Their names have now become household words in South Africa.

Correct the Perceptions
A mistaken belief among many white South Africans, and possibly foreigners too, is that black farmers moved to the southern parts of the country at the same time the European immigrants moved north. By implication then, their stake in the land was equal as allegedly neither group got there first. But recent research shows that this idea is fallacious as black pastoral farmers were farming at Table Bay (which is now Cape Town) some 2,000 years ago, and that the first crop farmers had entered what is now South Africa, from the north, by about AD 200—a wee while before the European immigrants arrived!

Very Different Approaches

Pre-colonial African farmers had a markedly different approach to land ownership compared to the Europeans who arrived from the 16th century onwards. Firstly, land belonged to the community and access to it was linked to membership of the group. The tribal chief, as head of the community, allocated the land to individuals as long as they used it. Land was not measured and no record of access rights were kept, but boundaries were pointed out so people knew who had rights of access to which particular piece of land. Right to use the land could be inherited, and its size could be changed as the needs of the family or another family developed or changed.

Immigrant Interference

The first European immigrants altered these African concepts vastly. They believed land was privately owned or rented and owners were individuals. Land could be bought and sold with total security of tenure. Farmers were allowed to mortgage their land to raise money to pay their debts. They also believed that land could be inherited as it was, or the owner could divide it for the heirs. And contrary to the African practice, land was measured with written records of transactions and ownership.

This meant that over the years, land ownership tended to be concentrated in fewer and fewer hands and many people became tenants or wage earners on land which by Western standards belonged to someone else—invariably it was black tenants and labourers on white-owned farms. This is of course changing rapidly now, as more black South Africans turn to farming in various forms—in some cases with the support of the process of land restitution.

These dramatically different concepts of land access and landownership sometimes caused a great deal of misunderstanding, bitterness and conflicts between the two groups in those early days. For example: chiefs willingly shared land with whites in their area, but the whites then settled on it and behaved as if they owned it. Neither party properly understood the others' approach to landownership, thus leading to conflicts. Certainly these early problems underscore the complexities involved in resolving the imbalance in land distribution faced in present times by South Africa.

A letter in the *Weekly Mail* (now *Mail & Guardian*) newspaper a few years ago expressed the opinion of Dobs Mfeka, and no doubt a large number of other Africans. He writes: "The land is a gift from God to the people…all land. It is not like a house. A house is made of man's things. Land is not for sale. It is like air. The land is my blanket. I wear it like my ancestors…Land belongs to the black people who were living here long before the settlers came."

Not All That Easy

For the early white farmers, it was not just a case of walking into the wilds and staking claim to a piece of farmland. The various governments at the Cape in the 18th and 19th centuries controlled the land, but immigrant farmers had easy access to it. Prior to 1813, farmers paid a small annual amount to the government for access to the land they farmed. But in 1813, the British effectively gave them tenure to it. By 1828, the Coloured, or mixed race people were also allowed to own their own land under British rule. The same deal was extended to some African farmers later in the century. In KwaZulu-Natal, under British rule, Africans could own land both in their specially designated reserves as well as in the rest of the province. These rights were continued into the 20th

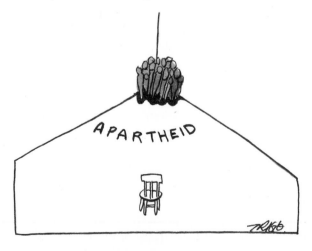

century and only came to an end with the promulgation of the 1913 Natives Land Act.

However, prior to 1913, in the Afrikaner republics, only whites were allowed to own land and black farmers were confined to the independent chiefdoms and scattered reserves—areas specifically set aside for them. African peasant farmers in the Transvaal and the Orange Free State had to enter into sharecropper arrangements with the white farmers.

The Horror Of The Natives Land Act

The 1913 Natives Land Act effectively prevented blacks from owning land outside of the reserves designated for them. It also forbade sharecropping and other forms of rent tenancy by black farmers on white land. Although it came into existence more than three decades ahead of the institutionalisation of apartheid, this Act was certainly the basis for the segregation policies that were to follow.

This Act and some 86 other land laws, proclamations and regulations have been used to keep all but whites from owning a share of their birthright until the pillars of apartheid were scrapped in the 1990s. All those rulings were then condemned to the scrap heap and land rights are again accessible to everyone!

Blot on the Landscape

One of the greatest horrors in South Africa's recent land history is that of forced removals. To enforce its policy of segregation, the Nationalist government forced more than 3.5 million people to relocate to areas designated for them by the authorities. This applied to people living in the rural areas, towns and cities too.

Soweto, an acronym for South Western Township, was formed in the 1950s when the government decided to move all blacks who were living in and around Johannesburg, and especially in the vibrant Sophiatown area, to their 'own' location or township, as these urban ghettos were called.

The forced removals have caused abject misery and poverty, dislocation and breakdown of family relations, and sheer degradation to some 10 per cent of the entire population. Besides these, the cost in monetary terms for the implementation of the Group Areas Act is estimated at Rand 4 billion—money that if well spent at the time could have made a major indent on the drastic housing shortage the country has faced for many decades, and still does.

Who Has What?

Under the apartheid system, 13 per cent of the country's land was set aside to make the homelands for the entire African population, which comprised around 74 per cent of all South Africans. To make matters worse, the homelands had only 16 per cent of the arable land in the country, and the majority of the rural Africans had no other way of earning a living other than by farming. Thus there is little wonder that the homelands and so-called independent states were never economically viable! At the time of the scrapping of apartheid, the population density in the homelands was over 150 people per sq km (389 per sq mile), and growing fast. In the rest of South Africa, there were only about 20 people to a sq km (52 per sq mile).

The Solution

With the scrapping of apartheid and the formation of the new democratic South Africa, obviously all the discriminatory land laws were also scrapped. In the years that followed many people have flocked to be near the cities from their rural homes in search of work.

This has brought problems for both local municipalities and the national government in the delivery of services and infrastructure, but the process is being managed and low-cost housing is a priority of the government.

The ANC's approach to land redistribution is pragmatic and realistic. There is no single model of land provision to the many who have been dispossessed over the years, nor does it entertain the simplistic approach of seizing land from whites and giving it to blacks. Instead it has put in place a process for land restitution that is looked at on the merit of each case. The process is complicated, but, in a nutshell, some land is returned to its original owners and the previous owner is compensated, and sometimes the African community seeking restitution is compensated. The process is far from finalised and no doubt will move along in various ways for decades to come. But land grabbing *al la* Zimbabwe has been seriously frowned on.

Although anyone can now live anywhere in the country, a large majority of the population does not have the economic means to buy the land of their dreams, but even this is slowly changing as the growing economy spreads wealth across a far wider base.

Land—Who Grabbed What and When

The discovery of diamonds and gold led to huge foreign investment mostly from Britain, Europe and the United States. The mines grew fast and economic activities developed which caused great changes to the lives of thousands, and later millions, of black South Africans. The whites owned, financed and provided the technical skills to open the mines while occupying the well-paid skilled jobs. The blacks did the unskilled work and were strictly controlled by the migrant labour systems.

These changes had a deep and lasting effect on the lifestyle and future of black South Africans. In 1867, when the first diamond was discovered, and despite the spread of the Boers and British across the land, most Africans still lived under the rule of independent chiefs and worked as farmers on their own land. By 1914, the whites had defeated most of the chiefs and taken possession of 90 per cent of the land. This move forced ever more blacks to work as labourers in the mines, towns and on white-owned farms.

The Boers vs The British

By the end of the 19th century, the Boers were again at war. The Anglo-Boer War began in 1899 and ended in Boer defeat in 1902. The reason, simply put, was that the British wanted control of the goldfields as it would ultimately give them control of the whole country.

During the war, the British decided to uproot almost an entire nation of Boers and place the families in relief camps. These later became concentration camps. By 1902, the Boer guerrillas were worn-out and finally agreed to the Treaty of Vereeniging, which brought them back under British domination. Ironically, it was British domination they had sought to escape when they trekked away from the Cape more than half a century before.

Although the scars of this war are still evident to some extent as white English and Afrikaan South Africans sometimes count their differences, rather than their similarities, the new multicultural moves in the country have swept such petty issues into insignificance for most.

Britain Hands Back Her Dearly Won Prize

At the instigation of Generals Jan Smuts and Louis Botha, stalwarts of the Anglo-Boer war, whites from all four colonies drew up a draft Act of Union which was passed by the British Parliament in 1910. The colonies were united in a self-governing dominion, the Union of South Africa. Black South Africans realised that if they were ruled by Afrikaners their chances of a fair deal were zero, but their objections fell on deaf British ears. Their struggle for a equality had begun. Black nationalism was in the making.

A split, however, soon developed in white politics. Smuts and Botha stayed with the more liberal and English-oriented South African Party (which has mutated many times since and is currently called the Democratic Alliance), while J B Hertzog led the National Party of dyed-in-the-wool Afrikaners, the forerunner to the current National Party and instigators of the apartheid policy.

The Consolidation of Apartheid

The 1948 election victory of the right-wing Afrikaner party, in the 'whites-only' general election, began an epoch of unbroken National Party rule. This was a turning point in South Africa's political history that ushered in more than four decades of institutionalised racial discrimination and white supremacy.

Although the Nationalist majority in parliament was not big, it was sufficient to define by statute, legislate and hence enforce the practice of apartheid. Hosts of laws segregating, separating and oppressing people were implemented during the period of National Party rule.

Some of the more vile ones, described by the United Nations as "crimes against humanity", include:

- Prohibition of Mixed Marriages Act (1949) which forbade marriages between whites and people of other 'colours'.
- Immorality Act (No. 21) of 1950 extended an earlier ban— the Immorality Act (No. 5) of 1927—on sexual relations between whites and blacks (meaning African) to a ban on sexual relations between whites and any non-whites.
- Population Registration Act (1950) which classified every person according to race, on a national register.
- Group Areas Act (1950) which enabled the government to implement physical separation between races, enforcing separate residential areas. Often Coloured, Indian and African communities were forcibly moved to different and usually inferior residential areas. Whites were rarely adversely effected by this.
- Reservation of Separate Amenities Act (1953) which prevented people of a different 'colour' from sharing public amenities such as toilets, cinemas, restaurants, hospitals, schools and more. This was aimed at preventing the different racial groups from mixing with each other. Supposedly each group had its own amenities, but in reality whites had access to all the best public facilities and the other groups, if they had anything at all, had second rate ones.

A major tenet of the apartheid blueprint was the Bantu Authorities Act (1951) which provided for the establishment of separate rural areas called homelands or *bantustans* where almost all Africans were forced to live according to their tribal identity. Homelands could gain 'independence' as separate countries. Some followed that path like Transkei, Ciskei, Venda and Bophuthatswana—but no other country in the world, except South Africa and the other so-called independent states would recognise their sovereignty.

BLACK RESISTANCE GAINS STRENGTH
The African National Congress

Black South Africans began to organise regional resistance to white rule in the late 19th century. The movement gathered strength, cutting across tribal lines after their failure to prevent the formation of the Union of South Africa, which meant the end of liberal British control of the country. In 1912, a nationwide conference was called of all African chiefs and leaders of political organisations. They agreed to establish the South African Native National Congress, later renamed the African National Congress (ANC). In January 1913, its headquarters was opened in Johannesburg.

In 1914, the South African National Party which had tried to unite English and Afrikaans-speaking whites, finally admitted defeat and split into two. The politically conscious black South Africans, ironically, had just established the first, and still thriving, nationwide African national movement in the country. Their first president, Reverend John Dube, had studied in England while early members of the ANC were African men who received their early education in English-run mission schools. Many of these members were later sent abroad by the missionaries for further education and training in various professions.

The initial role of the ANC was to attempt to persuade the white government to recognise all people as equals.

A More Radical Approach

The ANC Youth League was formed at the ANC 1944 annual conference. It was a much more radical organisation than the older conservative elements that dominated the ANC leadership. It opposed the white government with growing fierceness and quickly gained momentum when the Afrikaners took control of the government in 1948 and began to build the rigid systems of apartheid. The ANC had not been a militant organisation until this time.

In 1950, the South African Communist Party, always a close ally of the ANC, was declared unlawful by the Suppression of Communism Act. This law was used to full and brutal effect in later decades to suppress anyone or any organisation that resisted the apartheid government.

Ongoing ANC passive-resistance campaigns were organised against the exclusion of black people from the process of government. They were specifically against the laws which forced only Africans to carry identity documents at all times. Then in April 1960, the government banned the ANC, thus it was no longer a lawful political organisation. With this act, 50 years of non-violent struggle was brought to nothing and by mid-1961 the ANC decided that it would have to use violent methods of resistance to achieve its aims.

In 1961, the military wing of the ANC was formed. Called *Umkhonto we Sizwe*, it means Spear of the Nation. Its tactics of sabotage were at first aimed at damaging only buildings and property, thus avoiding loss of life.

In 1963, the top leaders of the ANC, including Nelson Mandela, were brought to trial and sentenced to life imprisonment. The organisation went into exile and continued its work. As the apartheid laws became more repressive, the ANC again changed its tactics and civilians became targets of sabotage.

In the 1970s and 1980s, the ANC had, with the help of many anti-apartheid organisations worldwide, built up a wide support network both in the East and the West. Because of internal and external pressure, Nelson Mandela, the movement's powerful figurehead and leader of the ANC at the time, and other members were released from jail in February 1990. The ban was lifted on the organisation which very quickly transformed itself into a very successful politcal party.

Under the leadership of Nelson Mandela it won the first ever democratic elections hands down —and so was born the new era of peace and relative stability for a country that had teetered on the brink of civil war for more than a decade.

Justice Through Trade Unions

For an outsider, the trade union movement in South Africa, and particularly its history, may not be as simple to understand as those in other countries. This is because during the more than five decades that the majority black population was denied any real political representation, the unions were the best, and often the only, avenue for airing grievances, and not only work-related ones. They represented in many ways the political aspirations and also political clout of people who were barred from formal political processes.

Today since the country is a fully-fledged democracy the need for this secondary—and in the decades of the 1970s and 1980s, often primary—political process has been removed. Unions are now more about the normal issues that unions deal with: salary, working conditions and the likes. But even today, the trade union umbrella body, Congress of South African Trade Unions (COSATU), and its general secretary, are closely allied to the current ruling party, the ANC, and play an important role in mustering political support during elections. With the South African Communist Party, the three organisations form what is called the Tripartite Alliance which to date has been supportive of the government in its need to forge totally new policies.

The union movement began in the 1880s, but began in earnest with the dire need for South Africa to manufacture products locally, both during and immediately after World War II and in so doing transformed the economy from one based solely on mining, to include a manufacturing base as well.

The Great Depression, the period between the World Wars, had been a desperate economic time for a newly industrialising country. A large influx of rural people no longer able to make a living on their farms moved into the towns and cities. This period which reduced many whites to dire poverty despite their more privileged status, resulted in much greater suffering for black people who were the poorest section of the population. Their lot was made even worse by deliberate measures to favour white workers over them.

Little wonder the first black unions were formed at this time. The African Mine Workers' Union was established with a commanding position in mining compounds at the end of the war and it has held onto this position ever since. Now called the National Union of Mine Workers, it is one of the biggest, most powerful and best organised in the country. But it is not alone. Most major sectors in the country are unionised to a greater or lesser degree and the unions generally play a powerful role in ensuring the generous labour laws are adhered to.

In the early days of unionisation as the aspirations of the millions of disenfranchised people increased, so did the political and union activities, but this soon led to a government crack down and certain organisations were banned, including COSATU.

The new union movement that burst into the 1970s and 1980s was more militant and politically driven. The divisions in the country were echoed in the unions. There were black and white unions, left- and right-wing ones. These upheavals led to the black unions winning the same legal rights as their white counterparts. Slowly labour laws were amended and improved, and by the late 1980s the black and white unions enjoyed equitable bargaining power.

Today South Africa has some 3 million trade unionists. The two largest bodies in the South African trade union movement are COSATU whose various member unions together attract well over 2 million members; and the Federation of Unions of South Africa (FEDUSA) which has over half a million members in about 27 affiliated unions.

There is now a greater realisation that all South Africans are mutually relevant to the growth of the economy and a spirit of cooperation is encouraged. Despite attempts to foster the notion that workers, capital and the state should jointly control the economy, union-management clashes are not uncommon and strikes are often the end result.

THE DECLINE OF APARTHEID
Sharpville Shootings—A Day to Commemorate
Under the system of apartheid all Africans were forced to carry a 'pass book': an identity document that listed all their racial particulars. In 1960 the ANC called for a nationwide defiance campaign by blacks aimed particularly at the hated 'pass laws'.

On 21 March 1960 in Vereenigning, a town just south-east of Johannesburg, demonstrators marched on a local police station. After calling for reinforcements, the panic-stricken police opened fire on unarmed civilians, killing 69 people and wounding 180. The tragic events at Sharpville, the neighbourhood where the incident occurred, evoked censure and revulsion from around the world. The Sharpville massacre was seen as a direct consequence of the system of apartheid, and thus condemned vehemently.

The date 21 March was called Sharpville Day and became a symbolic day to commemorate the horrors inflicted on the black community by the practice of apartheid. Today it is a public holiday with the generic title of Human Rights Day.

June 16, 1976, Soweto Day

For any newcomer to South Africa it is vital to understand the poignance and depth of emotions attached to the commemoration of 16 June 1976 each year. Now called Youth Day, it is an official public holiday. So how did this emotion-laden day come about? The government of the time arbitrarily instituted a new regulation stating that instead of English, Afrikaans was to be the medium of instruction for some subjects in African schools. This move sparked a tinder box of discontent in the black communities and especially its youth because, while both languages were 'official', Afrikaans was seen as the language of the oppressor while English was viewed as international. (Under apartheid, South Africa was a bilingual country where English and Afrikaans had equal status, while no African language was deemed official. Today we have 11 official languages reflecting a vast variety of cultures.)

The student grievances at this time against their inferior education in overcrowded classes with poorly qualified teachers were totally justified. Their white counterparts received a high-quality free education. Other grievances such as poor housing and lack of electricity and running water in most black homes also added fuel to this fire.

Resistance was strongest in Soweto, the huge black and largely poorer residential neighbourhood south-west of Johannesburg. On 16 June 1976, some 15,000 school pupils marched in a demonstration, defying a police ban on marches. They were stopped by police, but stood firm despite the warning shots and tear gas. Police then opened fire into the crowd, killing two of the youngsters and wounding several more. A now famous photograph of two students carrying the fatally injured 13-year-old Hector Pietersen, has come to symbolise this tragic event.

First, Soweto and then almost every other township in South Africa erupted with demonstrations, riots, destructive violence and confrontations with the police. When the violence eventually subsided in October 1977, the death toll was over 700, comprising mostly youths.

The Final Straw—The 1984 Constitution

"Sharpville was the revolt of the parents, Soweto (16 June 1976) was that of the children. Now it's both," said an experienced black press photographer in 1986.

In 1984, the apartheid government drew up a new constitution forming a tricameral parliament with three separate houses. It gave the Indian community and the mixed-race community, called 'Coloureds', some form of representation in the white government. But this was far from equality as the white government reserved full power to veto any decision made in either of the other houses. Thus many boycotted this sham system right from the start.

The tricameral parliament also deeply angered the Africans whose only form of political representation was in the homeland governments, which were mostly not recognised internationally and were seen as illegitimate, puppet regimes. Demonstrations were held across the country. They vented frustrations over other issues as well like steep rent rises, continuing forced removals, the abysmal condition of black education and many more. Police patrolling a funeral at the time, which, as always, was also a political demonstration, panicked and shot dead 19 mourners. Again, riots spread across the country.

Confrontation became ever more violent in the black townships between demonstrators and the police, aided by the military, the South African Defence Force. At almost every new funeral-cum-political-rally, more people were killed and the spiral of violence continued. In addition, added violence was experienced in what is now KwaZulu-Natal, blamed at least to some extent on the Zulu-ANC rivalries, but also on Zulu factions.

It was at this time that the dreadful 'necklace' method of murdering perceived spies and informers in the black community came into being. A motorcar tyre filled with petrol was put around the neck or body of a victim and then set alight.

International condemnation of both the rioting and the harsh repression of the apartheid regime did little to alleviate the violence.

In July 1985, the then State President P W Botha declared a state of emergency, saying the country was ungovernable—exactly the intention of the disenfranchised masses. Over 8,500 people were detained, many of them children. Thousands lost their lives, thousands more were banned or jailed. Both the international and local press were severely censored.

But tragically, the violence continued. Horror at what was happening to the country caused foreign banks to withdraw capital. The value of the South African currency dropped dramatically and the country faced economic and financial disaster. By 1987, the violence had subsided a little, but almost everyone, both black and white, was more politicised and polarised than ever before. Negative world opinion, disinvestment and sanctions were forcing South Africa to consider a peaceful route to democracy.

When F W de Klerk succeeded Botha as state president in 1989, he began a process of genuine reform, lifting the state of emergency, allowing black political demonstrations and releasing a number of important political prisoners. In February 1990, he ended the 30-year ban on the ANC and legalised a host of other anti-apartheid political organisations. To international acclaim, on 11 February 1990, the world's most famous political prisoner, Nelson Mandela, walked free.

And They All Came Tumbling Down Again

In a speech to the nation on 1 February 1991, President F W de Klerk finally buried the cornerstones of apartheid. The Group Areas Act, the various land acts, the Population Registration Act—the laws that had caused so much grief, suffering and loss of human dignity for more than 40 years—were nullified. Through a negotiated settlement, the tricameral parliamentary system and the homeland governments were moulded into a new democratic political system for all.

De Klerk's release of Mandela was an act of bold and unusual trust by both men. Mandela agreed to work with his arch political enemy while balancing the expectations of those who believed in his leadership. De Klerk on the other hand, had to try to fulfil his electoral promise to break down apartheid structures while working to protect the white, Asian and Coloured minorities.

They had given the country a chance to take a long hard look at itself: De Klerk had to persuade his constituency they had been following a false dream for over 40 years; the ANC had to adapt from being an activist, exiled, revolutionary organisation, committed to armed struggle, to being a political party and potential government in a democratic South Africa.

The momentum for the peace-making process of the future had been set in motion. It culminated in the first democratic elections in the nation's history being held over three days in April 1994. The historic event which saw South Africans of all races, colours and creeds standing together in very long queues, getting to know each other as some had never done before, sometimes for many, many hours and almost always in a state of peace and reconciliation, is now celebrated on 27 April each year as Freedom Day.

The Beginning of the Uphill Battle

The first tottering step on the road to political and social normality was set in motion at the end of 1991. Called the Convention for a Democratic South Africa, or CODESA to the glib of tongue, it was host to almost 400 delegates from 19 political organisations who met on Mondays, and sometimes Tuesdays too, to negotiate mutually acceptable ways of moving from apartheid to something entirely different.

CODESA drew up a declaration of intent committing the participating parties to a constitution-making process. They also had an effective say in national policies pursued during the interim period leading to the formation of a new government.

At first things went smoothly and this nation, blighted with political turmoil for hundreds of years, was euphoric. But not for long.

The two main contenders in the negotiations process, De Klerk's government and the ANC agreed that a constitution should be drawn up and adopted by a popularly elected national assembly. So far, so good.

But then three major bones of contention arose: they could not agree on the percentage majority needed to adopt the constitution; there was conflict over the role of the Senate or upper house; and also over the time frame for creating the constitution. The upshot of it all was that the ANC suspended talks at CODESA, and the first tottering step was halted, negotiations were derailed. Each side retreated to lick its wounds, rally its supporters and prepare for the next round.

The talks began again some months later at the same venue, under a slightly different guise. The notion of a negotiated settlement had not been abandoned nor had the concept of a constitution.

THE FALL OF APARTHEID

After years of home-grown resistance and ever increasing world censure, apartheid was finally dismantled. The culmination of that abhorrent era, and the beginning of the march to democracy, was heralded by the 'Yes for change' vote in the 1992 referendum where the vast majority of whites threw their weight behind the reform process already in motion. In the words of President F W de Klerk, "Today we have closed the book of apartheid. That chapter is over. We, who started this long chapter in our history were called upon to close it." And they did.

And Then....

But ending decades of apartheid on paper was vastly easier and more concisely clinical than it was and still is in reality. The system of racial division had permeated every level of political as well as social life. Of course a few people mixed 'across the colour line' as it was called before its demise, but all the structures, especially the physical ones like living areas, schools, government departments—absolutely everything—was divided along racial lines.

The process of integration had to happen as quickly as possible, especially after the first democratic elections in 1994, but simultaneously the day-to-day workings of government and business needed as little disruption as possible.

Transformation in all of the civil service generally happened slowly and steadily, and most systems work as well or as badly as they ever did, sometimes with emphasis on different areas or issues than before. Many people, because they had been excluded for so long, had no experience of the skills needed to make various sectors of government work, but it did not take long— sometimes with mentors and sometimes being thrown in at the deep end—for them to learn and implement their new civil skills.

The South African Constitution

Apart from the practical changes in government and the administration, one of the most urgent issues was to draw up a constitution that would forever protect the rights of every South African so that "never, never again will this beautiful land experience the oppression of one by another," as stated by Nelson Mandela on 10 May 1994 at his swearing-in ceremony as the country's first democratically elected president.

And just a little less than three years later, the Constitution of the Republic of South Africa, approved by the Constitutional Court, came into effect on 4 February 1997. Thought by many people at home and internationally to be one of the most progressive in the world, it is the supreme law of the land and no other law or government action can supersede the provisions of the constitution. It can only be changed if at least two-thirds of the members of the National Assembly and at least six provinces in the National Council of Provinces vote for it. It is said to have some of the most cutting edge provisions for socioeconomic rights, but it has also been praised for backing this up with the judicial wherewithall to enforce these rights. Rights which include the more usual civil and political rights, but also the less commonly enshrined social, economic and cultural rights.

Business Needed to Grow and Change and Grow Some More

Business was a more complex matter in some ways. The economy had been flailing for a number of years prior to the end of apartheid, mostly due to economic sanctions imposed on the country in an attempt to end the dreaded racist policy, but also due to the fact that a large sector of the population had been denied access to various jobs, levels of education and general economic opportunities leading to a dearth in skills and know-how among a large section of the population. This too put a formidable brake on the economy which, although vastly improved now, still hinders good growth in some business sectors.

Since the vast majority of business was solely in the hands of the white population during the apartheid era, it was necessary to speed up the spread of wealth creation to a broad spectrum of people.

BEE: Empowering The Way Forward

After many years of discussion, research and planning on how to address this issue, the government has adopted what is Black Economic Empowerment (BEE) programme. It is designed to redress the entrenched inequalities of apartheid by giving those previously disadvantaged by the race-driven policies of the past, a fast track to upliftment. In other words, creating an enabling climate for them to create their own wealth and thus to catch up.

It is not a process of taking from the rich (whites) and giving it to the poor (mostly black population), but rather a growth strategy that targets the economy's weakest link—inequality entrenched over decades. The government is hyper-aware that simplistic redistribution would just become a process of substituting a new elite where there had been an old white one.

In its very early days the empowerment process certainly appeared to be making a few black entrepreneurs very rich as they grew vast and successful business empires. Of course the reality of creating economic opportunities across the population was not, and is still not easy, and at times government rhetoric, especially at election time, did not address fully the reality, the long time frame and the difficulty of bringing a large country (more than 45 million people), most of whom were not wealthy, into the wealth creation fold.

The economic empowerment process was at first left to market forces. The sheer determination of people desiring a new life enabled the first wave of change, but once this began to slow, the government saw the need to embrace what is now called BEE.

In a nutshell it is a voluntary programme which encourages companies to use people from previously disadvantaged communities over those who were privileged in the past. Taken a step further, companies are encouraged to source goods and services from those who practice BEE, or from companies that have good BEE credentials. Similarly, government tenders and contracts will only be awarded to companies or organisations that are BEE-oriented. This process has the pebble-in-a-pond ripple effect empowering ever more people.

To determine who is BEE savvy, business credentials are evaluated on a scorecard system: each industry, with input from government, has drawn up a charter determining values for various empowerment actions. In this way, it is possible to establish a relatively true and fair reflection of an organisation's BEE street cred. In theory, this programme should work extremely well, but should it not be sufficiently successful in a given time frame, the ruling party has indicated it may use stronger legislation to enforce it.

Truth and Reconcilliation Commission

"... a commission is a necessary exercise to enable South Africans to come to terms with their past on a morally accepted basis and to advance the cause of reconciliation."

—Mr Dullah Omar, former Minister of Justice

A far more complex and emotive task was to address and redress the atrocities committed during the apartheid era, crimes committed by those on both sides of the apartheid government in the struggle for freedom.

In 1995, a special law enabled the Truth and Reconciliation Commission, or the TRC, to be set up to do this, although the concept had been mooted a few years earlier during the period of the Government of National Unity. Its role was to investigate and provide "as complete a picture as possible of the nature, causes and extent of the gross violations of human rights".

The remarkable lack of bitterness that characterised Nelson Mandela's attitude (even after more than 27 years in jail) to the road ahead, was embodied in the TRC's mandate. He and all who helped establish it hoped that it would give South Africa its best chance at reconciliation.

The whole process began in April 1996 under the chairmanship of Archbishop Desmond Tutu. Anyone who felt they had been a victim of violence could come forward and be heard at the TRC. Perpetrators of violence could also tell their story and request amnesty from prosecution—this was granted mostly to people who confessed their crimes in full and in public at the TRC hearings, as one of its main goals was to heal wounds that would otherwise fester into violence and recriminations, something many were desperate to avoid.

Most South Africans feel the TRC was one of the most valuable tools in the process of letting everyone begin to understand the complexities of the struggle for and against apartheid. Many feel it has helped a lot in normalising people's relationships with each other in a country that had lived under very abnormal conditions for many decades.

Practically it had three committees to carry out its three major roles:

- to investigate human rights abuses that took place between 1960 and 1994, based on statements made by people to the TRC;
- to ensure reparations are made to restore victims' dignity and help the healing process of survivors, their families and the communities;
- and to consider applications made for amnesty within the framework of the law.

Most of the TRC's work was completed by the end of July 1998 and a massive 3,500-page report was later published and handed to then President Nelson Mandela in a formal ceremony on 29 October 1998.

Where to Now?

Since the role of the TRC is over, it is now up to South Africans to continue the healing process in every way they know to ensure all the pain, suffering and hard work was not in vain. There is generally a quiet, and sometimes not so quiet determination and pride among ordinary people, after having taken such risks and reached such depths of horror to wrestle their rights from the apartheid regime, to defend them vigorously.

This means that in many ways the country and its people are pretty vociferous in their views, often testing out new-found rights with marches, demonstrations and a lot of media discussion and speculation. It makes for a lively existence and as a bit of an outsider you are likely to find it quite invigorating!

The younger South Africans—those who were young when the final process of transformation to a democracy was started in the early 1990s—are far out ahead in their multi-cultural pursuit of life, love and a common future and it is often from the youth that we get some of the most exciting and vibrant levels of creativity, not only in the world of art and culture, but across the spectrum of work and life in general. The Rainbow Nation is certainly rarely dull.

THE DESPERATE BATTLE AGAINS HIV/AIDS

Tragically one of the biggest social issues the South African government has to cope with at present is the prevalence of HIV/AIDS. The country has one of the highest levels in the world and it is spread across not only the adult population, but also many of the children. This high incidence is underscored by the UNAIDS 2006 Global Report estimate that at least 18.8 per cent of the population between the ages of 15 and 49 years old is infected. This means that

well over 5 million people are living with the virus and an estimated 1,000 die of it each day.

The government's response to the epidemic has been to draw up a broad national framework focusing on four priority areas: prevention, treatment, care and support. However the application of the plan has not been as speedily effective nor as easy to roll out as the severity of the epidemic requires. Social attitudes and poor levels of education, especially in the rural areas, and to some level, denial of the reality of the disease, has led to a less than perfect application of the scheme.

A Presidential Failure

One cannot but mention the then President Thabo Mbeki's rather bizarre stance on the biggest scourge facing South Africa: he indicated that he did not believe HIV was the cause of AIDS. This led to bitter confrontations locally and utter ridicule internationally. Worse is that South Africa, which has one of the highest levels of infection in the world, did not immediately embark on a sufficiently good or large-scale prevention and treatment campaign. The problem has been addressed more fully recently but valuable time—and an estimated nearly two million lives (by the end of 2006)—were lost.

Only in 2003, after sustained pressure from advocacy groups like the Treatment Action Campaign, did the government agree to the provision of anti-retroviral drugs and even then the process of rolling it out has been a slow one. A reason for this is that there is just insufficient infrastructure to cope with the demand across the country and partly because the health department continued to give out a mixed message implying that traditional medicine and nutrition would suffice. In addition, there are elements who disavowed the safety of the ARV drugs available (a disingenuous stance since these drugs are being used almost everywhere else in the world to good effect).

The effect on the economy is expected to be severe, but far more tragic is that there are vast numbers of children who have been orphaned because their parents have died of the disease, and in a growing number of cases there is no one else who can care for and support them. There are heart-rending stories on a daily basis of children, often not even teenagers, who are caring for their younger siblings. The longer term and wider social implications of this can only be imagined with horror. It is of course hoped that this and every successive government will do all in its power to address this situation.

WHO'S WHO IN POLITICS

As all of South Africa embraced democracy fully for the first time in 1994, there was a host of political parties, quasi-political organisations and fringe organisations. Three general elections later, there are fewer and only a very few who really play much of a role.

The fringe parties on both the left and the right have become less significant, either because their support base is so small, or because they have joined forces with one of the larger parties and been swamped almost into insignificance.

So, in case you should be in a position to vote, or are just curious to know who's who, here follows a potted rundown of the more prominent organisations—in alphabetical order least I be accused of political bias!

African National Congress (ANC)

Discussed in detail above, it suffices to say that the ANC, once a liberation movement and now a fully fledged political party, won the first ever democratic elections in 1994 under Nelson Mandela's leadership and retained the next two elections with an increased majority. It currently (at the time of going to press in 2008) still has the support of both the South African Communist Party (SACP) which does not contest the elections but puts its support in the ANC camp, and the help of the massive trade union umbrella body, COSATU, to sway voters in its favour. But recently there have been rumblings of discontent within this triumverite, the Tripartite Alliance, mainly due to the moderate and more market-led economic policies the ANC leadership has adopted.

Jacob Gedleyihlekisa Zuma (born 12 Jan 1942)

Jacob Zuma, South Africa's fourth democratically elected president since independence, had a volatile and uneasy rise to the ultimate political role in the country. But since finally coming to power after the May 2009 national elections, he has been relatively successful in his role of trying to appease and lead a culturally and economically divergent population.

From the impoverished rural area of Nkandla in KwaZulu Natal, his father a policeman who died when he was a child and his mother a domestic worker, he had very little formal education and took to politics at the age of 17 when he joined the ANC. Only a few years later, and just after the ANC was banned by the ruling whites-only government, he became actively involved with its armed wing, Umkhonto we Sizwe, which led to his arrest, trial and imprisonment for attempting to overthrow the existing government. He spent the next 10 years on Robben Island, the island prison used then for political prisoners, with other notable "comrades" of the ANC, including Nelson Mandela.

Once out of prison he played an active and ultimately very senior role in the external wing of Umkhonto we Sizwe until he was able to return legally to South Africa in 1990 when the ANC was unbanned and he and many other stalwarts of the organisation could begin the negotiations towards a democratic future for South Africa. He rose quickly through the ranks of the ANC in his home province Natal (now KwaZulu Natal) and then became the deputy leader of the entire organisation ahead of the second democratic elections in 1999. Given the ANC won the elections hands down, he became the deputy President of South Africa to the newly elected President Thabo Mbeki.

Continue Next Page

Jacob Gedleyihlekisa Zuma (continue)

The relationship between the president and his deputy, never an easy one due to vastly differing personalities, backgrounds and constant rivalry for ultimate leadership of the party and hence the country, broke down when Mr Zuma became involved in allegations of corruption and was charged, but not convicted, of rape. President Mbeki relieved him of his position in 2005 and appointed Phumzile Mlambo-Ngcuka as the new deputy President.

For many politicians that would have been the end of a career, but Mr Zuma bounced back from the ropes probably because of a mixture of his charismatic nature, his popular touch, a wily political nous and the fact that like some 70 % or more of South Africans, his roots are very humble. "JZ" as he is colloquially called is seen by many as a people's person, a champion of the poor!

As deputy president of the ANC it was assumed that he would eventually take over from Thabo Mbeki as the organisation's leader, which, as long as the ANC is in power, means president of the country too. After a very divided ANC national congress at the end of 2007 Mr Zuma was elected with the support of certain factions as its leader, although Mr Mbeki still had two years left to serve of his presidency. An unusual situation. Only a few months later the ANC decided to "recall" President Mbeki which effectively deposed him. The deputy leader of the ANC, Kgalema Motlanthe, became president until the national election in 2009. At this stage Mr Zuma was still facing corruption charges, but these were thrown out of court only a few weeks before the national elections. The ANC won the elections and Mr Zuma was sworn in as president in May 2009.

Although he joined the South African Communist Party in 1963, has called himself an economic socialist at times, on occasion talked about the redistribution of the country's wealth and came to power due to large support from the trade union movement, he has not altered the country's economic course very much to date. He has preferred to steer a middle road attempting to placate big business in return for the creation of much needed jobs and the fact that it generates tax revenue to spend on the upliftment of the poor. The global economic recession has made his job more difficult and the jury is out on whether he can retain this stance or will be forced to take a more worker-centric direction in the near future.

Like a fair number of South Africans, especially in the more rural areas, President Zuma is a polygamist. Although he keeps rather tight-lipped about his wives, fiancés and children, it is believed that at present he has five or six wives (one of whom has divorced him), two fiancés and more than 20 children, not all of which were born to his legal wives.

Democratic Alliance (DA)

This is a mutated political party. The ancestry of the Democratic Alliance can surely be traced as far back as the old South African Party which was formed in 1911. Although it has always been a relatively small party its contribution was important under the apartheid government as it kept issues related to liberal political values on the political agenda—and it still does.

Initially, its support was almost purely from within the white sector of the population, but in recent times it has grown its support base a little to include people from all walks of life. Although it is the major opposition party in parliament, it still has only about one-sixth of the vote that the ANC does. At the time of going to press the DA is in the process of merging with the Independent Democrats (see page 55).

Inkatha Freedom Party (IFP)

Inkatha was started as a Zulu cultural organisation in 1928. Since then its popularity has fluctuated until the mid-70s when its leader, Dr Mangosuthu Buthelezi, injected enthusiasm and boosted its membership, which a decade later claimed 1.5 million. Its support is almost entirely Zulu-based, but not all Zulus support it.

When, in 1990, it became evident that South Africa was en route to a democratic future, Inkatha changed into the Inkatha Freedom Party, a nationally-based political party open to all races. Although Buthelezi was a member of the ANC in his youth and supported it while it was banned, the two organisations clashed dramatically in the early days of democracy which led to sporadic violence and the resulting loss of life.

As they worked together in the first government, so tensions dissipated and it also slowly lost support. Now it is the third largest with only half the support of the DA.

New National Party (NNP)

This was the political party (initially called the National Party) held ultimately responsible for apartheid, and almost anything else wrong with the country in the past as well.

In retrospect, the coming to power of the NP in 1948 was the single most deleterious moment in the country's 20th-century history. They may have led the country to sovereign independence, and later even Republic-hood (the ultimate dream of the Afrikaner as a means of eternally shaking free of the British yoke), but they also gave it the horrific albatross—apartheid.

It is—or was—also probably the most ironic party since, as its support dwindled to almost nothing, it decided first to join the DA in an alliance which soon fell apart and then in 2004, it formed an alliance with the ANC! Of course being so insignificant, its policies are irrelevant and it is simply a stooge in the ANC camp where it helps them hold sway in the provinces of Western Cape and Northern Cape.

Independent Democrats (ID)

This party was only formed in 2003 as a break-away from the black liberation party, the Pan Africanist Congress, as it wanted to move towards a more open, non-race-based stance in government. It is vociferous on corruption problems in the ruling party and is a veritable and beneficial thorn in the side of the ANC.

WHAT'S IN A NAME?

Since 1994, South Africa has been steadily changing its face to reflect the rich variety of people, cultures and creeds that make up our vibrant new democracy. In the recent past, and even since the first Europeans arrived here some six centuries ago, the names of places—be they geographic or political, whether they are towns, cities, lakes or airports—tended to reflect the dominant or ruling powers, but not often that of the majority of inhabitants.

To address this issue in as unemotional a way as possible and also to ensure that those who had been excluded from playing a role in naming places in the past would now be fairly represented, the government introduced the South African Geographical Names Council Act 118 of 1998. It was enacted to unify communities and to address the imbalances of the past, with the aim of uniting people across the divides.

The intention of the Act is noble, but in the view of a wide spectrum of people involved in its application, it is not quite prescriptive enough to enable a smooth road to name change, and at the same time eliminate small-scale political point scoring which, sadly, divides rather than unites people. For this reason there is a call from some parties for the government to draw up a definitive set of rules and criteria (like those used in some African and European countries) to evaluate name changes. Stringent and enforced guidelines would also diffuse what, on occasion, becomes a petty but heated debate ending up in court time and again, and also costing the country way too much time and money.

It is felt that these rules would assist the South African Geographical Names Council, the organisation that advises government, in particular the Minister of Arts and Culture, on name changes, to cut out much of the unnecessary mud-slinging, both in the media and in court. Many name changes have smoothly fallen into place, but sadly a few have blown up into political or racial feuds. Some examples:

In Pietermaritzburg, part of the Msunduzi municipal area and the capital city in KwaZulu-Natal province, full consultation of a broad spectrum of communities was undertaken on all the name changes. Their views were seriously considered and the result is a host of new names that are the general consensus of a very high percentage of the people they affect. And so the act can be done in the spirit it is meant!

However, the attempt at the renaming the city of Pretoria, one of the country's three capital cities, has pitted old guard Afrikaner against their nemesis, the ruling ANC party. The greater metropolitan region around Pretoria, which incorporates a number of municipalities, was renamed Tshwane Metropole a while ago. According to the Afrikaners, they did not contest this as they were assured that the actual city would remain Pretoria (as has Pietermaritzburg), a name beloved to them as it was named after one of their *Voortrekker* heroes. However more recently, the Pretoria city council has attempted to change the name of the city to Tshwane too. At the time of going to press, this issue is still raging on with numerous court challenges and counteractions.

In Durban a similar battle is underway, but in this case, two rival black groups are pitted against each other. A few hundred street name changes have been proposed by the ruling ANC party in the eThikwine council, which oversees the greater Durban area, but unfortunately it was done with very limited input or consultation from the very diverse Durban population.

The result is that some of these changes are being opposed by the main opposition parties there: the Inkatha Freedom Party, headed by the traditional leader of the Zulu people, Mangosuthu Buthelezi; and the Democratic Alliance. The ensuing battle raised tempers to levels of violent street protest and rioting, much of which focused on the proposed change of the highway named for the Zulu leader. It is felt that the negative outcome and the host of court cases that follow could so easily have been avoided if the correct procedures had been followed.

NEIGHBOURS

During the apartheid years South Africa's relations with her many neighbours and near-neighbours in sub-Saharan Africa left a lot to be desired. Since the Nationalist government came to power in 1948, all these former colonies have gained independence. They opted for majority rule and, to varying degrees, have been supportive of the ANC in its struggle against apartheid and minority rule in South Africa.

In retaliation, the apartheid government conducted a destabilisation policy in the region. In effect, this meant South Africa attacked the ANC bases in various neighbouring countries, frequently killing large numbers of innocent civilians and damaging property, not to mention violating sovereign territory and enraging governments that were impotent in the face of South Africa's superior military might. South Africa also gave covert, and later quite open, support to anti-communist rebel guerrilla movements like Renamo in Mozambique (which was intent on overthrowing the Marxist Mozambique government) and Unita in Angola (which was fighting the country's left-wing MPLA government).

Now not only are regional links well established, especially as South Africa with its good quality infrastructure is seen as the gateway for trade to and from the rest of the region, but it plays a major role in the African Union and thus in the continent's politics.

A very potted history of each of these countries will be useful in understanding their roles in the region, particularly if you are going to do business with them.

Botswana

The British declared Bechuanaland a protectorate in 1885, but the local chiefs were allowed to rule their people with minimal colonial interference.

Later, having won their battle not to be incorporated into South Africa, their heir apparent, Seretse Khama, married a white British woman, Ruth Williams, in 1948. The major row this caused forced Khama to give up his right to rule. He lived initially as an ordinary citizen, but soon became active in party politics. In 1966, the Republic of Botswana was declared with Sir Seretse Khama (knighted at independence) as its first president. Khama kept the country on a stable, steady and politically moderate path until his death in 1980.

His successor, Dr Quett Masire, who had been vice president and minister of finance, maintained his intimate involvement in the country's economic development. His pivotal role in the country's economic success story led to an annual growth rate of some 8 per cent in the 1980s, substantially higher than the population growth rate. By increasing government spending to improve the infrastructure, Botswana hopes to encourage a strong manufacturing sector and tourism industry to stimulate future growth.

South Africa's relationship with Botswana was probably the most strained during the 1980s when anti-apartheid resistance was at a high point. Having the economic and military upper hand, South Africa could force Botswana to expel the ANC bases despite Botswana being a non-aligned country that was supportive of sanctions and the ANC.

Botswana is a member of the African Union (AU), the United Nations (UN), the Commonwealth and the Non-Alligned Nations. Its principled stand on issues like apartheid and its generally moderate approach have given it an effective voice in many international deliberations.

Zimbabwe

The Republic of Zimbabwe, the internationally recognised successor to the British colony of Southern Rhodesia, arose in April 1980 from the ashes of a 14-year-long civil war between the ruling whites and the African majority. International sanctions and internal guerrilla activity eventually led to the capitulation of the white minority regime, but not before the country was economically on its knees. Many thousands of white Rhodesians migrated to South Africa—at the time, the last bastion in Africa of white minority rule.

Zimbabwe, like Botswana and others, was affected by the instability South Africa wreaked on the region. And, being landlocked, the only route to the coast other than via South Africa was through the newly independent Mozambique. However, South Africa's support for the anti-government guerrilla rebels in that country meant they were constantly able to disrupt this vital rail link.

Unfortunately, the leadership of Zimbabwe's long-time President Robert Mugabe, once a skilled and generally fair leader, has deteriorated to what can only be described as megalomania. In only a few years he, his cronies and his not very democratic government have brought the country to its knees economically and socially with inflation reaching nearly 8,000 per cent by December 2007, the highest in the world.

In elections held in 2008 the opposition leader, Morgan Tsvangirai, was widely held to have trumped Mr Mugabe, despite massive intimidation at the polls by the incumbent regime. However Mr Mugabe would not stand down and a joint government was eventually established under pressure from other African leaders. A very unsuccessful result for democracy and for the resolution of the desperate poverty still facing millions of Zimbabweans.

Namibia

By the early 1890s, the Germans had secured the boundaries of what is now called Namibia. They colonised it and called it South West Africa. The Germans began to set up their administration, but not without resistance from the indigenous people including the Hereros, Namas and other groups. They introduced systems of pass laws and vagrancy laws which severely curtailed the freedom of movement of local people. They confiscated large numbers of their cattle and, as a final onslaught, embarked on a massacre of the Hereros.

At the beginning of World War I, South African forces, fighting on the side of Britain, ended the German occupation of Namibia. In 1920, Namibia came under the administration of South Africa as a League of Nations mandate territory. In theory, South Africa was supposed to promote the "utmost material and moral well-being and social progress of the inhabitants of the territory", but in practice it was administered as a South African colony. Thus when South Africa began to enforce apartheid on her own soil, Namibia got a dose of it too.

The United Nations tried for many years to coerce South Africa into ending racial discrimination and to transfer, progressively, full power to Namibians. But to no avail. Thus a UN resolution was passed in 1966, terminating South Africa's trusteeship of the territory.

At this time, the South West African People's Organisation (SWAPO), an indigenous liberation movement which until then had agitated non-violently for change, launched an armed struggle against South African forces. The battle continued for many years both in the UN and on the ground.

As most of Namibia's resources are in alluvial diamonds and mining (once controlled in large measure by South

Africa's mining mega-conglomerates), South Africa was obviously reluctant to part with this rich cash cow.

The saga is as intricate as a jigsaw puzzle: SWAPO had bases in Angola from which it attacked South Africans in Namibia. There was a civil war in Angola between the left-wing government forces, MPLA, and the guerrilla rebels, Unita. South Africa backed the rebels; and the Cubans helped the MPLA. The escalating cross-border raids led to South Africa invading Angola in 1983 and holding large areas in the south of the country for a prolonged period. Negotiations, five years later, brought to an end these years of conflict and led to Namibia's first general election. SWAPO leader Sam Nujoma became the independent nation's first president in 1990.

Mozambique

The collapse of the dictatorship in Portugal to the left-wing in 1974, led to her pulling out of Africa with major implications for her colonies, especially Mozambique and Angola.

When Mozambique gained independence in 1975 under President Samora Machel, some 90 per cent of the Portuguese population, who represented almost the entire skilled labour force, left the country. Some returned to the motherland, but the majority emigrated to South Africa. The new government formed by the Marxist liberation movement, Frelimo, strongly opposed apartheid and allowed ANC guerrillas to infiltrate and attack South Africa from bases within Mozambique.

In return, South Africa tried to overturn Machel's government by backing the resistance movement, Renamo. This group sabotaged road and rail links, hydroelectric power stations and oil pipelines, as well as waging an out-and-out war and guerrilla atrocities on the pro-Frelimo civilians.

By 1984, Mozambique, being politically and economically battered, signed the Nkomati Accord with South Africa. This was an agreement between the two countries that neither would allow 'enemy bases' on their territory. Two years later, President Samora Machel died in a plane crash many felt was South Africa's doing, although it has not been proven. He was succeeded by Joaquim Chissano. At the end of the decade, the two countries again tried to re-establish relations. South Africa agreed to assist in the rebuilding of the country's infrastructure and re-establish roads, rail and sea links.

One of most serious effects of the civil war, conducted primarily in the bread basket region of the land, is its exacerbation of the severe famine which first threatened some 4.6 million people in 1989. Between 1991–1992, another severe drought and continued hostilities between the Renamo guerrillas and the Mozambican government again led to severe famine and the need for large-scale international relief aid.

In 1992, the Portuguese added their weight to the peace effort and a very tenuous ceasefire began, and with it the rebuilding of the country. General elections have been held regularly and a stable democracy now flourishes which is slowly benefitting economic growth. With the assistance of foreign aid, infrastructure was refurbished and upgraded, the ports and some of the railways and roads again serve this long, narrow country and its landlocked neighbours. Because of its idyllic coastline and its vibey capital Maputo, Mozambique's tourist industry is beginning to flourish.

Angola

Angola, also once a Portuguese territory, gained independence in 1975 after the change of government in Portugal. An internal guerrilla war caused most skilled people to flee the country and left the ruling Marxist-leaning MPLA government with a destroyed infrastructure.

The MPLA refused to share power with any other groups, forcing the opposition to disband or fight. Unita, led by Jonas Savimbi, decided on an armed struggle. Cuban forces entered Angola in a bid to help the ideologically compatible MPLA, while South African troops backed Unita. This war involved varying degrees of intensity, the most severe being in the 1980s when South Africa occupied large tracts of southern Angola for an extensive period.

In August 1988, South Africa announced a ceasefire agreement in Angola. Both South Africa and Cuba slowly withdrew their troops from Angola. Despite sporadic breakdowns due to violations of ceasefire, by 1990, peace in Angola was more than a pipe dream. Both the former Soviet Union and the United States are believed to have exerted pressure for a negotiated settlement.

The multiparty Angolan elections were held in September 1992 with the MPLA winning by a narrow margin. Unfortunately, Unita claimed the elections were unfair despite the opinions to the contrary by a battery of international observers. Sadly, only weeks after the elections a major civil war erupted again. However in February 2002, Jonas Savimbi was killed in battle. This quickly led to a ceasefire in April 2002 and the end of 27 years of civil war.

Since the early 1990s, Angola has found ever larger off-shore oil wealth which should help the war-ravaged land recuperate, but the process is very slow.

Lesotho

Formerly a British protectorate called Basotholand, the independent Kingdom of Lesotho is entirely surrounded by South Africa. It is a parliamentary constitutional monarchy.

The country developed as an impenetrable mountain stronghold in the time of the Mfecane, the great migration of southern African people in the early 1800s. In 1868 Britain annexed Lesotho and from 1930 it became a protectorate run by the local people with minimal intervention. In the 1950s and 1960s Lesotho developed a political awareness and was granted independence in 1966. Chief Leabua Jonathan won the elections to become the first prime minister.

Although Lesotho became a member of the United Nations and the Organisation of African Unity, supporting their stance against apartheid, the harsh reality is that it is surrounded by South Africa and dependent on its economy. Lesotho felt strongly that South Africa meddled in its internal politics during the 1970s and 1980s, and a South African Defence Force raid on an ANC base near Maseru, the capital, killed some 30 ANC members and also 12 innocent civilians. The military coup in 1986 was also blamed on South African intervention as a means of attacking the ANC bases in

Lesotho. Only a week after the coup, ANC members were deported to South Africa and the blockade of the country was lifted.

In 1992, King Moeshoeshoe who had fled into exile due to internal strife, returned to Lesotho from the United Kingdom. His son is now head of state and the country elects a government every five years.

Swaziland

Once a British Protectorate, the Kingdom of Swaziland is a tiny independent country surrounded by South Africa on three sides, with Mozambique on its eastern border. Like Lesotho, its national unity was formed at the time of the Mfecane. Around the turn of the century, South Africa tried to gain control of Swaziland from the British, but no sooner had they negotiated this than the Anglo-Boer War broke out and Swaziland was returned to British administration.

In 1967, Swaziland was granted self-government and the following year, independence. The tribal leader, King Sobhuza, became head-of-state and in 1973 he abolished parliament taking all power into his own hands. A benevolent dictator, he ruled until his death in August 1982.

Although neither for nor against the ANC, Swaziland was used as a conduit for ANC infiltration from Mozambique into South Africa. This led to South Africa attacking the ANC in Swaziland despite requests to respect its neutrality and sovereignty. Simultaneously, Swaziland was used as an 'address' for South African sanction busting.

After the king's death, various groups jockeying for power led to a degree of internal instability which was halted when one of his hundreds of children, King Mswati III, was crowned in 1986. He has followed in his father's footsteps by taking many wives, but unlike his father is not a great leader, is not at all keen on sharing power or in embracing democracy in any way and has banned vocal opposition parties. He rules by decree.

Nevertheless Swaziland has a fairly successful economy, dependent in large measure on its extremely viable sugar industry.

OUR PEOPLE: A MULTICOLOURED TAPESTRY

CHAPTER 3

'My humanity is bound up in yours,
for we can only be human together.'
—Desmond Tutu, South Africa Anglican archbishop
and Nobel Peace laureate.

WHEN SOUTH AFRICA'S 'FIRST CLERIC' and moral barometer, Archbishop Desmond Tutu, coined the phrase 'Rainbow Nation'—made immediately popular by then President Nelson Mandela—he surely had no idea how quickly and willingly the country would adopt it as our mantra. Perhaps it was simple proof of how many had yearned for so long to be able to celebrate together their multicoloured tapestry of differences, their differences in creed, in origin, in their backgrounds, in cultural histories and contemporary culture, and to let go of the simplistic differentiation based solely on colour or race that had been used to drive wedges between people so forcibly in the past.

Most South Africans learned quickly to appreciate the diversity and cultural richness in the country and also how to benefit from the edge it can give us when we deal with the vagaries of our daily lives. More often than not, the focus now is on mixing, not dividing, and this is best witnessed among the younger generations. The younger people were in 1994 (when South Africa became a democracy), the more naturally they slipped into the new 'normal'. Just recently I saw a snapshot of the now, the reality: a friend's teenage son and some of his friends were walking down the street in our neighbourhood. The cameo could not have been more representative—some shorter, some taller, paler and darker, straight blond hair and curly dark hair, all wearing the ubiquitous teenage gear. They were jesting and laughing and horsing around, quite oblivious to the fact that for many of us this was light years away from what our teenager years looked like!

Some parts of cities and towns are more mixed than others and some towns and cities themselves are more multicultural than others, but generally in most public areas, especially urban areas, shops and malls, in parks and restaurants people mix and mingle easily and freely. Sadly this is less the case in most residential areas, mostly because it just takes longer for people to move home. Now, at least, when people do move home, their choices are made more on the usual grounds as it is anywhere else in the world—and not on where you may or may not live based on your race.

Many families prefer to stay in the townships as they like the vibe or would miss the network of friends, relatives, near-family and family. Others, often the younger ones, have chosen to move to new areas, often into new lifestyles. And in some cases, groups of people joined by some commonality move into a particular suburb. A wonderful example which could well be set for the Middle East, is leafy, peaceful Greenside in Johannesburg: once a predominantly Jewish neighbourhood, it now also has a sufficiently large Muslim community to warrant the building of a mosque in the area.

CELEBRATING OUR RACIAL DIFFERENCES

Although it may seem to be playing into the hands of that totally discredited and destroyed philosophy—apartheid—it is worth understanding the cultural heritage of South Africa's different people. We are as different as day and night, dusk and dawn, sun and moon, but are now forged into a new life where equality pervades.

Africans

The ethnic history of the many culturally diverse indigenous tribes in South Africa is so complex that it has inspired hundreds of books and research documents. It is totally beyond the scope of this book to even begin to do justice to this subject, but I will attempt to give you a very potted description of the different tribes and I hope you will get some feeling of how unique each is.

The Tribes—In Brief

The origins of the various tribes lie in the sub-Saharan indigenous people who split into two groups thousands of years ago. The *San*, or Bushmen, inhabited the southern portion of the continent and the Negroids lived in the forested areas of Central Africa. Later they migrated south and population movements over the years have resulted in the different groups being mixed to some extent.

The following is a quick description of some random cultural traits of the African tribes, some, albeit very few now, of whom still live in much the same way as they did thousands of years ago. This information is a way of superficially letting you in on conversation where otherwise words like Xhosa or Venda may draw a complete blank. But remember, however, that South African society is changing very fast and some of the traditions have been modified or dropped, especially by the city-dwellers.

Xhosa An oral tradition traces this tribe back to a mythological founder named Xhosa, but it is also possible the word means 'angry men'. Because their traditional area falls into the Cape region, they came into early contact with Westerners. Nelson Mandela and many other high profile political leaders come from this group.

To those Xhosas leading a traditional lifestyle—and there are ever fewer as people adopt modern ways through urbanisation—social groupings and marriage are very important. Marriage is more than just the bond between man and woman, it is the joining together of two clans. Hence members of the same clan are not allowed to be married.

Bride price, or *lobola*, is paid in this culture as it is in almost all traditional African tribes. Once married, the bride moves from her family home to that of her husband's and his extended family.

The huts in the *kraal*, or homestead area, are organised in a hierarchical order and the families living there are almost always related to the headman. As an outsider, a wife improves her status and secures her position in the extended family by having her husband's children.

Young children are treated with great tolerance by the older relatives and learn by imitating their elders. Once old enough they are expected to help with chores like cattle herding and bringing water from the nearest source, perhaps a river. Boys are initiated into manhood by a circumcision ritual where their survival skills are tested by living alone in and off the bush for a few weeks or months.

The chief is the head of the tribe, and he is invariably the wealthiest man and the main religious leader in the group. Tradition requires that he rule by consensus so his power is limited by his counsellors and public opinion.

Ancestor worship forms the basis of the Xhosa's spiritual belief and kinship relationships apply in the world hereafter. Xhosa diviners communicate with their ancestors in seances. Herbalists treat both people and animals through their intimate knowledge of natural medicine, rather than supernatural intervention as in some other tribes.

Zulu In the 18th century, the Zulus were a small group but rose to fame under Shaka who usurped the Zulu throne and, with the help of his mighty army, unified the many independent chiefdoms into one powerful nation. By his death in 1828, the might of the Zulus was well established. Today the Zulus still revere their king, who like tribal leaders in some of the other provinces, heads the House of Traditional Leaders in KwaZulu-Natal.

In very traditional societies, girls and boys go through many ceremonies to mark their passage into adulthood and their readiness for marriage. An example is ear piercing of children just before they reach puberty. This ceremony is accompanied by much festivity. Over the years, the holes in the earlobes are made ever bigger and often adorned with traditional earrings made of decorated wood. (You can

The House of Traditional Leaders was established at national level so that people living under traditional law and custom had influence in government and the way the country is run.

sometimes buy these colourful earings at the Mai Mai market in downtown Johannesburg.) Traditional marriage ceremonies will include the practice of *lobola*.

Traditional Zulus believe in an all-powerful being called 'Older-Than-Old' with whom ancestors act as intermediaries. For the treatment of medical problems, an *isangoma*, or diviner, is approached. In Zulu culture, this term refers to a herbalist or spiritualist.

Ndebele They have been settled in the northeastern part of the country among the Sotho tribes for many, many years and thus their culture and language have come to resemble Sotho in many ways.

Now divided into Southern and Northern Ndebele, their traditional ceremonies come from their Zulu/Nguni origin and some are also borrowed from their Sotho neighbours. Ceremonies play a major role as they can draw a whole village together in sadness or in joy.

Traditional homes are usually rectangular (but can be round too) with mud walls, thatched roofs and cow-dung floors. A distinct characteristic of the Ndebele homestead is the beautiful patterns and colours painted on the walls of both the homestead buildings and the wall surrounding it. These artistic skills are handed down by the women to the young girls before they reach puberty.

Very similar patterns, colours and themes to the wall paintings are used in making the beaded jewellery and garments worn during special tribal functions. The older beadwork and wall decorations tend to be more stylised and geometric in design, whereas some of the designs today incorporate modern technological symbols like aeroplanes or street lights. (Ndebele beadwork can often be bought in craft shops and markets in the bigger cities.)

Although beads are not as important to Ndebele men as they are to women, there are times when men are expected to wear them as charms. Also, by being passed down from father to son, they can symbolise the continuity of generations.

Ancestor worship is part of the Ndebele culture seen in the 'throwing of the bones' for divination. The diviner has a whole assortment of materials including sea shells, stones and bones of small animals which are thrown together onto the ground. The pattern they fall in is read, interpreted and used to provide solutions to problems or events that need explanation.

The Sotho Groups Together the Sotho groups make up about 30 per cent of the country's African population. Because of the many generations of contact between them and the other main group, the Nguni, many of the distinctions between the two groups are quite blurred. There are four main groups: North Sotho, Lobedu, South Sotho and Tswana.

North Sotho It is thought that they occupied a large area north of Gauteng mostly in what is now Limpopo province from about AD 400. A large group of this tribe, called the Pedi, live in Sekhukhuneland and have been there since about the 17th century. Their economy is based on agriculture and animal husbandry and they possess a detailed knowledge of soils and plants. Land is communally owned and most of the tilling is done by the women. Homesteads consist of one or more thatched huts with a verandah and mud walls around the circumference of each hut.

Both boys and girls have initiation rights where they receive instruction on the relative relationships between men and women, and are taught respect for their cultural values and customs. After these initiation ceremonies, they are welcomed into society as adults and allowed to marry.

The Pedi believe that the world was created by Kgobe and that his son, Kgobeane, created the human race. The power of ancestors is important to the Pedi, who also respect the role of diviners and herbalists.

Lobedu (pronounced lovedu) Unique to southern Africa is the fact that they have a woman ruler, Mujaji, the Rain Queen. Although she is the pivotal point and source of strength to the tribe, her powers rest not on military might, but on her ability to make rain—and on a network of political marriages. The queen is considered of divine origin and has a special affinity with nature. The role of ancestors is important in daily life and shrines of stones, earth mounds or sacred plants are made in their honour.

South Sotho Many South Sothos live in what is now the independent kingdom of Lesotho, a tiny mountainous country totally surrounded by South Africa. Homes in this mountainous area are made of stones and covered with thatched roofs. They are well known for their Basotho ponies which are small and extremely nimble on the rocky mountain passes.

Their kinship beliefs grant more recognition to relatives on the mother's side than most other southern African tribes. Polygamy, although permitted, is reserved for the wealthy and is on the decline. Initiation occurs for boys and girls and begins with a feast. The boys are circumcised and isolated for a while, whereas the girls receive instruction on the role of women in their society and their behaviour with men.

They believe in a supreme creator, Modimo, and ancestors play a pivotal role in their religious life. Bone-throwing diviners and herbalists form part of a complicated system to ward off evil spirits, induce rain and protect the tribe from natural occurrences like lightning.

Tswana Tswana traditions indicate that their ancestors came in several migrations from lands north of what is now South Africa. Due to quarrels in the distant past and also the vast amount of land in the areas they lived in, the Tswana tribe now consists of over 50 different groups. They lived in very large villages of up to 20,000 people, probably for reasons of defence as they are not naturally warlike.

They run a mixed economy of cattle farming and agriculture on commonly-owned land. The Tswana make excellent crafts: the men work with skin, bone and metal, while women make pots. Both are adept at making baskets. Initiation rites take place for both boys and girls after which they are allowed to marry.

The Shangaan Originally they lived in the Mozambique area (where many still do) and as far down the east coast as Durban, but they moved inland to areas in Mpumalanga and Limpopo provinces as well.

Their homesteads are individual units that are separated from one another, instead of being grouped into villages. The buildings are usually in a circle and often surrounded by some trees, one of which is considered to be sacred. This sacred tree is specially chosen and on which they nail the skulls of the cattle slaughtered in rituals. The entire area is then enclosed by a fence which is sometimes made out of living trees.

Children are taught the customs of their culture as early as possible and after completing their initiation they are allowed to begin courting. Marriages are marked in three stages: a go-between calls at the chosen girl's village, the *lobola* is negotiated, then the young girl makes a show of reluctance, but then joins her husband.

Venda The Venda, who live in the northern part of the country, have a culture and language quite different from the other southern Africans. As their oral tradition explains, they may have moved into this area from around Lake Malawi before the 17th century.

They live in relatively large villages strategically placed on hill sides, with fencing or walls for protection. Traditional huts are made of stakes or built out of stone, with thatched roofs and verandas for protection from the sun and also for added storage space. The Venda are one of most accomplished groups of traditional potters in the whole region. Pots are made by women without a wheel, and the quality and designs are excellent. Men do metal work and used to use ant hills as forges and animal skins as bellows to make everyday-work items like hoes.

Ancestor worship is central to their religion and they believe in a complex system of ancestral spirits. Diviners, herbalists and medicine men play a vital role in protecting people against witchcraft.

Coloureds

The origins of the Coloureds, or people of mixed race, go back to the Cape region around the 17th century when many of the *Khoikhoi* mixed with and married the early Dutch sailors (who were of course all men). At the same time, Malay women were brought to the Cape as wives for Dutch sailors and settlers. Thus the Malay cultural heritage was also added to this community. Recently, some in the community have looked more seriously to their Islamic roots, following the Muslim faith more closely.

In the latter part of the 1800s, the Coloured people found their skills as craftsmen, artisans, fishermen and farm labourers in great demand as the Cape Colony developed. They also had the vote because the British ran the colony on a colour-blind franchise. But this 100-year-old right was ended by the apartheid government in one of the most despicable acts of constitutional gerrymandering. The right was removed despite a long, bitter and determined struggle in the courts by the Coloured community and the opposition whites.

Coloureds Aren't White?

One of the enduring myths of racist South Africa was that the Coloured people were a separate group like the Africans or Indians. In reality they spoke the same languages— Afrikaans and English, practised the same religions—mostly Protestant—and had the same aspirations towards Western culture and values. The only thing that made them different from the whites was the status that apartheid and its racial cornerstone, the Population Registration Act, gave them— based on the darker hues of their skin. Today, a growing number of the Coloured community, particularly those of Malay descent, are embracing the Islamic faith.

Coloured Heritage

To experience some of the wit and exuberance of the Coloureds in Cape Town, just stop and chat with the flower sellers or fruit and vegetable hawkers in Adderly Street. You may not be able to keep up with the speed of their chatter, but their humour is unique and their laughter is totally infectious. In fact, this wit was one of the things I was often homesick for in the years I lived abroad.

Every year the community holds a minstrel carnival which begins at New Year and lasts into January where groups of brightly clad minstrels, many made up with clown faces, dance and sing traditional folk songs. A lot of merriment is made by participants and spectators alike.

The Coloured community has contributed some superb literature to the South African culture, with Adam Small, Sol Plaatjies and Don Mattera being a few of their best known.

Chinese

The current Chinese community, one of the smallest minority groups in South Africa, developed from sporadic migrations from 1891 onwards until racist laws in the 1960s put a stop to it, except spouses of Chinese-South Africans. Then in the last decade or so before independence there was quite keen immigration by Taiwanese. Taiwan was one of the few countries which had overt trade relations with South Africa during the dying days of apartheid.

The Early Arrivals

The early immigrants were mostly of Cantonese origin, traders who arrived via Madagascar and Mauritius. With the discovery of diamonds and then gold, many moved towards Kimberley and the Johannesburg area, but then moved again to the seaports and the interior with the onset of the Anglo-Boer War (1899–1902). Today there are Chinese in most major urban centres with the Johannesburg area having the biggest community.

In 1904, when the country needed additional labour for post-war reconstruction, many thousands of Chinese labourers were recruited for this and also to work on the gold mines. However, the present Chinese community did not originate from these labourers as they were all repatriated by 1910.

Neither Here Nor There

Under apartheid, the Chinese occupied a strange and demeaning position. Although classified as Asian and hence 'non-white' with no vote, they could access white privileges by applying for permits to live in white neighbourhoods or to attend 'whites-only' schools and hospitals. This left them in a no-man's land as they were informally accepted by the white community but not officially part of it, nor were they formally part of the black community that comprised all those fighting for political rights.

Chinese Heritage

The earlier generations were mostly traders—wholesalers and retailers—and their driving ambition was their children's entry into university. One of the strongest Chinese values still existing in the community is the respect for education and career success. Today, most Chinese are successful professionals or business people living in good neighbourhoods, while their children go to good schools.

Most of them retain a respect for traditional Chinese values and customs especially for major events like birth, marriage and death; but other Chinese customs are not rigidly followed. Many have lost contact with Buddhism and are now Christians. Also, few of the younger generation have much more than a tenuous grasp of any of the Chinese languages.

If you take a stroll in the Chinese area of Sydenham in Johannesburg as well as the much older and now very tiny Chinese area in downtown central Johannesburg, you will still find old, traditional Chinese folk running some of the provision stores that stock a wonderment of culinary and other domestic Chinese delights.

Indians
How They Came

In the mid-19th century, the European sugar cane planters needed labour skilled in this area of agriculture, so they recruited workers from the Indian subcontinent. Most of these initial immigrants were Hindus, but there were also a number of Muslims, Christians and other religious groups among the arrivals. Although imported primarily to work on the sugar plantations, they had an assortment of skills and soon a number were absorbed into other businesses. Over the next five decades, some 150,000 Indians were attracted by the prospects of trade in the new colony and emigrated to South Africa. Most of them came to the country under contract and were indentured to their employers for periods of at least three to five years before they were free to work as they pleased. Conditions on the plantations were harsh and often the Indians were seen as units of work, not human beings.

Indian Influence

Today the majority of the million-strong Indian population still lives in Durban and other areas of KwaZulu-Natal. Some have spread throughout the country, mostly to urban areas where they are successfully involved in the professions, business and commerce, and trading.

Classified as 'Asians' under apartheid and forced to live and trade in segregated areas, the most wonderful Indian markets and bazaars have developed within these communities. There, traditional food and spices add exotic colour and aroma to a buzzing atmosphere. Garments, particularly *saris* (the traditional dress of Indian women); traditional household goods; and jewellery and trinkets are imported from the motherland and sold alongside normal day-to-day fare.

Civil Rights: A Burning Issue

Not all the Indian immigrants were labourers. Some of higher caste came on their own as traders and merchants. Very soon they were selling not only to the Africans and Indians, but to the white community as well. Wealthier, more confident and ambitious, they formed an elite group that soon drew together to fight for political and civil rights.

In 1893, Mahatma Gandhi was thrown out of a train in South Africa because he refused to move out of a 'whites-only' compartment. He had come to South Africa to defend a court case but ended up spending 20 years in the country, being a key figure in the Indian protest movement.

A crucial event in Indian political history was the formation of the Natal Indian Congress (NIC) in 1894, which was set up to fight for their rights. The NIC and the Transvaal Indian Congress were very active in the struggle against apartheid and very active within the ANC. They were totally against the formation of the tricameral parliament—where the Indians and Coloureds each had a separate and inferior House to the whites.

A number of very prominent Indian politicians have been appointed to positions in the post-apartheid governments.

Whites

The white population of South Africa is as diverse as the others. Its heritage is mostly European, with a wide variety of cultures from the north, south and west of Europe. Nevertheless, it is fair to say that although they are proud of and indulge in their Portuguese, British, Greek or whatever heritage, they are first and foremost South Africans.

Wipe The Stereotypes Away

An internationally stereotyped and sometimes inaccurate view of white South Africans is that the Boers or Afrikaners are the baddies, the racists and the perpetrators of apartheid; while the English are the goodies, liberal in their political views and keen for the best deal for all South Africans. This can often be correct, but beware.

There are the liberal English, the Helen Suzmans of this world. She spent 36 years in Parliament, 13 of them as the sole representative of liberal democratic values, tirelessly fighting the apartheid government. But there are also the Afrikaners who have fought for human rights and a world view of democracy. Look at internationally famous author Breyten Breytenbach who spent seven years in jail for working with the ANC, and then had to live in exile until the apartheid walls came tumbling down. Karl Niehaus is another white Afrikaner who is a high ranking, highly regarded member of the ANC, as is Alec Irwin who has been a minister of the post-apartheid government.

Then you will find the occasional rural white Boer farmer who may even refer to his black labour in unacceptable words, but will rush them hundreds of kilometres to the nearest doctor when they are ill—and his kind is not that of the affluent land baron, but rather salt of the earth people, struggling to make a meagre living. Once I heard of a woman in the Free State who does the farm labourers' washing and ironing for them because, "Ag shame (a colloquial expression of sympathy), they don't have any electricity so I have to help them." I don't know any city-slickers who would go to those lengths. But these are the exceptions.

On the flip side of the coin, there are numerous stories of 'liberal white English' families treating their domestic workers like slaves, paying them peanuts for working hours that went out with the Dark Ages—and then when they couldn't cope with the situation in the country or the transformation to majority rule, just walked away from their staff leaving them with no pension or means of support after some 20 or 30 years of service.

It cuts both ways so it's best to ensure you are not drawn into either faction inadvertently. And another word of advice: you are sure at some stage to hear people, usually whites, referring to others as "them", often with a capital T and in snide tones. This is just a slightly more subtle way of using racist slander and gossip and it is still just as discriminatory and hurtful. Again, my advice is: Don't be drawn in.

RACISIM DOESN'T DIE OVERNIGHT

Unfortunately, it is a universal fact that racism still exists all over the world no matter how hard we try to eradicate it. In a land where it has been institutionalized and ingrained in people for more than four decades, mindsets are even harder to change. So don't be surprised if you run into it, or even if you find it directed at you. But equally, don't go about looking for racial insults as this may lead you to interpret things wrongly. As always for a newcomer, the best route is to walk away from it, but remember that the vast majority of South Africans will be only too keen to jump to your defence. Don't let the small minority spoil it for you.

Racial animosity in South Africa is not just the often discussed white/black issue. In the past there were any number of clashes between various groups which still fuels problems. For example, the Boer War led to most English and Afrikaans South Africans of the time detesting each other;

there was, in the 1990s and to some extent still is, little love lost between the ANC and the mainly Zulu Inkatha Freedom Party; and some of the Afrikaners have split into groups that are irreconcilable.

But under South Africa's new dispensation, these gripes of the past have become so much less significant as most South Africans are trying to put their differences aside and get on with creating the so-called Rainbow Nation. The constitution also enshrines peoples' rights to their differences and laws can come down harshly on racist behaviour.

COOL DUDES OF THE TOWNSHIPS, HIP MALL TRAWLERS

There are numerous counter-culture youth groups spread across the sprawling townships. They are young and hip, cool dudes who wouldn't be seen dressed in anything other than that dictated by their peers—it might be trousers with an immaculate crease down the legs, or two-tone black and white brogue shoes which could be the flare of the moment. They speak in jargon, fast and fun. Some revere the life and times of Sophiatown (Johannesburg's African township in the 1950s, the forerunner to Soweto): a hotbed of artistic creativity, life and love, music, music and more music. Miriam Makeba, one of South Africa's most famous singers was discovered in Sophiatown.

Of course as racial barriers fall—far more quickly among the youth as they are all at school or university together—so they adopt what is cool, new and trendy in attitude, lifestyle, clothes and music from across the local and, of course, international spectrum.

IGNORANCE IS BLISS, BUT IT'S GETTING BETTER

Don't be too surprised if you meet a South African who doesn't even know that your home country exists, unless it is one of the biggies. International and geographic isolation in the past due to sanctions, added to a less than perfect education in many cases, has led to some fairly under-informed people. Not all, of course, and far less often than in the past now that South Africa is exposed to much the same barrage of information as any other country, and of course the Internet is here. In addition, the government is often very active in African and international politics.

And just because some people are ignorant of factual information doesn't necessarily prevent them from having a lot of strong, and strange opinions.

THAT SOUTH AFRICAN-NESS

Despite apartheid, or perhaps because of it, a South African-ness exists about all the people living here, not the least of which is a deep affection for the country, the land itself. Sometimes this is reflected in rather nationally chauvinistic ways. You may well hear a South African telling the crowds that "we have the best beaches/beer/soccer players/climate in the world". If you should be so silly as to try to discuss the virtues of say Sydney's Bondi Beach, or Munich's best Bavarian brew, France's Zinedine Zidane or southern California's blue heavens, you may well find your words falling on deaf ears. This is partly because the person making these wild and gauche statements doesn't want to know that anything better or even comparable exists, and partly because they are quite likely to have never left their home turf or perhaps never even left their hometown. Bear with them. They usually mean well.

A far less pleasant trait is the often vehement xenophobia meted out to other Africans who dare to cross our borders in search of work or a better life. They are often blamed for the high crime rates even though there is no evidence that they are more or less involved than their South Africans counterparts. Some South Africans defend their views saying that these other Africans "take our jobs". Rarely do we hear how our country benefits from the different skills and trades they may bring with them. Hopefully, as the economy creates more jobs, so will their vehemence against fellow Africans fall away.

To really get to know South Africans don't let stereotypes get in the way. This way you will make a wonderful, motley crew of new-found friends.

> **Discrimination is a No-No At Any Level**
>
> Section 9 of the Constitution of the Republic of South Africa, entitled 'Equality', states: "The state may not unfairly discriminate directly or indirectly against anyone on one or more grounds, including race, gender, sex, pregnancy, marital status, ethnic or social origin, colour, sexual orientation, age, disability, religion, conscience, belief, culture, language and birth."
>
> This sentiment also applies to individuals, organisations, companies, corporations —absolutely no discrimination is tolerated—and this can be enforced by law. That is not to say there is none! Simply that the law is totally on the side of someone who is being discriminated against.

THE 'FAIRER SEX'—DON'T EVEN GO THERE

Until South Africa embraced its new constitution in 1997, women, no matter which group in society they belonged to, were less than equal to men and often discriminated against. Now equality of all people is entrenched in the constitution and enforceable by law. This is a substantial change from earlier days where discrimination was rooted in the legal system. A man was deemed the automatic head of the household and this most often permeated all areas of society including the workplace.

In a large part of the white society, such opinions were further entrenched by the views of the dominant Calvinistic churches, while in African society tribal tradition rarely accorded women the same status as men. This meant women had to strive far harder than men just to find employment, let alone be acknowledged in their careers or as experts in their fields.

Rooted In The Law but...

Even though the law protects women fully from discrimination and in theory anyone can reach any position—in the workplace, in politics, the home—it is a much harder task to ensure that all people think, act and behave in accordance with the law! But views and attitudes are changing, again often more quickly among the young.

EQUAL RIGHTS

Ever since the 1994 democratic elections, the country has had an admirably large number of women in parliament and government in general, more than most other countries. Sadly the same cannot be said of big business. Here to a fairly large extent the new black elite have followed the route of their white predecessors with far fewer women than men in really top jobs. But the imbalance improves continually and ever more women push their way to the top. At least this is the case in the urban areas.

In the rural areas it is a little different and a lot more complex, as African women are able to elect to live by customary law and many still do as they feel it is their cultural heritage. Customary marriage laws, however, can disadvantage women as, for example, they allow for polygamy and a fair amount of male dominance, but at least now under the constitution these women have recourse to the law if they are unhappy with their lot.

GAY AND LESBIAN RIGHTS UP IN LIGHTS

Gay and lesbian South Africans were the first in the world to have their right to equality entrenched in a constitution. This is because our constitution is the first in the world to prohibit unfair discrimination based on the grounds of 'sexual orientation'. These words were specifically included in the section prohibiting discrimination, alongside race, gender, ethnicity, religion and the likes, because it was recognised that they too had suffered injustices in the same manner as many other groups had.

In the past sex between two people of the same gender was a crime and public displays of affection could—and did—lead to abuse and violence. Gay people were often harassed, blackmailed, refused employment and could lose custody of their children in a divorce.

Now even gay marriage has been legalised. At the end of 2006, the Civil Union Bill was passed into law, after the government was forced to address this issue by the Constitutional Court. This gives gays the right to a full, legal marriage—the only country in Africa and one of only five in the world where this is permitted at present. And the first couple to wed under this new law were game rangers who had their wedding on the first day after the law came into effect—International Aids Day, 1 December 2006. The couple, who run a guest lodge and an animal rehabilitation centre, Tony Halls and Vernon Gibbs, wore traditional game ranger outfits—khakis and leather boots. Said Vernon, "South Africa has the most progressive constitution in the world which protects all people against discrimination. No gay could wish for a better constitution."

But as with so much in a country making so many changes in a relatively short time, not everyone has caught up with the law. There are still South Africans who oppose homosexuality and gay marriage and who vociferously denounce it is un-African. People are still discriminated against and abused; but at least the law is on their side!

From a lifestyle point of view, there is a lot going on in South Africa for the gay community: clubs, forums, film festivals, specifically gay media and websites, and

Game rangers Tony Halls (*left*) and Vernon Gibbs: the first gay couple to marry legally in South Africa. The couple runs Arendhoogte Guest Lodge and an animal sanctuary near the town of George.

like elsewhere in the world, gay-friendly establishments often indicate their hospitality with the rainbow symbol. Most big cities have a thriving gay community, and Johannesburg and Cape Town have an annual great Gay Pride march and celebration. In addition, Cape Town's cloudy tablecloth that so often envelops the world famous Table Mountain now often has a glorious pink glow, well at least metaphorically, as the city has gone out of its way to embrace gay tourism too.

A NEW SOCIETY: JOIN IN, FIT IN

CHAPTER 4

'Knowing the past helps you imagine the road ahead.'
—Alpha Oumar Konare, former president of Mali

South Africa has undergone one of the most exciting phases of political and social change in its entire history over that last decade and more, discarding structures, some of which had existed for over 300 years. Some of the old laws have been thrown out and with them the legalised discrimination, racism and in many instances, the narrow-minded bigotry that underscored so much of life till the last decade of the last century. Now South Africans are discovering that the generally deep-seated moral or ethical values that make up the backbone of almost all societies in the world, are certainly prevalent across the board in this country too. It is mostly only culture or religion that differentiate various groups and this creates an exciting tapestry of diversity.

Generally, the deep-seated human values like concern for the under-privileged, the need to protect our environment, or parents' responsibility to their children and their desire to see their children have the best education they can, are similar across all cultures.

But there are differences in attitudes to matters like divorce, single-parent families, premarital sex and extramarital children; and differences in customs at weddings, funerals, and birthdays for instance. People's approach to life can also be quite different in the urban compared to the rural areas—the latter usually being more conservative, but often also more friendly and generous with their time.

In addition, as South Africa carves a whole new image for itself, so there are trends, mannerisms, ways of talking, of being, of living, that are being developed, changed and improved on, on an ongoing basis and this makes living in the country right now very exciting. Challenging too, but never dull.

MAKING FRIENDS

South Africans are a very mixed bag. We have a very wide variety of indigenous people, but add to the melting pot the new and not-so-new immigrants from almost every country in the world and you are almost reaching United Nations' levels. To really know and enjoy the country it makes a lot of sense to try to meet, mix and socialise with as wide a section of society as you can. This is not always as easy as it should be as the remnants of apartheid still separate people residentially to some degree, but it is well worth the effort of transcending these geographic boundaries.

Put shyness, preconceived ideas, fears and prejudices aside. Try to communicate with anyone and everyone you meet—in the street, in shops, at work, everywhere. Mostly you will be pleasantly surprised at the easy rapport you will establish with the most unlikely of people. If you have a moment, ask them about their lives, their homes, their families. Explain that you are a newcomer to the country and want to learn to love it, all of it! Always be a ready listener as you can learn so much that way which may be invaluable later in a work or social context. Also remember that your accent may be much harder for us to understand than you imagine, and likewise, our many different accents will certainly confuse you at times, so just laugh and try again!

THE MANY FACES OF COMMUNICATION
Greetings

There are ever so many different ways of greeting people in South Africa and much of it depends on the culture and language of the person concerned. But as a general rule, do greet people whenever and wherever possible—99 times out of a 100, it is worth the effort.

Any traditionally Western person is quite accustomed to the quick "good morning" or "good afternoon" as you rush by. But for almost all black people—urban and the more traditional—such a greeting is seen as pretty impolite. Much more importance is placed on greeting someone and exchanging a few pleasantries, so it may well be necessary to say a bit more (and mean it) than a rushed "good day" by adding a few questions like "How are you doing?", "Is all well today?", "Is your family well?" or anything else that crosses your mind—and do remember to await the reply and to answer the questions that are put to you. It costs very little time, yet builds strong bridges and working relationships. They of course will greet you in the same way.

For example, when you walk into someone's office to begin a meeting with them, or walk onto a factory floor to issue an instruction, it is courteous to first have a discussion with the person about their family or some other matter of social intercourse and only then launch into the business of the day.

The Handshake and Beyond

When meeting a person for the first time, men are almost always expected to shake hands —just grasp right hand to right hand and shake. More often women meeting men follow this ritual too, while women meeting women may shake hands or may verbalise "good to meet you" or a similar expression, and also nod an acknowledgement.

In a social situation, once you are much more familiar with people, you may find that men will greet women friends with a kiss on the cheek, while they will greet each other with a handshake, and some will give each other a hug. In a business environment it is appropriate for women to greet male colleagues with either a nod or a handshake. A kiss would of course be way too familiar for the business community.

The African Handshake

This is more often used in the black community, so you would use it more particularly when meeting or greeting black people, to indicate solidarity and affiliation with the non-racial ethos and politics of the country. For example, I tend to use it when I meet and greet all black friends, colleagues or people new to me. I have also noticed this handshake more and more among those whites who are clearly (overtly or not) keen to indicate that our differences are melting away and we are all becoming so much more at ease with our non-racial life.

How is it done: First you shake in the Western way, then without letting go slip your hand around each other's thumbs, then back again into the traditional grasp. Give it a go. But if, by mistake, you forget or get it wrong, don't worry! No one would hold it against you.

Swearing is a 'No-No' But...

Generally swearing is not acceptable in 'polite' South African society, but that is not to say you don't hear a fair amount of it. Swearing in front of women and children is certainly frowned on, especially the more vulgar kind, while in all-male company swear words are more frequently sprinkled into conversation. But circumstances and situations vary according to the group you are with, the age, your familiarity with each other and a host of other factors. A safe rule is not

to swear at all until you know the people you are with well enough, then you will be able to gauge for yourself.

On the odd occasion you may be shocked to hear someone using quite foul language in a situation where it seems certainly inappropriate. Your best route is to ignore it, as very often people are not speaking their mother tongue, and may thus use swear words they have heard but have very little grasp of the real meaning, implication or offensiveness. As always, things are more easy-going among the younger generations.

Words like 'damn' or 'blasted', 'Oh god', and 'Jesus' which is often pronounced 'jeez' do not usually cause major offence; but left out of your conversation will certainly make integration easier. The F-word is certainly a 'no-no' until you are very familiar with your crowd, and even then it is best avoided. That's not to say you won't see and hear it used both in company and in the media and movies, so if it offends you be prepared to shut your ears a little.

The When-We (Were Back Home) Saga

One of the easiest ways to lose new-found friends and alienate yourself from your new community is to harp on, too loud and too long, about all the good things you left behind. Keep comparisons or complaints about what you don't have, can't get or have left behind, to yourself. Such feelings are natural to newcomers, but your hosts won't necessarily understand that, and are unlikely to be too sympathetic. Focusing on what is new, fun and positive in South Africa will be of far more use to you and will ingratiate you with your hosts and your host nation.

Remember many South Africans will be much worse off than you are, especially financially and materially. Their options, choices and quality of life may be far more limited than yours. Many may never have had the opportunity to leave South Africa, some may not even have left their home town, even for a holiday.

South Africa is geographically fairly remote from many parts of the world and so most people will be naturally curious about your origins. By all means discuss your country, your home and your culture to bring about understanding, but it is best not to use it as a comparison to put South Africa and South Africans down.

NAMES THAT DIVIDE...IF YOU MUST

Even though the apartheid era is over, race is often still a sensitive issue. And because it can be near impossible to avoid using racial descriptions on occasion, do exercise tact and sensitivity. Since it might be necessary occasionally to describe people by colour or creed, it's best you know which words are acceptable.

Black When used as a political term as in 'black liberation movement' or 'black economic empowerment', it applies to Africans, Indians and Coloured people. 'Previously disadvantaged' is totally PC in South Africa and is used often, as in "BEE is used to benefit the previously disadvantaged people". Black can occasionally refer to Africans only as in 'black culture', but as the lines between groups blur so does the word and you could just as easily just leave it out or use some other form of description. There is no harm in using it to describe a person, as in 'black woman', but ONLY if there is reason to distinguish colour, otherwise using just 'woman' will win you many more friends.

White Refers to anyone of European descent and is quite okay to use if you need to. However, the apartheid engendered 'non-white' which meant everyone else in the entire county is a total 'no-no'.

Coloured Refers to people of mixed race, a group made distinct by apartheid despite their very similar heritage to the Afrikaners. Also occasionally referred to as the 'Bruin Afrikaners' or Brown Afrikaners, more so in the southern parts of the country.

Asian Now Asian is used in descriptive ways as in the population census, but rarely is there any other need to use it collectively. In the apartheid race classification, 'Asian' was used to refer to almost anyone with roots in the Indian subcontinent and Asia. Many Indians and Chinese find it extremely offensive, especially as it takes no cognisance of the vast diversity of nations in that region.

Derogatory words NEVER EVER use 'Kaffir' to refer to black people, even though sadly you may still hear a local use it. No matter its dictionary meaning of 'unbeliever', here it embodies everything that is morally and racistly abhorrent and is deemed hate speech, which is illegal. Sadly, you may be subjected to other similarly abhorrent words referring to blacks, like *moents* or *houts*—walk away from them literally and metaphorically. Using *coolie* to refer to Indians and *hotnot* to Coloureds is also in the hate-speech league.

ASPIRATIONS
Many South Africans aspire to the traditional lifestyle patterns of finding a partner, getting married and probably raising a family. Different groups may go about it in slightly different ways, but the sentiment is the same—the desire to have a home and family life.

For the more affluent this is the norm, taken for granted, but for the less affluent and the many Africans who have homes in the rural areas and work in the cities or on the mines, family life is plagued with problems. These migrant workers sometimes only go home once or twice a year and some even take city-wives, quite legitimate under tribal marriage customs, but often very hurtful emotionally and financially to the rural families.

ATTITUDES TO SEX AND BABIES

The different communities in South Africa have widely differing views on premarital sex and extramarital babies. Many Afrikaners and the more conservative English communities frown on premarital sex and actively discourage it. Babies born out of wedlock are seen as bringing shame on the families. If a young woman does become pregnant, she is often pressurised into marrying the child's father before its birth. Quite often these are not stable relationships and lead to divorce. Abortions are now also an option and there are very few homes for unmarried mothers. However a fast growing number of young people do live together before getting married and a few don't bother to marry at all.

In African societies, both rural and urban, there are few taboos concerning sex before marriage or premarital babies. It is not unusual for the more traditional African men to say they want proof of their would-be wife's fertility ahead

A poor rural grandmother looks after a host of grandchildren

of their marriage as children mean additional manpower, possess income potential, and will ensure a secure old age, although this view is certainly changing especially in urban areas to mirror attitudes in the developed world where smaller families are the norm.

The number of single-mother households is increasing all the time as rural women are deserted by their husbands who go to work in the cities or on the mines, and then never return to their tribal homes. Also a growing number of urban women have opted for single-parenthood because of the stressful chauvinistic attitude of some African men who expect their wives to feed, clothe and care for them and the children in addition to working.

Some young women, forced to seek jobs in the towns and cities to survive economically, become pregnant without much commitment from the father and often send their babies back to their rural homes to be raised by the child's grandmothers or other members of their extended family. Although this is very much part of African lifestyle and shows a wonderful generosity of spirit, it often puts even greater strain on the poverty-wrecked rural families and communities. In addition the HIV/AIDS epidemic in the country makes this task ever harder as more and more children lose their mother, or often both parents, leaving ever less adults to care for them.

HIV/AIDS: OUR GREATEST TRAGEDY AND OUR GREATEST CHALLENGE

Because the incidence of HIV/AIDS is extremely high in South Africa you are quite likely to hear a great deal more about it both in the media and in general conversation than in many other parts of the world. But at the same time, you may come across any number of myths, or even downright falsehoods about the illness, its causes and most tragically its cures.

What is not a myth is that unprotected sex is deadly dangerous unless you are totally sure of your partner's HIV/AIDS status. Among the sensible people here it is not uncommon, once you have decided on a totally committed, monogamous relationship, to both have a test.

Despite a pretty progressive and multi-facetted information programmes, there is still a great deal of ignorance about the illness, as well as a huge stigma, in some communities. So getting the message across is not always straight forward, nor is it always successful. There are still many people who are unhappy dealing with this national problem, and I have often heard from other women how some men will just not use condoms, despite having more than one partner. It is a complex issue and the reasons run deep, being, in a nutshell, a mixture of cultural views and male chauvanism/male dominance. The government's initial ambivalence on the subject has also not helped matters. But what ever the reason, the risk of infection is just not worth it.

DIVORCE

South Africans are certainly not proud of having one of the highest divorce rates in the world. In some parts of the country as many as one in two marriages ends in divorce. In the past women tended to get a pretty bad deal in a divorce settlement, but recent legislation and of course the constitution has made the stakes between husbands and wives a little more even. Tribal African divorces are not conducted in court, but are handled by the male-dominated tribal authorities, hence these women can get a very raw deal, often being left with nothing but the burden of looking after the children on little or no income.

In spite of the high divorce rate, strangely there are still a number of conservative people, particularly the more Calvinistic whites who see divorce as bad or wrong. Consequently they may even discriminate against a divorcee.

TRIBAL CUSTOMS

The difference between rural African tribal life and city life is even greater than in the white communities. Most of the African people in the rural areas practise tribal customs to some degree. The importance of the group is utmost and individualism is not as highly valued as in a Western society. The continuity and growth of the group is of prime importance. It is impossible to do justice to the many and varied rituals in the scope of this book, but for anyone with a keen interest there are many interesting publications on the subject. It is also worth noting that these tribal loyalties are sometimes expected to hold sway in government and business, like employing members of ones extended family instead of the best person for the job. But law and the government try hard to curb this.

Polygamy

Of the most hotly-debated tribal issues in recent years are those of polygamy and the bride price, or *lobola*. Because of the imbalance in the ratio of men to women in tribal societies of the past, caused by many men being killed in tribal wars, polygamy had valid historical reasons for existing. Today it is felt by many, especially women, that polygamy has outlived its use and has lowered respect for women. They say that in a monogamous marriage where partnership is emphasised, women command equal respect with men. Some, however, argue that they prefer an open form of polygamy rather than a pretence at monogamy while indulging in prostitution, promiscuity and infidelity on the side.

Bride Price

Bride price, or *lobola*, is a very complex issue not easily understood by people unfamiliar with tribal ethics. Simply put, it establishes a bond and mutual responsibilities between the two families and involves the bridegroom giving cattle to the bride's family. It is a guarantee of his economic status and is compensation to the bride's family for the loss of her services. But most importantly, the *lobola* is the proof of the seriousness of the man's intentions—cattle are very valuable both economically and traditionally in a tribal culture. It is a promise that marital duties on both sides will be carried out.

However this system does not always adapt well to a Westernised lifestyle. Quite often in an urban environment, the bride price is paid in cash and other consumer items which, of course, offer little or no protection to the wife once it is spent. In a modern urban society some women feel it is demeaning to be viewed as goods that can be bought, and that bride price has lost its relevance in cases where women work and can take care of themselves.

MALE CHAUVINISTS—NOT A DYING BREED

Male chauvinism is alive and well in South Africa—in all communities. So if you come from a society where MCPs (short for 'male chauvinist pigs') are scarce, you are in for a bit of a shock. On one level most men are overtly polite and courteous to women, and as with chauvinism, the courtesy comes in different forms depending on the person's cultural heritage. My advice is to accept gracefully the fact that men may open the car door for you, stand up to greet you when you enter a room, or let you proceed them through a door.

But there are other acts of a more overtly belittling kind, such as referring to businesswomen as "girls" or addressing a member of staff, even a senior one, as "my dear girl", or "my young girl". In a meeting, men may expect the woman who might be their equal, if not their senior, to serve them tea.

Of a more serious nature, a number of women in companies and corporations report often being deliberately excluded from discussions where their input is essential, or where the decisions being made will directly affect the division they are responsible for.

MALE CONFERENCING
One very senior woman in a major computer company related a very amusing, if irritating experience. She, the only woman, and a number of male colleagues were having a major strategy planning meeting. When they adjourned for a tea break, the men continued the discussion in the toilet while they were relieving themselves. When they reconvened the meeting, she was generally confused and felt that she had been left behind in the discussion!

But as the number of women, especially from previously disadvantaged groups, enter business, this behaviour is less likely to hold sway. Government has many more women in parliament and at senior levels than in most other countries and this must filter down to the business community over time.

Who Holds The Reins?

In all fields in South Africa—business, politics, home life—the proportion of male decision-makers in relation to females is still skewed. In the past fewer women pushed to be in the front line, but today things are improving, not least because there were many black women involved in the liberation struggle who now expect and do take their place in society as equals. Of course the constitution also backs them up!

Men in the Home

Many South African men are unwilling to do domestic chores, household shopping and the like. Some of this is because, especially in white homes, they have wives who perhaps don't work and hence they feel it is the wife's job. But more often the resistance goes deeper as men feel it is 'women's work' and therefore beneath them to get involved in it. It's a perception that is changing and today you do often see more men or couples sharing the chores.

WHAT'S A MAN TO DO WHEN HE'S OUT OF TOOTHPASTE?

A single businesswomen friend recently related a humorous story. The man she has been seeing for some months (who is divorced) ran out of toothpaste. Instead of going to the nearest emergency pharmacy (since it was after working hours), he drove right across town to borrow some from her. He did this two nights in succession! In the past, no doubt, his wife was responsible for all domestic matters including seeing that the toothpaste did not run out. Imagine his surprise when my friend did not rush out to buy him more toothpaste.

A Deep-Rooted View

Among some South Africans and particularly men, there is a deep-rooted belief that women only work 'if they have to'. It often comes as quite a shock to them when they learn that many women, just like the men, work for personal fulfilment;

to support or help support their families; to make their own decisions, and to be in control of their own lives.

If you are from countries that have long since closed these type of debates, you may find having to reinvent the wheel, so to speak, is rather trying. For the good of all, don't hold your tongue—educate the ignorant!

The Women's Front

Today there are many women's organisations in South Africa stretching from the overtly political and politicised to the most apolitical charity fundraisers. They include those from the ultra-left to the radical right, some have memberships in the thousands, others are very much smaller, but they tend to offer something for almost anyone interested.

Once settled in the country you may want to join a group either as a way of meeting more like-minded women or to add your helping hand to the many and varied charities and organisations that can always do with extra assistance in their projects. My suggestion is that you start your search by asking friends and on the Internet, although your choice will no doubt also be determined by where you choose to live.

Useful Internet Sources

The first two websites listed below are international sites so click through to South Africa and then find what you are interested in. The third one is a local businesswomen's site which may be useful too.

- Go to www.peacewomen.org and click your way to South Africa or use http://www.peacewomen.org/countries_and_regions/africa/southern-africa/south-africa

- Sangonetpulse, an NGO news and information site found at: www.ngopulse.org

- South African businesswomen's association: www.bwasa.co.za/

THE GREAT RURAL-URBAN DIVIDE

In both black and white communities there is a vast difference between the value systems of rural and urban people. The majority of the whites living in the rural areas, or *platteland*, are farmers and a high percentage of them are Afrikaners. With their lives centred around the conservative Calvinist churches, their views are often very narrow and somewhat unworldly. But as a countermeasure they often have very sound values, putting less emphasis on materialism and more on human decency.

In the small country towns, people make more time for social niceties. It is still customary for drivers of passing cars to give one another friendly greetings, as do pedestrians and drivers of animal drawn vehicles. Especially among the black people, a friendly smile is almost always returned.

If racism is taken out of the equation, rural folk are known to be friendly, hospitable people always prepared to pass the time of day with you. If, for example, you lose your way along some dusty country road, and call in at a farm house for help, it would not be unusual for them to offer you a meal, perhaps even a bed for the night, or at least drive miles out of their way to put you on the right track.

Of course their city-slicker siblings say it is merely because they have the time. But it is really because they can be bothered to make the time. Making a buck is of slightly less importance.

In the big city, however, the opposite occurs. I remember how my father's rural neighbour lost his way and ran out of petrol in an elite Johannesburg suburb late at night. He rang numerous door-bells on numerous high walled properties and not a soul would assist him. In fact many threatened to call the police if he did not leave immediately. A little, but not all, of the blame for this attitude has to do with fear of the high crime rate in the city.

City-dwellers in South Africa have developed a much harder attitude to life as they live in the fast lane. Sadly, so often their values system is based on what people own, earn and drive. Their exposure to world trends is greater than their country cousins, which means they tend to lead the country in all the fads and fashions from abroad.

CENSORSHIP
Prudity Towards Nudity

One of the guardians of South Africans' morals is the Censorship Board which is charged with the task of deciding what degree of salaciousness is permissible and to whom. Under apartheid the board was so conservative and Calvinistic—not surprising since it was made up almost entirely of conservative white Afrikaner men—that even a hint of sex on screen was frowned on. Films were cut to ribbons or not allowed to be released at all, men's girlie magazines were heavily censored and pornography was a complete 'no-no'.

These days a much more enlightened attitude towards censorship is taken, not least because of the freedoms enshrined in the constitution. Of course films are rated for their suitability to young audiences, just as they are in most other countries, and cinemas are unlikely to allow underage youngsters to view such films. The result is that the quality and variety of films on circuit and in the dvd/video rental stores has vastly improved.

One of the more amusing ploys of the old-style Censorship Board was the insistence that white women's nipples were taboo, but not the breast. This meant that girlie pin-ups South African style were blessed with star-shaped nipples as every nipple had to be covered with a star! Today there is a far greater tolerance of bare breasts, even in ordinary women's magazines. And those that border on softcore pornography tend to be sealed in a clear plastic bag so that inquisitive youths (and miserly adults) in supermarkets and bookstores are not able to flip through the magazines, but have to buy them to read in the privacy of their home. Hardcore pornography is generally only sold in sex shops, more commonly called "adult stores".

The Written Word

In the past, the censors also had a go at the written word, more often from a political perspective. For many years one was just unable to get any literature on anything that was vaguely 'red'— that is anything that showed communism in a favourable light. Criticism of the South African regime, be it in a scholarly work or a novel, could lead to the book being banned, but today such silliness is long since gone and the only restriction on books you may encounter is that they are not stocked here. Not a problem as bookstores will order them for you, or you can use the Internet to buy your more obscure books.

A classic urban legend about the old-style Censorship Board is that when it first heard about the classic English children's novel *Black Beauty*—the life story of a horse—they immediately banned it because they were convinced, without reading it, that it was salacious and disturbing to public morals. How far has South Africa moved towards normalcy under democratic rule!

FAMILY PLANNING

Family planning is accepted more readily among whites and urbanites than among the rural communities, particularly the traditional Africans. All forms of contraceptives are available and most can be obtained free-of-charge from state clinics.

There is a strong resistance from some African men to the use of contraceptives, partly because they see children as proof of their virility and manhood.

Sadly, the resistance to contraception extends to the using of condoms, with dire consequences for the spread of HIV/ AIDS, but there are now educational programmes, some government run and funded, particularly as part of the HIV/ AIDS prevention programme. They tend to be conducted in the media, on billboards and now also in schools and universities, and attempt to normalise the use of condoms especially as a means of preventing the spread of HIV/AIDS and other sexually transmitted diseases.

Family Size

In South Africa like most countries in the world, there is a definite correlation between the standard of living and the birth rate—the higher the quality of life, the smaller the family. Among the urban affluent, two- and three-child families are now the norm; but in the rural families, particularly the tribal communities, larger families are still common. Since it is the children's responsibility to look after their parents in their old age, they believe that the more children they have, the better care they will receive in their twilight years. Even today in many traditional African families, it is the duty of the youngest child to stay home to look after the aged parents, while the other siblings contribute financially to their parents' well-being.

Before the days of easy access to contraception, many white families, especially in the rural areas, were 10- or 12-children strong; but this is fairly rare these days.

ENTERTAINING—SOUTH AFRICAN STYLE

Most people here are friendly and hospitable and invitations like "you should come round for a drink" or "pop in any time" are often meant sincerely. Casual invitations to a meal, a barbecue *(braai)*, or perhaps to have a drink with friends on your way home from work are common. So don't be a shrinking violet—take them up on their offers. But do it thoughtfully.

If you are unsure that the offer was a serious one, confirm it ahead of time. Because South Africans are very casual, it is wise to phone a day or two in advance. Nothing could be more embarrassing than to turn up on their doorstep and find that they are not expecting you, or worse, not to go then later find out that they had gone to great lengths to invite others to meet you. If the invitation is extended to you on the spur of the moment and for immediate use, just ensure it is not inconvenient and then jump at the chance to enjoy new company.

Many people will invite you to 'pop in' whenever you like. Some will even suggest you need not bother to phone first. This is often well meant, but until you know their family routine, call ahead. Arriving at the children's bath time can be a bit of a strain on your host, or just popping in when they are about to sit down to a meal could be embarrassing to both of you.

Generally, entertaining South African-style revolves around a lot of chit-chat and some 'breaking of bread'. If you are invited to do something more formal like play tennis or a game of bridge, you will usually be told in advance. Since there is such a high number of private swimming pools in the country, you should take along your swimsuit and a towel, especially in the summer.

A Gesture Of Appreciation

If you are being entertained in someone's home for the first time it will certainly be appreciated if you bring a tiny gift along—a bunch of flowers, a box of chocolates, perhaps a bottle of wine. If you come from a land uncommon to your hosts, one of your local delicacies may well be appreciated. Don't go to great lengths or expense, it is not necessary and not expected. Once you are visiting your friends on a much more regular basis it is not necessary to take a gift on each occasion, but often good friends tend always to offer to bring something to contribute to the dinner or lunch party. If they want you to do so, most people will simply suggest what you can bring. If they absolutely insist you don't, either do their bidding or take a bottle of wine. This way they can use it or put it aside for some other occasion.

Social Etiquette: Some Random Pointers

Social mores and what is viewed as polite and by whom are very different depending on the community or the company you are in. Most people, especially in the urban and business environment, will follow international norms of polite behaviour, but there are also many little nuances from each different culture that you will surely come across and pick up once you are living and working in South Africa.

- Always call an employee by his/her name. If you don't know their name ask for it. Many South Africans are more sensitive than you may expect on this issue because of the disrespect experienced in the past. Never just say "Hey you". Some names may be difficult to pronounce, but if you explain that you are foreign and not familiar with names here, people will understand.

- Never call a person by the name of an animal, as it is seen as very rude, even though you may mean it in a friendly way. For example, do not say, "Oh you silly monkey, why did you not tell me there was a problem." In Western society this may be seen as a gentle rebuke, but to many an African this is considered very rude.

- Quite often it is expected that when you hand something to someone, you should do it with your right hand. This is not always the case but it is worth knowing. Sometimes more traditional people will give or receive things with both hands. It is not expected that you should do the same.

When to Leave

It is sometimes not easy to know just when you should take your leave if you are new to the land and the culture.

If there are other guests, you can follow their lead, but at the same time, it is not always necessary for you to leave just because the others do. A safe guide is to remember that South Africans are early risers and 11 pm is usually considered a late night, particularly during the week. That's not to say that they don't go carousing till the wee hours of the morning, but it's not the norm on a weekday night. Over weekends—Friday and Saturday nights—people go out and stay up much later. A strange South African habit is to walk you to your car. Now don't misconstrue this as thinking they are escorting you off the property to ensure you have really left—it is just a very courteous and friendly gesture. Accept it as that. Another strange, but perhaps slightly less common, South African habit: when you have decided to leave, you will all walk to the door for your farewells, but then stand there or at the car and become involved in yet another conversation. If you are keen to leave, just politely say as much, and indicate you can continue the conversation the next time you meet.

LIFECYCLE MILESTONES

Celebrations of lifecycle events are always interesting and usually great fun too, but as an outsider you may feel a little ill at ease if you are not sure what to expect or what to do. It really does no harm to ask as, with the wide variety of cultures making up the South African tapestry, no one would expect a newcomer to know all the ropes.

Birthdays

If birthdays are celebrated at all, it is usually informally—perhaps a special dinner at home or in a restaurant, or a party at home. Of course special years like turning 21 or hitting the big 40 and the likes are often celebrated with much more aplomb. A birthday gift is the norm, particularly if it is a special birthday, and my advice is, until you know the person well and know their likes and dislikes, give them something consumable—it's hard to go wrong with that.

Weddings

Most often weddings are more formal affairs. The vast majority of urban people have traditional Christian-type weddings with a church ceremony followed by a reception to celebrate the event. Some people choose to get married in a civil ceremony, which is usually held in a registry office (part of the law courts), and followed with a reception similar to a church wedding. In most cases you will receive a formal printed wedding invitation which will state the time and place of both the wedding and celebration.

Men are usually expected to wear suits for the more traditional weddings, or, if it is a more cool or hip affair, something casual but smart. The same rule of thumb would apply to women—dresses, skirts or suits are the norm, as are smart trousers. In the past, more staid dress was common but today an exotic array of dress is the norm especially as people come from a wide variety of backgrounds. Some African women wear forms of traditional dress which can include wonderful bold prints and headwraps. Others wear Western high fashion or just something simply elegant.

It is the norm to give a wedding gift, and mostly they are taken along to the reception and left for the bridal couple to open in their own time. For quite a few weddings now, a list of what the couple would like as gifts is placed with a number of department stores and you are able to go and choose something affordable which the bridal couple want and need.

Weddings with a Difference

The more traditional communities (particularly the Indian, Malay and some Africans) often have culturally specific wedding ceremonies. If you should be invited to a wedding and are not sure of the procedure, ask your host or someone else who is familiar with the ritual exactly what is expected of you. No one will be offended that you don't know, and you will enjoy the occasion so much more if you feel at ease.

Funerals

Like weddings, many funerals follow Christian traditions. A notice is often placed in the local newspapers stating the date, time and place of the funeral. It is up to you whether you want to attend or not. Usually relatives, personal friends, family friends, and colleagues will attend. If you are a little uncertain, ask someone for advice.

Black dress is rarely expected at a funeral today, but modest clothes in quiet colours are generally preferred. Many people are cremated, in which case a service is held in the chapel at the crematorium. If there is a burial, there will be a service in the church and then a trip following the hearse to the graveyard.

Quite often tea, drinks or even a meal may be served after the funeral. In some cases only close friends and family are invited to the reception so watch others for your cue, or wait to be invited, if you are not sure.

Tribal Funerals

Tribal African funerals follow very special rituals, particularly as ancestors play a major role in most traditional beliefs. The whole funeral and mourning process is complex and often takes days or even weeks. Africans in the cities take leave from work and go back to the rural areas to bury a relative. If you are the employer, it is important to understand the significance of this request and thus the person's need to take time off.

Also remember that many Africans do not think of family relationships in the same way Westerners do. This means that a person may refer to someone as their brother or even father but, in the strictest sense of blood relations, does not actually hold that relationship. Do not fall into the trap, as other unthinking South Africans have, of feeling the person is trying to con you. I have heard of cases where employers have become very angry when an employee has asked to attend the funeral of 'yet another sister or father'—the important thing to remember is whether or not it is a blood brother or a brother by some complex tribal link, it is important for that person to attend the funeral.

Today there are also a great many funerals for people who have died from AIDS related illnesses. This can be a bit of a tricky situation for an outsider as there is still a lot of taboo surrounding AIDS deaths and friends and family often do not admit it is the cause of the death. In such circumstances to save embarrassment it is wise just to go with the flow of what is being given as the cause of death.

Christmas

Christmas is a major celebration especially because it falls in the middle of the school and summer holidays. Even the most irreligious tends to celebrate it by giving gifts and enjoying a special meal with family and friends. Newcomers to the country and the community are often invited to join in the family festivities of their newfound friends.

It may feel rather strange to many, especially anyone from the northern hemisphere, to celebrate Christmas on a hot and sunny day, but that's the way it's done here. And more strange still, is the fact that some South Africans try to approximate that special winter-Christmas feeling with cotton wool and polystyrene chips, the most common imitation of snow. Many South Africans may rarely, if ever, have seen snow! Homes and shops are usually decorated with Christmas trees, baubles and tinsel. And Father Christmas is a myth enjoyed by all children.

Giving of gifts is certainly part of the Christmas ritual, especially to children. The type of gift depends very much on your relationship with the person you are giving it to, but generally something small is appreciated. Don't bankrupt yourself buying gifts—with a little effort and imagination you will find a number of interesting, inexpensive gifts in the shops and also in the plethora of outdoor or informal markets. Even by the roadside in some parts of the country you may find interesting craft work.

Although sending Christmas greetings cards to friends, family, and business colleagues and contacts is certainly part of the festive spirit, the habit seems to be dwindling as costs climb and Internet Christmas cards gain their place. There are charities that sell a wide variety of cards, but buy them as soon as you see them in the kiosks or stores as the good ones tend to sell-out very quickly.

The major celebration is held during either Christmas eve dinner or Christmas day lunch. And for many, especially in the white communities, a fairly traditional British Christmas meal of roast turkey and ham with vegetables is served. Dessert includes the traditional Christmas pudding with brandy sauce, mince pies and other sweet meats, nuts and dried fruit. This feast is washed down with a celebratory drink like champagne, wine or anything else that takes their fancy.

Certainly a fair number of South Africans have adapted their Christmas meal to suit the summer climate and may perhaps eat a cold meal al fresco around the pool, or have a *braai*. The day after Christmas is also a public holiday, giving everyone time to recover from their over indulgence, or to continue the festivities with other friends and family members.

RELIGION

Freedom of worship is practised and upheld by the state and the constitution. Restrictions, however, apply to extremely destructive cults which, if deemed harmful would mostly not be tolerated.

All the major world religions like Christianity, Judaism, Islam, Buddhism and others are practised in South Africa. There are also some home-grown Christian churches, the two most prominent being the Dutch Reformed Church and its various branches which caters predominantly to the Afrikaner and is based on the Calvinist beliefs Dutch settlers brought to South Africa in the 17th century; and the Zionist (not to be confused with Judaism) type churches which are supported almost entirely by the African population.

In the days of apartheid, a number of Christian leaders took up the cudgels against the inhumanity of the system and at some levels, especially in the Christian churches, politics and religion became fairly interwoven. There is now no need for this role and most churches have reverted to their traditional role.

The Calvinist Route

The Dutch Reformed Church is one of the larger churches in the country. It is Calvinist in origins and, even today, is still fairly conservative, especially in the rural areas where the churches play an important role in the community. As an example, you are quite likely to find the *dominee*, the Dutch Reformed preacher, in prominent positions on school committees and the likes as he is held in high esteem by the community. There are various branches of this church, some more conservative than others.

African Independent Churches

The African Independent Churches (AIC) is a huge grouping of indigenous Christian churches started by Africans themselves because they did not agree with some of the teachings of the European missionaries. They are indigenous and not linked to other European style Christian churches.

Members of one of the African Independent Churches.

Most of these Zionist-type churches have a characteristic form of dress worn to all services by members—long dresses in bold, plain primary colours and capes which are usually white and often decorated with figures like crosses, stars, rings or angels. Divine healing, triple immersion and the imminence of Christ's second coming is taught within the pattern of doctrine and worship in these churches. The laying-on of hands is practised for the purposes of healing as well as for driving out the powers of witchcraft and sorcery.

Some of the AIC followers mix Christian religion with traditional African ancestor worship. Most followers honour and respect ancestors, but do not worship them. Even very Westernised Africans, more often than not, will observe a few rites and customs in acts of remembrance and thanksgiving to their ancestors.

The Zionist Christian Church has by far the largest following of any of the AICs and is financially self-reliant. The ministering of healing and the promise of prosperity to members is seen as one of the main reasons for attracting adherents, as is its acceptance of polygamy.

Every Easter thousands of supporters flock to Moria, the church's headquarters near Polokwane in northern Limpopo Province. Over this period, the roads in this area are extremely congested, particularly with buses and taxis, and best avoided unless you are in no hurry!

CHAPTER 5

SETTLE IN, MAKE YOURSELF AT HOME

'It is far better to forgive your enemy
while he is still alive than to try to shake his hand
when either of you is long dead.'
—Zulu proverb

THIS CHAPTER GIVES YOU AN OVERVIEW of what it's like coming to South Africa either as an immigrant or expatriate and offers some ideas on how to settle down and become 'one of the crowd'. It may appear that life in South Africa, at least urban life, is quite similar to almost any Western lifestyle you may know or have become accustomed to. You may even speak one of the many languages many South Africans speak. Probably English. But look further, and dig deeper. It's not always that simple to settle in and the smallest or simplest of things can cause you enormous amounts of unnecessary stress and aggravation until you remember it may be done just that tiny bit differently here.

The people who find it hardest to adapt to their new environment are often those whose lifestyle in the past has been quite similar to life in South Africa. You expect things to work like they do back home and when they don't, you're thrown quite off-balance. Sometimes people coming from dramatically different cultures are better geared for the differences. Whatever your position on the 'sameness' scale, take heed of some of the little 'smoothers' and your adjustment will become easier.

But once you have decided to take the 'great leap', it is essential you contact the correct authorities for detailed guidance and information. Policies, laws and customs duties change continuously. The South African embassy or consulate in your country is the best place to start and you can find the details on the Internet.

Locating the Nearest South Africa Embassy
The Department of Foreign Affairs website offers a full list of all the South African missions abroad, and for each one you will find a comprehensive list of contact details, names and addresses:
www.dfa.gov.za

HOW THINGS HAVE CHANGED

In the past, many people did not wish to come to South Africa because of its racist policies, many more were not welcome by the authorities because they were deemed 'not white' so would rarely be granted a visa. At various stages during the 40-odd years of apartheid rule, Indians, Chinese and other Asians, for example, were unwelcome despite their being large, well established communities of those people living in the country. Of course most people from the rest of Africa received the same very cold shoulder too, except for those who came to work on South Africa's mines, but then they were never immigrants. Once their contracts were completed they were sent home, and their families were never allowed to join them.

In fact I recall in the mid-1980s the hard time the authorities gave an African-American friend of mine who was sent out as a foreign correspondent for an American media company. He stood his ground, but it was a very unpleasant introduction to a country he later came to love.

Bizarre as it may seem, the Japanese were deemed 'honorary whites'! No doubt their economic might and the vast amount of trade they did with South Africa in the early days had some role to play in their 'honorary' title. But in the 1980s, when practically the whole world united against apartheid, the Japanese joined in and cut their links too.

...FOR THE BETTER

Now South Africa's immigration policy is more pragmatic and needs driven. Two of its basic tennets are: to promote the future growth, expansion and diversification of the economy and to facilitate the process of skills transferral—and prospective immigrants are mostly judged on these merits.

Other more general things like being of 'good character', being 'a desirable inhabitant', or 'not likely to be harmful to the welfare of the country' are important, but one of the more crucial aspects of the law is to ensure that new immigrants do not follow an occupation in which there are already more than enough locals who can do the same job.

DO YOU HAVE WHAT IT TAKES?

In the turmoil of the student uprisings in the 1970s and the anti-apartheid violence of the 1980s, many South Africans emigrated, leaving the country with a dearth of skilled manpower and management personnel, then to make matters more difficult still, as the economy began to prosper under the new government so there was an even greater need for skilled people.

Of course there are always particular categories of skills that are most needed at particular times and immigrants in these categories are naturally given preference. Science and technology in its broadest sense rates pretty highly right now and will for a good while to come. But with the ebb and flow of people arriving and leaving the country, and also with the dynamic process of an emerging economy, the type of skills needed changes continuously.

If you have loads of money (so that the government is sure you and your family are financially independent), they may also look favourably on your immigration application. Industrialists and entrepreneurs are also in great demand as they are seen as prime producers of jobs, a scarce commodity in our land.

In other words, anyone who will genuinely benefit the economy and the country will be hailed heartily. And remember, the skills needs do change with the country's changing needs so it is essential you find out which ones are in demand at the time you are considering moving to South Africa.

The Work Permit Way

Simply put: to work in South Africa a foreigner needs a work permit of some description or another. The process may be long and tedious, it may require piles of documents, tons of tenacity and bucketfuls of patience when dealing with all the red tape and bureaucracy, but then show me a country where it does not!

And if patience is not your strong point, there are a wonderful array of entrepreneurs who will 'Q4U'. Outside most Home Affairs offices is a motely crew of small caravans manned by people who know the system, understand the exact needs of bureaucracy and are armed with oceans of patience and know-how. They are extremely helpful, officially authorised to do the job and take the 'Q' out of queueing—but you do pay for it! Worth every cent in my view.

Generally a work permit application is an application for a temporary residence permit, but the two are not identical things! And it does get even more confusing than that as there are different types of work permits depending on the way in which you will be employed. A potted list follows, but before you make an application it is essential you get up-to-the-minute information from your nearest South African embassy or consulate, or someone very well qualified to assist you in this process.

Types of Work Permit

General Work Permit Here, the most relevant issue is to prove that no South African can do the job you are applying for. To do this, potential employers need to advertise for the position in the national print media for a specific period. Then they need to give details of those who did apply and the reasons they are not suitable.

Employers also have to show that you, the foreign national, are not prepared to work for a salary or work conditions that are inferior to what would be paid to a local resident. In addition, they have to agree to tell the Department of Home Affairs if you leave their employ or change your job description.

Exceptional Skills Work Permit This category of work permit is for those who are seriously well qualified in areas that South Africa is very short on. If you can prove you are in this league, there is not much else you need to provide to the Department of Home Affairs and you can be exempt from many of the formalities needed for other work permits. Each case is handled on its individual merits.

Quota Work Permit Between them, the Ministries of Home Affairs, Labour and Trade and Industry draw up an annual quota categories list where they determine not only the type of skills needed at that time, but also the number of people needed to do them. If you have these skills, well you're in luck!

Intra-Company Transfer Permit This work permit is issued to a foreign national who is employed permanently outside South Africa by a company which has a branch, subsidiary or affiliate business here and who is required to work in South Africa for a period of time. This work permit is valid for a maximum of two years and cannot be extended. Its upside is that the application process is somewhat less stringent as it is clear you will not be here for very long.

Immigration: How to do it

Usually people apply for immigration to South Africa while in their country of residence. To do it this way you apply to your nearest South African embassy or consulate and once it is granted, well you are off. You can also apply if you are already in the country under certain conditions, in which case you approach a Home Affairs office. These include being in the country on a valid work permit; married to, or the child of, a South African citizen or permanent resident in South Africa on a valid temporary residence permit; or sponsored for immigration purposes by a blood family member who is permanently and lawfully resident in South Africa and you have a valid temporary residence permit.

There are Home Affairs offices, part of the Department of Home Affairs, in all the major cities in South Africa. You can also find loads of information on their website http://www.home-affairs.gov.za

Visas Like most countries in the world, South Africa requires citizens of some countries to get a visa before the head off for our sunny shores. It is important to check if you fall into this category as this has to be done before you head for the airport as almost all airlines will not let you on board if you need a visa for entry and don't have one. Visas are usually associated with things short term—holidays and tourism, or coming to the country to conduct business. And not to be confused with temporary residence permits!

Temporary Residence Permit This allows you to stay in the country for a limited period of time which can be anything from 30 days to three years depending on what you are applying for. Some of the grounds include: visitor's permit for up to three years, study, work, business, a retired person (with their own means of support), or spouse or life partner of a South African or a permanent residence holder. Often this procedure is used as a forerunner to something more permanent (although not always), like a permanent residence permit. And it is good to remember that if you have decided to make the change from one to the other that you can only do it while you are actually in the country.

Permanent Residence Permit You should only apply for one if you intend to live in South Africa on an ongoing basis, rather than for a specified time. In other words it has no specific time frame and is not dissimilar to being a citizen bar the fact you can't vote. Nevertheless you still need to apply for it in one of the categories similar to that of the temporary residence permit such as work, business, spouse or life partner of a South African, or a permanent residence holder, a retired person, or a financially independent person.

When you actually come to make any of these various applications, it is essential you get advice from the embassy or consulate, Home Affairs if you are in the country, or someone well qualified to assist you.

What to Submit for a Temporary Residence Permit

- Passport valid for no less than 30 days after expiry of the intended visit.
- A full medical certificate.
- Full birth certificate.
- Full marriage certificate/ affidavit proof of spousal relationship.
- Divorce decree, where applicable.
- Proof of court order awarding custody, where applicable.
- Death certificate, in respect of late spouse, where applicable.
- Written consent from both parents, or sole custody parent where applicable with proof of sole custody.
- Proof of legal adoption where applicable.
- Legal separation order, where applicable.
- Police clearance certificates in respect of applicants 21 years and older, in respect of all countries where the person resided for one year or longer.
- A vaccination certificate, if required.

And if You Want That More Permanent Feeling…

- A full set of fingerprints.
- Marriage certificate / Proof of spousal relationship, if applicable.
- Divorce decree / proof of legal separation, if applicable.
- Proof of custody / maintenance, if applicable.
- Death certificate of late spouse, if applicable.
- Consent of parents for minors, if applicable.
- Proof of judicial adoption, if applicable.
- Police clearance certificates for all countries in which you resided for a period of one year or longer, since your 18th birthday.
- Valid temporary residence permit, if already in South Africa.

Please note: I really do advise that you check with the relevant authority that these lists are correct and entire and also the exact nature of the documents required for any application before you submit it. It will definitely ensure a smoother ride, and probably a much quicker one if you have every 'i' dotted and 't' crossed. Also be absolutely sure you have at least one if not more copies of ALL the documentation you submit.

PRE-IMMIGRATION ADVICE

Visit it First

In the words of a Hong Kong Chinese immigrant friend, who has made South Africa his home for over 30 years, "I caution anyone I can to come and look first before you make that big leap. Not everyone is suited to the complex socio-politics of South Africa." He is quite right!

And socio-politics is not the only side to this complex country. There are so many issues, cultures, creeds, attitudes, landscapes and seaboards that it really is wise, if finances permit, to plan a visit to South Africa to see for yourself the lie of the land. Unless you know you are destined for a particular city or town, try to see as many different areas of the country as you can, or at least the following major cities:

- Johannesburg: The hub of the business community. A hard, fast and exciting city. Not always pretty, but stimulating and often cutting edge, especially in cultural terms. Most business emanates from Jozi, Jo'burg, or Egoli, as it is often nicknamed.
- Durban: Sub-tropical, balmy and by the sea. Fast growing, exciting and always abuzz, both socially and now also from a business point of view. It is South Africa's major port city too.
- Cape Town: Also called the Mother City, it is the most refined of South African cities or so it likes to think. A harbour city, it is certainly the most beautiful city as it hugs the sides of Table Mountain and has a glorious coastline. It is a little sleepy, but some corporates do have their headquarters there.

Read All About it

If you don't manage a trip, get as much reading material as you can from as many sources to try and get a balanced view. All the promotion blurbs from your closest South African embassy or consulate will give you the rosy hues—factual but rosy. Also try to get information from other sources: there is a lot on the Internet, but since there is a great deal of 'opinion' about South Africa, to be sure of its factual accuracy I suggest you try some of the newspapers' online archives—international ones like London's *The Guardian* (http://www.guardian.co.uk) or *The New York Times* (http://www.nytimes.com), both of which have had correspondents in South Africa for decades and so do give a balanced view from an external perspective.

Each major South African city has its own newspapers, while some of the Sunday papers are national, as is *Business Day* a daily carrying business and general news, and *The Mail & Guardian*, a weekly which is hard-hitting and critical with a very lively team of investigative journalists. It also carries a good arts and entertainment section. Most local newspaper groups have websites too. By far the best in my view is *The Mail & Guardian* (http://www.mg.co.za) which also has excellent archives. Others include the Independent group (http://www.iol.co.za) which owns a lot of the regional papers, *Business Day* (http://www.businessday.co.za), or The Sowetan (http://www.sowetan.co.za). The broader your pickings the more balanced a view you are likely to get.

A wide range of non-fiction books, accounts of the country's history, politics and socio-economic situation are published locally and also by most of the major international publishers. They will add to your overall understanding of the country and its people—and in the long-term it will make your settling in easier.

A Quirky Cost of Living

It can be hard to get a handle on the cost of living (COL) in South Africa. And don't be wooed by the fact that the Rand is fairly weak against some of the major developed world currencies as this has positive and negative sides. If you earn in a good foreign currency then you are better off than most South Africans, but the downside is that if you earn in Rand some foreign imported goods, particularly at the luxury end, can be quite costly.

Imported goods are much the same price in dollar or pound terms, sometimes a little more, than in the developed world, and the variety of goods and goodies is pretty extensive, especially in the consumer market. So when you hanker after a bit of home, whether it is Lindt chocolate or Twinings Earl Grey Tea, it's there for the picking. If your tastes are a little more demanding, say from the Middle East or the Asia, well you are pretty likely to find your treat, but it will take a bit longer.

If you consider the COL in relation to earning a local, Rand-based salary, a good quality lifestyle in South Africa's major cities is probably almost as expensive as say earning and paying pounds in England, or US dollar in Los Angeles.

Currency Exchange Control

Remember, at least at the time of writing, that there are still some levels of currency exchange controls in South Africa, but they are a very pale version of their former selves.

South Africa in the past, like many developing and often politically unstable countries, needed to stop huge outflows of capital at times of intense turmoil. Now that those days are gone there seems much less need for this rather pesky process. And to be fair to the current government, it has reduced the strictures of currency control allowing businesses and individuals far greater leeway and limits on the amount of money they can take and spend outside of the country.

Nevertheless, the rules and regulations, especially for businesses, are still quite complex so expert advice is essential not only if you need to purchase goods abroad, but also if you want to repatriate money. The controlling authority in such matters is the central bank, the South African Reserve Bank, and it is a good place to seek advice as are the big accountancy and auditing firm which are up-to-date on the latest laws and changes, or even your local South African bank.

But for small transactions, like buying a book or some CDs from an online website, there is in reality no problem at all if you use a credit card.

Dealing with Bureaucracy

Do take note before you head off to a government office that the civil service and anything government-related can begin work as early as 7:15 am or 7:30 am, but remember this means they may close anytime from 3:30 pm to 4:30 pm. This also includes the semi-government organisations, many of which have been semi-privatised recently like Telkom (the telephone department), Spoornet (the railways), Portnet (the harbours) and a number of others.

So when you are trying to organise your life on first arriving in the country and may need to visit government or local authority departments to collect documents, or even if you need to telephone them, just check the time they close.

City and town councils also operate on civil service type hours and remember, especially in the smaller towns and villages, almost everything including banks and the post office may close for lunch between 1 pm and 2 pm. This gets ever less common, but it still does happen so don't get caught out having to kick your heels for an hour in a town where there is usually not much else to entertain you for that hour!

Ship it

Once you are set on coming to sunny South Africa, you will need to decide on what and how many of your worldly possessions you are going to bring with you. It is not always an easy decision as having your familiar things around you helps you and your family feel more at home, but there is a cost implication that may not be worth it if you are coming for a short period or are young enough to enjoy the challenge of starting afresh. Only you can weigh up the pros and cons.

Ride the Ocean Waves

The best way to get your goods to South Africa is obviously by sea—unless you are bringing very little with you. If you are bringing an entire household of goods, try and fill a container. It makes it much easier for shipment and certainly helps prevent loss or theft of your possessions. Also be sure goods are shipped door-to-door, especially if you will be living inland in South Africa. Distances are vast and you may find yourself living many hundreds of kilometres from the port of entry. It could become a major undertaking to 'just pop down to the port' to fetch your cargo. Also, it is unlikely to save you any money by trying to do it yourself.

The shipping companies strongly recommend you insure your goods under a 'marine all-risks policy' that covers goods from the door of your old home to the door of your new one. When you choose a removal company, check who their counterpart is in South Africa to be sure the handling at your destination is as good as on your departure. If you are not using a door-to-door removal service, then you will find it well worth the cost of using a clearing agent to help you through the maze of import and customs procedures.

Ocean transport, as we all know, is neither speedy nor particularly precise on timing. So it's going to take all your organisational skills and some luck to ensure your goods arrive at the door of your new home at about the same time that you do. If you get this wrong and need to stay in a hotel for too long it could be a costly mistake. You certainly can get furnished, serviced apartments on a weekly or even daily rental, but it just adds to the costs of the move, always more costly than you expect.

The actual ocean voyage from say Europe takes only about seven to 10 days, while from East Asia it takes about two weeks, even more if it is a less direct service. Most good shipping lines will give you a fairly accurate estimated departure date. Far more vague is the arrival in South Africa since right now most of our ports are experiencing delays, sometimes pretty substantial ones, due to the fact that they are just too busy for their capacity. They also have known peak periods where delays can take almost as long as the voyage, but this is the exception rather than the rule. One such is the period leading up to Christmas when importers are readying for the holiday spending spree.

Having yet again moved a household back home, I can vouch for the joy of having a good removals company on this end as they smooth your way through the piles of documentation, keep close tabs on the real-time arrival date of the vessel and also facilitate the delivery and unpacking of your goods—if you shipped 'door-to-door'.

Customs Regulations

Generally, immigrants and people applying for permanent residency do not have to pay import duties on bona fide 'household effects and removable articles' as long as the customs officials have no reason to doubt the goods belong to you and that you have no plan to sell them. 'Household effects' includes anything that is normally necessary to equip a self-contained home, such as furniture, curtains, linen, crockery, and electric appliances like fridges and stoves as well as TV, video and hi-fi. 'Removable articles' refers to large items like boats, trailers and caravans.

Before you pack up your home, it would be wise to contact a South African embassy or consulate to check the up-to-the-minute customs duties and regulations as they are often changed and updated. Also note that South African ports charge cargo dues which are calculated on the volume rather than the value of your goods. It is not excessive, but must be factored into your costs.

There are certain goods you are not allowed to bring into the country, like unnumbered firearms, automatic rifles and pistols, any honey bee product, drugs, and 'indecent, obscene or objectionable goods including books and publications'—simply put, hardcore pornography. The list is long and worth enquiring about as its contents are not always obvious, and are frequently changed. The country of origin of your goods can also have a bearing on what you may not bring to South Africa.

There are other items which you need to get a special import permit in advance of your arrival here. These include firearms, plants and seeds, unwrought or semi-processed

gold, live animals and more. Again, try and get as much help as you can, including all the forms needed from the nearest South African mission.

What To Bring From Home

Because South Africa may be many thousands of miles away—physically and emotionally—from your home, and so you may not have had first-hand experience of it, many are surprised at how close it is in some ways to a typically developed country like Australia, the United States or parts of Europe. Often would-be visitors and immigrants have an image of life in South Africa based on media news from the whole continent, which for obvious reason shows a very different and much poorer side of African life. In many African countries it certainly is hard to get many of the consumer goods you take for granted if you come from a developed country. But in this respect, South Africa is very different from most of its continental neighbours. So if it took your fancy you could literally waltz in here and set up home from scratch with very little hardship—except of course on your wallet!

My recommendation on what you choose to bring with you is based on the length of your stay. If it is only for some weeks or a few months, don't burden yourself with possessions. In fact you are sure to want to take a whole lot of things home with you so save the space and weight in your luggage. But if you plan to stay for years or immigrate then the choice is vastly different and very individual. All you really need to know is that if you don't bring it you almost certainly will be able to find a relatively similar equivalent.

One thing I do think worth noting is that our voltage is 220V so North Americans should think hard before bringing electrical goods. Transformers are available but rarely is this process of stepping down the power to the 110V level of your appliances worth the effort. South African electrical plugs are also unlike most anywhere else so be prepared to have to change all your plugs when you get here, or use adaptors which you can buy here.

Because the climate is temperate when compared to say North American winters or Middle Eastern deserts, you don't need to bring any weather specific gear other than your day-to-day clothes. But don't be fooled by the mild temperatures in winter—they don't often go below zero—but central heating in homes is not as common as it could be so you may find some parts of the country, especially Johannesburg and its surrounds, a lot colder than you expect in the short winter season.

A good variety of books are readily available here and if you are looking for something very specialised the bookstores can order it for you or of course you can order it on the Internet.

Your Own Wheels

Unless you can't bear to part with your car, or are sure you will be staying in South Africa for a fairly long sojourn, it is rarely worth the hassle and cost of bringing a vehicle with you. The high cost of shipping it, the insurance and the customs duties make it a fairly expensive move, while the import procedures make it a complex one. You may also need to get certification from the South African Bureau of Standards. New cars in South Africa are pretty expensive, but there is a good used car market where you always find a good deal. If you do wish to bring your car, you must get all the relevant documentation from the embassy or consulate or contact the South African Revenue Services (somewhat unfortunately, although cynics say appropriately) called SARS in South Africa (http://www.sars.gov.za).

HOUSING: THE PRACTICAL TIPS

No doubt you've chosen the city or town you plan to live in, so your first move on arrival is to find a home. Generally this should pose no problem at all in the middle class suburbs of most towns and cities. South Africans tend to be very mobile, moving home fairly frequently which means that there are always loads of homes available on the rental and purchase markets.

Where Will You Live?

Unless you know the suburb you wish to live in, or have friends and acquaintances who can help you choose, there is no better way than driving or walking around to see what appeals to you. If you have children, you need to find out where the schools they are likely to attend are, where the closest shopping centres are, and also how far the attractive suburbs are from your place of work. Distances in South Africa, even in the cities, are often greater than you may expect. Also, the cities and towns are generally served by fairly good highways and road systems, but traffic congestion is getting heavier by the day as the economy—and thus the number of private vehicles on the roads—grows in leaps and bounds.

What to Choose?

There is ample rental accommodation in South Africa—both houses and apartments—and even more on the market to buy. The choice is yours. It may well be advisable to rent a home on a short-term lease if you are not certain of the city you've chosen or need to give yourself time to find out how things really tick. There is a limited amount of furnished accommodation which can be very useful if your possessions are in transit. But check exactly what 'furnished' means as I have heard of some folks who found out, after signing the short-term lease, that there was precious little in the apartment even though it was rented to them as 'fully furnished'. In fact I wouldn't rent something unless I had inspected it thoroughly first.

The Rented Option

You should be able to get short-term leases for three or six months at a time (I am not referring to the serviced, furnished suites mentioned above which you can rent for days or weeks at a time), while regular rental agreements usually run for a year or longer. After that time, either party has the right to give a month's notice to terminate the contract. Some people prefer three months' notice for termination, but most often you can negotiate your preference with the lessor.

If you are legally in South Africa you can rent a property without having to produce any further documentation other than your passport or some other legal form of identification.

Once the lease has run out, if you wish to stay on and the landlord is happy you do, you can continue to rent the place

An old Cape Dutch house that is beautiful to look at
but could cost a great deal in upkeep.

on the same 'expired' lease. Once in this position both lessor
and lessee have to give only one month's notice to terminate
the agreement. This is called 'tacit renewal' of the lease. If
you wish to get a new lease you certainly can, but there are
costs involved.

Stamp duties are payable on all leases at 0.5 per cent
(half per cent) on the aggregate rental, that is the rental for
the total duration of the lease. So if you signed up for 24
months at R 10,000 per month, you will pay 0.5 per cent of
R 240,000 in stamp duties. There is a rebate system: if the
stamp duty payable is less than R 500 then it will be waived.
This explains why people (and the law) are happy to let their
leases run on 'tacit renewal' once they have reached the end
of the stipulated term.

If you choose to rent, be sure you have a well drawn-up
lease from a good estate agent, and if possible get a lawyer
to give it the once-over before you sign up. There should
be nothing complicated in a rental agreement, but be sure
you understand your responsibilities. For example: you are
responsible for the electricity and water bills, as well as the
telephone bill (which usually arrive monthly); but you are not
responsible for the rates and taxes which should be paid by
the owner. Of course you can undertake to pay them, but
ensure that this is then reflected in a lower rental.

Your Rental Responsibilities

Once you are ensconced in your rented home, you may well be held responsible for drains that become blocked or other plumbing problems (this is quite legal), so be sure that you check these are all in order before you sign the lease. Some of the older cities like Johannesburg or Cape Town have beautiful old homes built in the late 1800s and before—a sheer delight to look at and very wonderful to live in, as long as you ensure that as a renter you are not responsible for the quirks and foibles of an old house which can be quite costly, such as very old electrical wiring or plumbing from the Dark Ages. Many of these homes have been modernised—just ensure this is the case with the one you rent.

Rent is almost always paid monthly in advance and it is quite legal for the lessor to ask for a deposit prior to handing over the keys, sometimes as much as three months, but more often one or two months rent.

Something that will most surely crop up in various ways when you are settling in, such as when setting up a relationship with a local bank, is the Financial Intelligence Centre Act, or FICA as we all call it. In essence, this Act is designed to combat money laundering and other similar abuses of the financial systems here (dare I suggest you have already come across some form of this in many other countries as the concept is ever more widely used to combat and prevent crime.) Under this law 'accountable institutions' such as the banks, or your estate agent even, are responsible for carrying out a "Know-Your-Client" check.

In essence it is their responsibility to let the authorities know if they feel their clients' funding is in any way suspicious. Of course this would not apply to any normal law-abiding citizen, but little things may get misconstrued if you are not aware of them: for example, you may be forced to pay the deposit in cash if you have not yet got your bank account established. This in turn could look suspicious if it is a huge amount of cash. So just be aware and all should go smoothly.

Just for additional support, you can contact the Estate Agency Affairs Board (EAAB; website: http://www.eaab.org.za), the body that governs all estate agents, and for more information on FICA, visit its website at http://www.fic.gov.za.

Rent or Buy? It's Your Choice

Your decision to rent or buy a home is based on so many factors, many of which are personal. But it will certainly help to have a local person highlight some of the pros and cons of the two options.

Once the initial rental period is over, you can usually move out of a home at a month's notice. Quite useful if you are likely to be transferred in a hurry or if you find something you like better. It is also so much easier to rent if you are only going to be in the country on a short-term basis. But as a renter you are paying the mortgage for someone else, something you could be doing for yourself with the benefit of getting your foot on the first rung of the local property-market ladder.

The residential property market, like in most other countries, fluctuates, but mostly seems to move steadily upwards. If you intend to be in the country for a medium to long duration, it is quite wise to buy your home as it is a fairly sound investment.

How To Pay For It

Almost all people buy their homes with a bank mortgage or housing loan, called a bond locally. As a foreign national legally living in South Africa, you will be able to get a mortgage from a local bank, but you are required to put down a deposit of 50 per cent whereas locals can get a mortgage of up to 80 per cent of the value of the property. The bank granting the mortgage may also ask to see your work or residence permit simply as proof of how long you plan to stay in the country. The application process in all other respects will be just the same as for a South African, where between the bank and the estate agent you should be guided through the process.

Mortgage rates are mostly not fixed—they fluctuate with the bank base rate which is driven by the inflation rate. At present, they are fairly reasonable and relatively stable, but be aware that if inflation rises above its targeted level (set by the

central bank) then interest rates will also rise. Don't be caught overextended. However the banks are fairly cautious about giving out mortgages and they will scrutinise your financial status thoroughly. There is no harm in asking them what they feel the interest rate trend is likely to be for a year or two.

If you and your spouse both work, the bank will take your joint income into account when assessing the size of loan they will grant you. They also send evaluators to look at the home you plan to buy, then immediately tell you if it is an inflated price in relation to current market values. This is quite comforting in a new environment.

Beware of The Pitfalls When Buying

Almost all homes are sold through an estate agent who takes a commission from the seller. You, as buyer, do not have to pay the estate agent a cent! Some estate agents are competent but, from personal experience, I would advise that you are tough with them from the start. Make it very clear exactly what you are looking for and let them know, in no uncertain terms, when they show you houses that do not fit your description. It can save you hours of wasted time.

When you do find a home that you think you like and can afford, DO NOT let the estate agent push you into making a snap decision. In South Africa, an offer to purchase a home is a legally binding contract. If you change your mind once you have signed it, it can cost you a great deal of money to nullify it. There is a horror story, doing the rounds here, of a foreigner who did not realise what the contract meant and had signed eight before he realised his expensive mistake. The onus is on the estate agent to explain the finer points of the buying market to you, so be sure they do, and ask as many questions as you can.

Once you have actually made an offer to purchase a home that has been accepted by the seller, the whole process of ownership transfer clicks into action. In some cities this takes only a few weeks, but don't be surprised if it takes more than a month or two. There is nothing to stop you moving in as soon as a convenient date is agreed between you and the seller. You will pay them what is called 'occupational rent' until the property is legally transferred to your name. Once your name is on the title deeds to the property, it is legally yours and security of tenure is assured.

You may have read about land claims disputes where previously disadvantaged groups or individuals make a claim on a property which they say was taken illegally from them in the past. To date, almost all of these have been settled amicably and I certainly do not know of any that have happened in an urban area. But it is a good question to ask your estate agent just to be sure.

Almost without exception houses are sold *voetstoots* which means that any problems regarding the structure of the building are yours as soon as you take ownership of it. There are exceptions, but it usually means going to the law courts. The best way to avoid drama is to check for things like rising damp (not common in a dry country like this, but it does occur), leaky roofs and gutters, rotting wood floors, and as I mentioned earlier, the electrical wiring and plumbing. If you discuss these issues with the seller, it is wise to note their answers and put them down in writing with their signatures and/or the estate agent's as proof of witness. This will ensure you a better chance if you do feel you have been misled and have to take the issue to court. The law now requires the seller to have a certificate ensuring the electrical wiring is up to safety standards when the property is sold.

The North-Facing Syndrome

South Africa is fairly far south in the world, so the sun strikes the earth and your home at an angle from the north—more so in winter when it is way up in the northern hemisphere. Thus the saying 'a north-facing home' means it is sited with the main living rooms facing north to make maximum use of sunlight and warmth. Although South Africa has a warm and sunny climate, homes that are not north-facing can be cold and dreary, especially in winter.

Another pointer to be aware of: winters never get desperately cold, so homes here can be very badly insulated and usually not centrally heated at all. People tend to huddle round electric or gas heaters in certain areas of the house while the rest remains rather chilly, especially at night. I have heard many a European immigrant say they feel colder in a Johannesburg home in winter than they ever did in London or Munich.

Freehold Rights

Most homeowners aspire to free-standing houses which almost always have freehold rights, or purchase rights that make you the sole owner. Cluster houses are also usually sold on freehold rights, but you are also bound to pay into a kitty for the maintenance of the communal gardens, exterior of the building and the like. However townhouses, which are generally a duplex home joined by communal walls but usually have their own private gardens, are sold by sectional title. This means that a corporate body, elected by the owners, governs or manages the entire complex and its surrounds. Owners normally pay a levy which finances the upkeep of communal areas. A sectional title means that you own the home and can do as you please with the interior, but may not alter the exterior without permission from the management. It is however, as secure a title deed as a freehold.

In the past, apartment blocks were seen as one unit and mostly only available for rental. But in the 1980s, the laws were changed and apartments can now be purchased singly, although the legal structure is marginally different from a freestanding home. As with a townhouse, all apartment owners will also pay a levy for the general maintenance of the building. Of course, you are responsible for the interior of your home.

A third way of buying a property is through a share block. This is similar to sectional title, but more communal since you buy a share in a company, rather than a title deed to a specific property. The share you own allows you to use a specific section of the property i.e. your flat or a house in a complex. It can be a more risky option as it depends on how well the company is managed. In a worst case scenario, if the company was maladministered and went into liquidation you could lose your home. This form of ownership is far less common so you may not even come across it.

Foreigners can buy property in South Africa and the status is not expected to change. However, if you have set your heart on buying your own home in South Africa, it is wise to check with your nearest South African embassy or consulate at a date close to your departure to ensure there have been no changes in the law.

Pointers for Buying a House
DO's

- make a careful inspection of the house and fixtures as houses are sold voetstoots. Remember that some fittings may not be included in the house sale so always ask if specific fittings are part of the deal as the law varies a little from province to province.
- remember that north-facing homes are much warmer, especially in winter—and don't under estimate how chilly winter can be in many parts of the country.
- If you need a mortgage, do be sure to speak to a bank before you make the offer to purchase, or be sure there is a clause in the offer making it subject to your getting a mortgage.
- use a lawyer as it means all the paperwork, especially for the transfer deeds, is done correctly making the whole process quicker and easier.
- ensure you have agreed an occupational rental price in advance of making an offer should you want to move in before the transfer into your name is completed

DO's

- do check the credentials of the company, if you are buying a home in a share block or other communal ownership situation, to ensure it is financially secure.
- familiarise yourself, in a share block situation, with all the rules set by the body corporate that govern all properties and the communal areas in a block of flats or a cluster development, such as number of cars you can park there, whether you can keep pets, any building or decorating restrictions and many more.

DON'Ts

- let an estate agent push you into making a decision before you have considered all the issues carefully—remember an offer to purchase is legally binding! Don't make it lightly.
- immediately offer to pay the asking price as there is almost always room to negotiate a lower price.
- forget to include all the costs of buying a home—lawyers' fees, transfer costs and the likes—into your overall financial calculations as they can mount up and give you a nasty surprise at the end, especially if you are pushing your resources to the limit.
- pay anything to an estate agent as the seller is responsible for the entire commission paid to an estate agent for the sale.
- stretch yourself too far on a mortgage as interest rates can fluctuate fairly quickly here as they are used by the central bank as one of the main tools to control inflation.

Sunday 'Cult'

As I have said, South Africans are ever so keen to up and move home if they see something they like better. In more recent years this has led to a whole new Sunday occupation—house hunting. It starts on Saturday in the bigger cities. The major Saturday newspapers have hundreds of pages of 'Houses For Sale' listed in alphabetical order with a photograph of the home's best face, and a flowery (and often very inaccurate) description of the home. Most of the listed houses will be on show that Sunday from about 10 am to 5 pm.

This means that an estate agent will sit in the home and anyone can walk in and have a thorough look at it, as the owners will not be there. The estate agent should be able to answer most of your questions and will know what sort of price the seller is hoping to realise. Often they have leaflets with the details of the house. These come in very handy when you have seen 10 or more homes in a day and the images start to merge with each other.

Prices quoted are almost always quite a bit higher than the buyer expects. This is why they will always ask you to make an offer. There is always room for bargaining, but if you really do want the home, remember that there are others who may have made an offer on the house too. It is the seller's right to choose the offer they prefer. If you have set your heart on a home, try and persuade the estate agent to let you know if there is someone else interested in it. Once you have decided you are keen on a home the estate agent will always arrange for you to view it as many times as is needed before you make that final binding offer.

This form of Sunday entertainment—a jaunt to view homes on the market—not only by keen buyers but also by the curious, has become an urban way of life for some. For a newcomer, this ritual has two major benefits. Firstly, you can get a very good idea of what South African homes are like in the space of only a few Sundays, and secondly, you can quickly discover the relative value-for-money in the different suburbs.

Any Shape or Size

Urban accommodation comes in almost any shape and size. Houses are built in almost any architectural style and also from a mixture of styles. Size depends very much on your bank balance and also your needs. In the past, the more affluent sought huge homes surrounded by huge lush gardens on large properties. They employed a host of domestic and garden workers to help run the show. Today many are changing to compact, easy-to-run homes but the emphasis is still very firmly on outdoor living space.

The Sad State Of Crime

Because of the increasing level of theft and violent crime, security is a major consideration when deciding the type of home and the suburb to live in. Many properties now have high surrounding walls, often topped with an electric fence, which may seem imposing and unfriendly, but it does help keep criminals out.

Burglar bars, electronically-operated gates or garage doors, and outside lights that are activated by movement are also common. Most houses have burglar alarm systems which are usually linked up to an armed response company. This means that if the alarm is triggered, even while you are out, they will speed out to your home and investigate. If an intruder comes into the house while you are there, you can also hit a button to alert them and they will come to your assistance.

A number of people, particularly the elderly, are moving out of bigger homes into townhouses as these do afford more security.

Parts of certain towns and cities tend to have a heavier crime rate than others. Some of the reasons for higher crime rates are the proximity of affluent suburbs to poorer ones. This juxtaposition seems to cause increased burglary, as does easy access from a wealthy suburb to the maze of a nearby township. Ask your estate agent for advice on crime levels, but the most knowledgeable will be the residents in an area you are considering.

WORK TO RULE

Early Bird Working Hours

Most people begin work fairly early in South Africa, so if you're not an early riser, beware! Actually, early morning, especially in summer, is often the most pleasant part of the day, and many people take advantage of it to enjoy outdoor exercise like jogging, cycling or mountain biking, or swimming. Golfers also tee-off very early.

It is not uncommon for business people to be up, showering and having breakfast not long after 6 am and some are in their offices before 7 am 'to get things done' before the work day officially starts, which is usually at 8 am or 8:30 am. Most office workers stay until 5 pm, and with the early start you may often find that 4:55 pm is not the most appropriate time to begin a long-winded business discussion. Of course there are exceptions who stay at the office much later, but don't bank on it.

A few businesses do start and end later, say 9 am and you may still catch them at work at 6 pm, but only if you have a direct line. To the best of my knowledge, there is not a switchboard open one second after 5 pm! Factories and labourers in many industries like the building industry also begin work very early, quite often at 7 am and finish by 4 pm at the latest.

Make Your Own Safety Net

South Africa is not a welfare state. There is no dole queue and very little other social security. Old age and disability pensions are paid to people who have no other means of support, but the amounts are not large. Many people who can afford it, organise their own pension schemes or retirement programmes either through the company they work for or privately, or both. It is a wise move.

Most bigger companies offer subsidised medical insurance schemes to their employees. If this is not part of your package, it may be wise to look into private medical insurance. At present, South African private medical care is expensive, but not as high as in Europe or the United States. However costs are rising. There are a number of state hospitals which are free or nearly free to the poorer members of our society where a 'means test' determines how much you pay for their services. However, anyone who can afford it goes private. For more complicated procedures, many people prefer the private health care route as the hospitals tend to have some of the most up-to-date technology—but you pay for the privilege!

The government has tried to improve the levels of social security, which it has done, especially in areas such as child support and education among others, but this really only kicks in at a very low level so is unlikely to apply to you.

A Five-Day Work Week

Monday to Friday is considered the working week, thus as a rule, businesses do not operate on a Saturday, nor do most government offices. Almost all shops are open on Saturday and often on Sunday too, although their opening hours vary. These days many of the larger stores, mall shops and department stores are open on most public holidays, but often the smaller or privately owned shops are closed.

Leave Periods

With South Africa being in the southern hemisphere, our summers run from about November to the end of March. This means that the long summer holidays fall over the Christmas–New Year period. And be warned, almost everyone goes on leave at this time, especially as it coincides with the long summer holiday that schools and universities have. From early in December to the middle of January, it appears as if the entire country has shut down! Most inlanders migrate to the coastal resorts for the summer holidays which also means that the roads, as well as the resorts, can be very congested. Other peak holiday periods are over Easter and, to a lesser extent, during the winter school holidays that come around in the middle of the year.

Generally people in senior positions have four weeks or 20 working days of leave a year, while others range from two to three weeks. There are also 12 national public holidays spread fairly well across the year, which help spread out your allocated leave quite well. Should you be working in the retail industry it may be worth knowing that shops, supermarkets and the likes are open on most of them, but businesses and some smaller shops close.

The Spouse: To Work Or Not To Work?

Each person applies for a work permit in their own right, thus there is no reason why as a spouse you should not work in South Africa if you choose to. If you are a dual-career family you may well both wish to pursue your career. Finding a job, for most professionals, will not pose too much of a problem as long as you are not in a field where there are plenty of locals who can fill the post.

If you find the casual lifestyle too appealing and don't want to commit yourself to full-time work, there are numerous NGOs, charities, self-help schemes and fundraising organisations that will welcome any help or professional skills you can offer.

Business: The Toughest Barriers

Although a number of the more affluent women have chosen to be homemakers, (not too strenuous a task as many are able to afford full-time child care and domestic help) the role of professional working women has become ever more important to the economy. This was first felt in the boom years of the 1970s and early 1980s when demand outstripped supply of skilled professionals, and also because of the emigration of large numbers of professional people due to the civil unrest at the time.

Today the constitutional equality afforded everyone in South Africa makes it much easier for women in the workplace—at least on paper. And the government has been pretty good not only in having one of the highest number of women in parliament, but also in encouraging women into the workforce. Built into the Black Economic Empowerment process (BEE) is the ability to gain additional points on your company's BEE scorecard for employing women. Although attitudes to women in business are changing, in reality South Africa still lags a bit behind much of industrialised world in fully accepting the essential role of women across the entire workforce and not just at the lower levels.

Most companies still have very few women in senior management or at board level and from discussions with women I know in senior positions, they still find a fair number of male colleagues belittling and patronising. Women say that the 'glass ceiling', an undeclared barrier to the highest ranks, does exist and they confirm that to succeed equally they have to do better than their male peers. At least women now have the law on their side and if they feel they are being discriminated against there is good recourse under our laws.

HOUSE HELP

Even with the growing economy there is still a high rate of poverty and unemployment in South Africa, and thus also a huge unskilled and semi-skilled labour pool. This means many people, predominantly women, are willing to work as domestic workers, nannies or child minders. Men in this category often work as gardeners. Depending on your needs you can employ full-time live-in domestic help, or you can employ someone who helps you a few days a week. Full-time staff are usually paid by the month while part-time workers can also be paid monthly, or by the day or week.

Since help in the home is very much a part of the lifestyle in South Africa for anyone who can afford it, it makes sense to employ some help if you can. Service staff will enhance your lifestyle by giving you more free time, and you can enhance theirs by creating jobs and helping them learn skills. Minimum wages and working conditions have been set for this kind of work by the Department of Labour, and this includes the need to enter into a proper, if simple, work contract with people you employ, especially if it is on a full-time basis. But even if you only employ someone for a few days a week, it is wise (and legal) to give them a written contract. Of course both parties must sign it and fair wages for fair work will inevitably lead to good results and a good working relationship.

DOMESTIC WORKERS

Most working women are there because their income is essential to the well-being of their families. In the rural areas, African women find their major source of employment as farm labourers; and in the cities a great many are employed as domestic workers, although an ever increasing number is entering the retail, manufacturing and service industries too.

Domestic workers are mainly employed by the affluent middle class. Many work full-time for one family and usually live with the family they work for, while others work as part-timers, or chars, working one to two days a week—in two or three different homes. In rural areas, domestic workers are employed in farm homesteads too.

Despite the stringent labour laws and the drive to encourage membership of the South African Domestic Workers' Union, they are still among the most exploited group in the country. Very long working hours, unfair dismissal and very little annual leave are some of their major grievances. Until the demise of apartheid, laws even forbade live-in domestic workers from having their children or husbands live with them if they were working for white families. This often led to a situation where women cared for their employer's children while their own children were looked after by grandparents or other relatives in the townships or homelands. Thus, they may only have seen their children a few times a year.

Many domestic workers still do this, but at least some of the reasons are that they feel happier with them in stable rural extended families than living in the cities.

You should set out your terms of employment before someone begins working for you, explaining carefully what you expect of them, the hours they are expected to work, their time off and, of course, the salary. Don't forget that many people in this land are only semi-literate so be clear, precise and, above all, polite and patient. The rewards are immeasurable.

Many homes in South Africa are geared to having live-in maids or nannies, but sometimes the quarters are barely fit for human habitation, so if you are going to have live-in help, and are buying or renting a home, check these quarters yourself—don't just take the word of the owner or estate agent.

Nannies in South Africa are most often exceptionally good with children, patient and understanding and usually err on the side of spoiling them. So you must set the parameters of what your children may and may not do, and also insist on their respect for their nanny.

Depending on the size of your garden, you may need a gardener a few times a week, or perhaps only once every week or two. There are many gardeners who work for a different family every day of the working week, and the best way to find someone is to ask around in your neighbourhood. Often you will find someone who has a day or two free per week and can be recommended by another employer.

Because of the high unemployment rate, many people may knock on your door seeking some form of work or even food. Be cautious. The crime rate, especially in the bigger cities, is high and it is essential to get some form of reference before you employ someone. However, do not fall into the trap of paranoia common to many South Africans, by thinking every person who knocks on your door is a criminal-in-waiting. But also don't let a stranger into your home until you know exactly who they are.

UNEMPLOYMENT INSURANCE FUND (UIF)

The Unemployment Insurance Fund (UIF) was set up to assist people who are earning lower incomes to keep body and soul together for a period of time should they lose their job. Various categories of workers based generally on income earned fall into this safety net, including domestic workers. It also includes part-time house help if they work for you for 24 hours per month or more.

The responsibility is on the employer to register their domestic worker for UIF and also to pay the contribution directly to the Department of Labour. The total contribution is 2 per cent of the employee's salary, but does not form part of it. The employer is supposed to pay 1 per cent and the employee 1 per cent, but I have found the easiest way to manage this process is to pay the full 2 per cent myself to ensure it is all quick and simple. If you choose you can of course reclaim the 1 per cent from your house help.

Continue on next page

Continue from previous page

Of all the chores and paperwork tasks one is faced with when moving to a new country, I find the UIF registration and payment process one of the less onerous and easiest to accomplish since it can all be done telephonically and/or online. The first step once you have employed the house helper is to get yourself registered to pay UIF for your employee and almost simultaneously you can register your domestic worker.

To do this you can download the forms from the Department of Labour website: http://www.labour.gov.za, and click on the UIF link. You need form UI 8 D for yourself and form UI 19 D for your employee. Once filled out you can email them both to: domestics@uif.gov.za. You will then get a registration number from them which you use when making the payments. You can also fax these forms to (012) 337-1636, but my recommendation is to do it electronically if you can. It's quicker, easier and less likely to go astray.

You can also register telephonically by calling the UIF Call Centre at (012) 337-1680 and they will tell you exactly how to proceed with the registration. For this you will need your employee's Identification Number (all South Africans have an ID book similar to a passport which has their full name and ID number) and your own passport number.

Or you can follow a similar process by registering online. On the Department of Labour website, you can fill in an online registration form where you will then get a log-on name and password. This will all be activated within 48 hours and then you can submit your information online. From experience I suggest the email route.

Once you are registered you can pay the contribution monthly, quarterly or annually. You can pay by cheque or bank transfer, but recently the uFiling electronic system (website: http://www.ufiling. gov.za) was set up, which is so much more efficient and easy. You can also call uFiling for assistance at 0860-345-464 from anywhere in the country.

Remember that you may need to register your gardener too, but only if they work the requisite 24 hours a month or more.

THE SCHOOL SYSTEM

Under the apartheid system, most schools and other educational institutions were racially segregated. Education for whites was the best by far since the state spent the most money per student on whites. By comparison, African education was very poor with some teachers not having much more education than their students. One of the most serious results of the discriminatory education is that a very large percentage of the black population is very poorly educated and as a workforce, lags far behind their counterparts in other parts of the world. Education for Asian and Coloured people was better than that given to Africans, but not nearly as much money was spent by the state on either of these groups as on whites. Most of the good facilities found in these schools were provided by the communities themselves.

Today, of course, they are not segregated, but there is still a lot of discrepancy in the quality of schools so if you plan to send your children to a state school, called public schools here, it is essential you find out from other parents which schools offer a good level of education. The vast majority of schools are state schools and they do accept foreign children on the same terms as local ones. You can register your child at any public school if there is a vacancy. Most schools have a feeder zone, a geographic area around the school and children from this area are given preference for admission. Parents need either to work or live in the zone to qualify for this preference which is why it is essential to look into schools at the same time you are looking for a home—as mentioned earlier. Any places at the school which are not filled in this way are allocated to children on a first-come, first-served basis.

South Africa has a good tradition of private education with the missionaries being the earliest educators in this field. Today, there are also a fair number of private schools—called independent schools—which are generally considered to offer a superior education. They are privately governed and can choose the type of curriculum and hence type of examinations they wish to offer, but it does have to be within the broad guidelines laid down by the state to ensure consistency and quality of education.

Fees are much more expensive than at state schools, but there is no feeder zone system. They are in high demand from those who can afford the fees, so it is wise to make applications well in advance of the new year (which begins at the beginning of the year after the long, summer holidays). There are also private schools like the Japanese, American, German or Greek schools, which are funded by specific immigrant groups.

Your Child In School

Education is divided into three blocks: primary school which begins with grade 0, a reception year and ends with grade 7. After this children go to secondary or high school for a further five years which culminates in the matriculation year, colloquially called 'matric'. At the end of this in public schools children write an examination called the National Senior Certificate.

It is compulsory for all children to attend school from the ages of seven to 15, or until they have completed grade nine, after which it becomes voluntary.

Because independent schools can choose their type of curriculum, they of course can also choose the type of examination: they can do the same exams as the state schools, or they write exams set by the Independent Education Board, which bases its exams on the state curriculum, but feels its method of examination reflects better children's ability to use their learning rather than just dish out exactly what they have been taught. Other types of examinations include the Cambridge certificate, Higher General Certificate of Education (HIGSE) or the International Baccalaureate. If you wished your children to take any other form of final school examination it would be wise to ask the Department of Education how to go about it as I am sure it can be done.

For reasons inexplicable to me, South Africa has decided to refer to all youngsters who are at school or university as 'learners'. I don't think anyone would be too worried if you used the normal generic words like scholar or student, but you may be a bit confused when you hear the word 'learner' for the first time.

It is also worth noting that schools, like work, tend to start much earlier in South Africa so don't be surprised it you child needs to be at school by 7 am or 7:30 am. Some may start a little later, but by not much. Schools do also thus tend to end earlier, with the younger children finishing round about midday or a bit later and the seniors staying a few hours more. Also many schools offer a good range of sports which are generally practised in the afternoon after academic school has been completed.

The Third And Final Round

Tertiary education refers to all universities, technical colleges and other forms of post-school education. Although all universities do receive state aid, fees are still relatively high and climbing continually. University education in general is of a high standard and in many fields—especially medicine, dentistry and some of the sciences— compares favourably with much of the developed world. A National Senior Certificate or equivalent private or foreign certificate is needed for a student to be eligible to apply for university entrance. The university then applies its own screening process to the applicants, based on merit.

DOCUMENTS NEEDED FOR SCHOOL

To enrol your child at a public school you will need the following documents:

- the child's birth certificate
- the child's immunisation card
- a transfer card or last school report, if the child has already been to another school

If for some reason you do not have them at the time of registration, your child may still be registered provisionally and the parents must be given a reasonable time to submit them.

Children With Special Needs

There are over 380 public and independent schools for children with learning disabilities or general disabilities, although the national education department has a policy of trying to 'mainstream' the special-needs children where ever possible in an attempt to prevent discrimination or marginalisation. Sadly at this stage there are still insufficient resources to implement this policy to its best advantage and so children who have been mainstreamed do not necessarily get the specialised attention they need.

However, a fairly high number of the better public and independent schools do offer remedial education in one form or another, usually using special teachers and much smaller classes, so your choice could be somewhat wider depending on the needs of your child and the area you are living in.

Child Care Facilities

There are very few child care facilities in South Africa and of those that there are, most are privately run. The reason is probably because there is a culture of having nannies in individual families to care for children. Much like schools, the best way to find out the whereabouts as well as the quality of what are often called 'creches' is to ask people in your neighbourhood.

A Very Special School For Very Special Girls

A very special school opened its doors in South Africa at the beginning of 2007. It's called the Oprah Winfrey Leadership Academy for Girls and was set up in a very hands-on way by the famous American talk show host and business tycoon.

When she visited the country some years ago to meet the then president, Nelson Mandela, she promised to build the academy because, as she said, "When you educate a girl, you begin to change the face of a nation." The school's mission in Oprah's words "will teach girls to be the best human beings they can ever be; it will train them to become decision-makers and leaders; it will be a model school for the rest of the world." Because of her own disadvantaged background, Oprah is very aware that education is the door to freedom.

Situated just south of Johannesburg on about 20 hectares (49.4 acres) of property, it will eventually cater for 450 girls who show outstanding promise, but who come from very impoverished homes where the family cannot support their education needs and costs. The school, with 28 buildings, cost about US$ 40 million to build and has state of the art classrooms which include computers and science laboratories.

How Your Kids Will Fit In

It is certainly not easy for any newcomer to settle down in a new environment, so expect your children to be a little unsure of themselves at first. One of the best places for them to make new friends is at school, so if possible try to move at a time that will coincide with the beginning of a the school year or, at least, a new term. South African academic institutions start their year with the calendar year.

What many parents have told me is that once settled, children tend to adapt to their new home far quicker and more easily than their parents. Often they tend to take on the social values of their peers to be 'part of the crowd', rejecting their own and probably quite different cultural values. Although this may be a little disturbing to parents, especially if you are finding it difficult to adjust to a culture quite different from your own, there is not much you can do about it. Frankly, it is better to let your children feel part of their new environment and more often than not, as they grow older they will take a renewed interest in their roots.

THAT FOUR-LEGGED LOVE OF YOUR LIFE

The four-legged love of your life—that faithful mutt that is always so pleased to see you when you get home from work, or that aloof and self-contained pussy who needs tender loving care as well as her steamed chicken bits—can't bear to hand them to the neighbour? Well, you don't have to! As long as they have had a microchip implanted, you certainly can bring your pets with you to South Africa, but whether it is worth it is a very debatable question.

The facts are thus: Pets can be imported free of duty, but they may be subject to a number of quarantine restrictions depending on the country they are coming from. They may need to stay in quarantine for a number of weeks, so you must obtain details of the procedure and necessary documentation from the nearest South African Embassy or Consulate months in advance of your and their departure. The reason for the very early start is that, depending on the country you live in, there may be any number of health certificates, a list

of vaccinations and checks that need to be compiled and completed before you can get an import permit.

Probably the greatest advantage of bringing your furry friends to your new home is that they are a link with home and the past, and will be of great comfort to you in those early days when you feel, which you will at times, that you are totally alone in a strange world! I have friends who have immigrated with small children, and the family dog provided that all-important continuity link until the children had re-established a lifestyle and circle of friends like they had back home.

There are several disadvantages, though. The costs of flying an animal are very high and the experience, especially on older pets can be traumatic enough to shorten their lifespan dramatically. The head of one of the quarantine stations told me that some of the older dogs died of things like kidney failure soon after arrival—they were just not able to deal with the shock adequately. There are also a number of fairly virulent pet diseases in South Africa, and newly imported animals, not having a natural immunity, will obviously be susceptible to them. This means that you have to take special care until they have developed an immunity. You can vaccinate against some of the diseases, but not all of them. If your pets are out of quarantine before you have found a permanent place to live, they can hamper your movements and may even become upset by the unsettled lifestyle, or even get lost.

Getting A Pet In South Africa

If you decide to leave your pet behind to minimise its trauma, you could always get a new one in South Africa. The Society for the Prevention of Cruelty to Animals, or SPCA, is a wonderful place to find yourself a pet. The national body based in Johannesburg can be contacted for a list of branches near you. If you prefer a pedigree dog, the best route is to phone the Kennel Union of South Africa, KUSA, who can put you in touch with the relevant pedigree breed societies. Since almost all breeds of dogs are available in South Africa, you can have your pick from champion bloodlines which are brought in from overseas.

Useful Contacts

- National Council of SPCAs
  (Based in Johannesburg) Tel: (011) 907-3590
  Website: http://www.nspca.co.za
- Kennel Union of South Africa
  Tel: (021) 423-9027
  Website: http://www.kusa.co.za
- Animal Anti-Cruelty League
  Website: http://www.aacl.co.za

Working dogs are very popular as guard dogs, for example German Shepherds, Rottweillers or Dobermans. Gun dogs, like Labradors or Pointers, are also very popular for hunting and for pets. There are a number of clubs, especially in the urban areas, where you can take your pooch for obedience training—a worthwhile effort especially if you have a big dog in a city garden.

From The Wilds

There are strict laws regarding the keeping of wild animals in captivity. If you are considering doing this, I would strongly advise you to get in touch with the Department of

Environmental Affairs and Tourism before doing this as it is strictly forbidden to keep certain wild animals in captivity. For others, there are stringent regulations concerning cage size and the like. Many do not thrive once taken from their natural habitat and it can be a costly and futile exercise if the animal dies. You are not allowed to 'take' a wild animal from the wilds unless you are in possession of a permit. And remember NEVER even touch a wild animal in a game reserve as the penalties are huge.

STAYING CONNECTED
Telecommunication in South Africa is not as good as it could be! Costs are high and service can be slow and sometimes less than perfect. Unfortunately the fixed line environment has been in the grasp of a single operator, Telkom, a semi-privatised government-owned organisation for decades. Admittedly in the recent past, Telkom has spent time and effort in bringing about an attitude and image change and generally improving its level of service. But costs remain way higher than they should be.

However in 2006, the government finally granted a licence to a second telephone network operator, Neotel. At least now there is the opportunity for some real competition which, it is hoped, will bring down the costs, especially of Internet access, to something more in line with the rest of the world. It is felt that the high cost and slow roll out of Internet access in South Africa when compared to other countries at a similar level of socioeconomic development, such as Egypt or China, is certainly hampering economic growth.

Most of the international telecommunication from South Africa is routed via a satellite, but some destinations still rely on the undersea cable. Either way, connections are usually fairly good.

Today the specifications of many phone instruments are international, but if you don't already own your phone and/or answering machine, it is much easier to buy one on arrival since on rare occasions the specifications may be slightly different. And do remember that if you are arriving from North America, the voltage here is 220V (yours would be 110V, so anything that needs power, like portables or answer phones will not work here).

The Wired World

Apart from the high costs and the slow supply of services, it is fair to say that urban South Africa is up there with most of the more developed countries in terms of the type and quality of telecommunication product on offer, such as high speed ADSL lines, medium and fast wi-fi delivered Internet access, Internet access delivered via satellite, or VOIP (voice over Internet) products. However if you are not in a major urban centre, your telecommunications, and more especially your Internet access, could seem to come from the Dark Ages. For example, in the village where one of my brothers lives, the only access to the Internet he can get (at the time of going to print) is a simple domestic landline! Not what many of you have come to accept as the norm. But things are changing.

There is a wide range of service provider companies offering various forms of Internet access, email accounts and also a host of business-related options. My best advice is that you do a bit of research once you are in the country to see which package suits your needs. For the occasional email to communicate with friends and family the landline option is no doubt the cheapest, but more frequent Internet access and a fair amount of net surfing or for VOIP such as Skype and the likes, you will definitely need a faster line.

It is worth noting that because of the constantly changing face of the telecommunication sector here, you should do a fair amount of research, including taking a look at what the near future holds. This is because some service providers are offering what seems to be a good deal if you sign up for a longer time, say two years. But you may discover that within that period an even better option is going to come on stream in a different format or from a different service provider. Always check the escape clause and the financial penalties in your contract before you sign it.

Mobile phone internet access is also widely available from all four providers (see below), but is usually a little more expensive than the others, although this can also depend on the amount you use

Public Phones: Don't Bank On Them

Although most middle class South Africans have telephones in their homes, a large number of the poorer population does not. Public telephones are few and far between and do not always work. But in recent times, with the semi-privatisation of Telkom, sharp township entrepreneurs have set up businesses supplying public telephone services. They charge a bit more than a regular Telkom public phone, but they are guaranteed to work.

A Real Success Story: Mobile Phones

As a counterpoint to the fixed line problems in South Africa, the mobile phone industry has been hugely successful here. Not only is holding the most trendy cellphone to your head just too cool, it has also empowered millions of people who in the past had virtually no access and certainly no quick and easy access to phone and internet communication.

There are currently four operators: the original two—Vodacom and MTN, and the newer entrants, Cell C and Virgin. Early on in the game, the first two operators rolled out massive coverage which is available over almost all urban

A familiar sight, particularly in Johannesburg, is artificial palm trees used to disguise the very high antennae that provide mobile phone services. A quirky nod at our modern life.

and semi-urban areas and along much of the country's fairly well developed road network. Coverage slips a bit in rural areas, but access is still relatively good in quite a large part of the rural areas. Service is also intermittent in the more mountainous areas.

Useful Contacts

- **Vodacom** Website: http://vodacom.co.za
- **MTN** Website: http://mtn.co.za
- **Cell C** Website: http://www.cellc.co.za/content/home/home.asp
- **Virgin** Website: http://www.virginmobile.co.za

You can access the world of cellular phone and/or internet communications either with a long-term contract with one of the service providers, which like in most countries, normally includes a handset, or you can just pick up a pay-as-you-go deal. This latter option has been hugely successful for people with low incomes and/or little or no credit rating and is one of the fastest growing sectors of the cell phone business at present.

Remember the South African system is GSM and also note that, at least on a contract, you can migrate your number. Also remember to take your passport and proof of residential address when you purchase a sim card to comply with the new mobile phone law commonly called RICA.

LIGHT UP YOUR LIFE
Electricity, Water And Gas Suppliers

The supplier of electricity, water and gas varies depending on where in the country you live. Almost all city and town municipalities do supply these services, but the government is also encouraging the privatisation of service delivery in some areas. For example in Johannesburg, I get my electricity and water supplied by the Johannesburg City Council, although the actual reading of meters, usually once a month, has been outsourced to private companies. In reality, the electricity is supplied to the City Council by the national government owned electricity generator, Eskom, and passed on to you by the council.

Water is usually managed and supplied by the city council of each town and city, but of course there is a national water policy, and health and safety standards are set nationally; however they are implemented by the councils. Generally, tap water in South Africa, at least in cities and towns, is quite safe to drink. Should you be living or travelling in the deeper rural areas, I would suggest drinking bottled or boiled water just to be on the safe side.

Gas supply is a little different. There are some neighbourhoods in Johannesburg, mine is one of them, where piped gas was laid on many years ago. If you are lucky enough to live in one of these areas you can usually still get piped gas supplied to your house. This used to be supplied by the City Council, but a few years ago Egoli Gas (website: http://www.egoligas.com), a private company was formed to handle the supply and I can attest to their very good, efficient service. Should you love to cook with gas (I do!) but not live in an area where gas is piped in, it is quite easy to get bottled gas supplied. It is slightly more troublesome as you have to remember to replenish the bottles! But it is certainly an option a number of people use.

When you rent or buy a house, as a first-timer in South Africa, the estate agent should be able to help you get your services connected. The process is usually simple and requires that you pay a deposit to the service provider, usually the city council, and within a short space of time—it should only be hours or a day—you should be connected. When paying your deposit or filling out the application forms, make sure you ask whoever you are dealing with for an exact time frame for the services being connected, and try to ensure you have a contact phone number for them too.

BANKING

Banking in South Africa is highly developed and closely regulated to protect the interests of the investors—namely you. The Registrar of Banks is the controlling authority and banks have to submit monthly and quarterly returns. The banking system revolves around a central bank, which is the Reserve Bank of South Africa. It sets rates, keeps a watchful eye on money supply, tries to control inflation in co-operation with the Ministry of Finance, and is ultimately responsible for all foreign exchange matters.

Spoiled for Choice

To bank in South Africa I recommend you use one of the four or five financially strong high-street banks—ABSA, First National Bank (FNB), Standard Bank and Nedbank, and Investec for high net worth individuals—which have merchant bank divisions as well. There are a few banks that are solely merchant banks, as well as a number of foreign or international banks in the country, which rarely operate as high-street banks, but are there more to serve the financial services sector.

Useful Contacts

- **ABSA** Website: http://www.absa.co.za
- **First National Bank (FNB)** Website: http://www.fnb.co.za
- **Standard Bank** Website: http://www.standardbank.co.za
- **Nedbank** Website: http://www.nedbank.co.za
- **Investec** Website: http://www.investec.com/SouthAfrica

The South African high-street banking system is very sophisticated, particularly in terms of electronic banking. All the high-street banks offer online banking with very good levels of Internet security. In fact, there is almost nothing you cannot do online once you have established your bona fides in person with your bank (See FICA below). All the banks also have ATMs (automatic teller machines) which are linked to most of their competitor banks too. This means you can do simple transactions like drawing or depositing money at almost any ATM of any bank. For more complex transactions you may need to use the ATM of your specific bank.

You can draw cash out of your foreign bank account with your cash/debit card or use your foreign credit card to draw cash at most ATMs in South Africa, as long as your bank is part of the international system—and you remember your pin number. However, if you should travel in the rural areas, do not expect to find ATMs on every corner—and remember, some small town banks close at lunch time!

Most ATMs are situated in safe areas in shopping malls and the likes and often have a security guard on watch, but always be aware that there is a level of ATM fraud here. Sometimes the machines are tampered with and so appear to swallow your card. Usually this is perpetrated by someone seeming to be kind and trying to offer you assistance, or just distracting you from what you are doing. Should you feel anyone is being intrusive or hanging around too close, be very firm and tell them to move away from you as you do not need help. If your card does not reappear as it normally should after a transaction DO NOT move away from the machine. Phone the help number of your bank which you should have on your mobile phone and which sometimes is also provided on the ATM itself. They will immediately put a stop on your card.

Having said how good the banks are technically, many memories come flooding back to me of occasions when bank clerical errors, delays or personnel incompetence have driven me to levels of wild rage—such rage that I have threatened to move all my accounts to another bank, only to hear someone say, "NO DON'T! I have just moved away from *that* bank." These frustrations, though personal, stem both from the lack of a service culture here and also the fact that banks are over-stretching their capacity. In the last few years, the quality of service has improved as a great deal of emphasis is now being placed on training personnel in customer service. We have a long way to go, though.

My strongest advice for a happier relationship with your bank is to get to know your bank manager personally. Don't tolerate bad service from day one, but at the same time remember that your accent is as foreign to most people working in the bank as theirs is to you. If you misunderstand one another, just try again and do try to be polite and pleasant. It gets you a very long way here as most people respond very positively. Also, make as much use of the electronic banking systems as possible!

> **What is Required When Opening a Bank Account**
>
> To meet the requirements of FICA, banks in South Africa are obliged to get certain very specific information from you that proves you are who you say you are. So to open a bank account in South Africa, the following is required:
>
> - Your passport from which they will be able to verify your full names, date of birth and work permit.
> - Proof of your residential address, so you will need to take an original telephone bill or utility bill or something of that nature which shows your home address and your name.
> - Your contact details.

Slap it On The Plastic

Urban South Africa is a very credit card friendly place. All major stores and most others too, accept credit cards. Mastercard and Visa, both local and foreign, are always accepted, while Diners Club International cards can be used at almost all the same places as the first two. American Express cards can be a problem in smaller establishments, as with their higher charges some stores are not keen to accept them. I have always kept two different cards just to be sure I am not thwarted on a spending spree!

Don't forget that interest charges on credit cards if you don't pay off in time are based on our bank base rate, which may be a lot higher than yours at home. Check this out before you find yourself spending more on paying off your debt than on your purchases!

Keeping Our Money Clean

In South Africa, our banking laws are modern and strict. This is to safeguard you and also to safeguard the country against those who may choose to launder their ill-gotten gains here. The most relevant law that will affect your banking procedures is the Financial Intelligence Centre Act, always referred to as FICA. It came into effect in 2001 and its aim is to combat money laundering, which I am sure will have no relevance to you. But it does affect you simply in the way in which the banks are obliged to verify who you are, as the onus is on them to ensure they do not bank dirty money and also to tip off the authorities if they feel someone (or their money) is acting suspiciously. They are also obliged to retain client information, but equally obliged not to make that information available to anyone except the relevant authorities should they request it.

PAYING YOUR DUES

My most candid advice for anyone who is going to be living and working in South Africa for any period of time beyond a few months is that you get good tax advice from a reputable firm and don't just rely on your friends' hearsay. It is not worth the hassle of getting it wrong and then getting on the wrong side of the tax authorities, called SARS here—it stands for South African Revenue Services. It can be a fairly complicated thing due to South Africa having instituted tax on worldwide income for residents (also called ordinary residents), as opposed to temporary residents who only pay tax on their local income, but not on income they may have elsewhere in the world.

As the laws are also updated or amended quite frequently, a good adviser is worth the cost. This could be one of the large multinational financial services companies, but in my own experience a smaller more hands-on local tax adviser is ideal. If you are being transferred by your company, they may well help you get sorted on the tax front too.

What makes it difficult is that there is not really a clear-cut definition of 'ordinary resident', but it is based on your intent to stay in the country for a long time and/or to make it your home. A temporary resident is someone transferred for a period of time, but who has every intention of leaving again and is treated for tax purposes as a 'non-resident'. But it is not quite as clear as that since if it appears to the tax authorities—because you have been in the country for a number of years and you really appear to have put down roots—that you are more permanent than you say, they could challenge your tax status.

When a foreigner comes to live and work here, you are asked to make a list of all your assets and to undertake not to make them available to South African residents during your time in the country. As a temporary resident, you do not need to remit earnings from your loot back home to South Africa, although you can of course do so if you want or need the money here. And you can send reasonable amounts of the money you have earned here back home—that is, if you have any left after you have been enjoying life here! If you do save you can take that money away with you when you leave too.

As a temporary resident you are taxed on any and all income derived in the country—salary, fees for services, rent from property, interest on your bank balance, interest from loans you may have made and the likes. If you did decide to become a permanent resident, you would need to declare all your assets and of course pay tax on income derived from them; you would fall into the net of capital gains tax on things like equities or property you may purchase, when you sell them.

You can get some general advice and an overview from the SARS website at http://www.sars.gov.za, but I would still highly recommend help from a professional.

CRIME WATCH

No doubt if you have done your homework on South Africa well, you will have read about the high level of crime. I am the first one to say that there is a high level of crime, higher than it should be and higher than we would like it to be. But I will also say that it has become the national pastime of some to constantly harp on the level of crime and the fact nothing is being done about it. Sadly I sometimes detect an overlay of the old racism in these criticisms. My advice is twofold: try not to get drawn into such negative discussions since they are rarely of any benefit to you at all from a practical point of view, and are on a par with any other form of gossip—salacious! Secondly, take note of some of the tips listed below, and generally practise the same level of sensible caution that you would anywhere in the world where things are not familiar to you and where you don't know your way around, or haven't yet developed a sense of local street smart.

Where and Where Not

There are areas that are less safe or even unsafe to visit on your own be it day or night. My advice is that you ask your friends and work colleagues when you are new to the country, and once you have been there for a while I am sure you will instinctively pick up what is ok and what is not. I am reluctant to make lists here of good and bad as things change and your attitude also affects how and where you feel comfortable. But don't get spun into a web of other people's fears! You will miss out on so much and be unhappy to boot!

We have a North American friend here sent out to work in his company's newly formed Johannesburg office. Sadly one of his colleagues (a South African who had emigrated many years ago and then come back after a decade or more's absence) put the fear of Hades into him about anything outside a walled gated community or a huge indoor shopping mall. When his wife and children came to visit him, with a view to coming to join him in South Africa for a few years, they were made very afraid by his colleague's attitude as he insisted that the company driver whisk them from the highly secure apartment complex to the boring shopping malls and back. And not much else. Needless to say they had a miserable time and never returned.

Street Smart Tips

- Take more caution at night than in the daylight, but still be cautious during the day as muggings and the likes are not solely the preserve of darkness

- Don't walk around areas you don't know at night on your own. Wait either until you are sure of the type of area it is (I walk around my own neighborhood at night, but there are some where I would not), or if you choose to it's better to be in a group

- Be aware of where you are and what you are doing: in some places wandering around yacking on your mobile, or with music plugged firmly into both ears is not wise, as it means you are not taking note of what goes on around you. It also indicates to a would-be mugger that you have a nice phone and mp3 player up for grabs!

- Don't keep your entire life in your handbag/briefcase—rather, keep things like your passport and maybe some of your bank and credit cards at home. This way should you be the unlucky victim of a mugging, you will have less to replace and have some form of ID to indicate to the bank or other authorities who you are

- Have a photocopy of all your vital documents stashed somewhere at home in case you lose the originals

- When driving around in your car, it is wise to lock all the doors (most cars these days have central locking) and put anything valuable in the boot, i.e. out of sight. It is not wise to leave it in full view on the front seat next to you, so I usually slip mine under the front seat if it is not in the boot.

- Park your car in a place with lots of light at night, under a street lamp or in a busy street. There are car guards (formal and informal ones) who offer to watch your vehicle for a few Rands which you give them when you return. Most of them are ordinary folk trying to earn a living and do a fairly good job.

Violent Crime

But it would also be remiss of me to dismiss the fact that South Africa does suffer more than some countries from violent crime which include armed robbery and rape. This is way less common than your gossips will allow, but it does happen and sadly, there is a tiny chance you could be a victim. Thus it is wise to know where your nearest police station is. It is also good to know where the nearest hospital is (for any emergency for that matter), and also should you have private medical insurance what you need to produce in an emergency to be admitted to a private hospital.

In the case of rape, it is important to remember that HIV/AIDS is a very real problem here and getting access to anti-retrovirals as quickly as possible is essential. Your best route is through a private hospital if you can.

In our home, we have a level of domestic security which is sufficient for our needs but does not make us feel like we are living in a prison. Each person has to set their own limits and much will depend not only on where you live, but also the type of accommodation. Living in a house means you will need to sort out your own security, such as a burglar alarm (most homes have them)—many people have this linked to a security company which sends armed security people to the property if the alarm is triggered. If you live in an apartment block there is usually a level of security on the entry points to the building, mostly run by security guards, sometimes simply an electronic gate that you can open with a remote control.

Women Alone

Women can certainly travel in most areas and on most forms of transport on their own, especially if they take normal precautions. It is quite normal for women to drive around going to work, doing chores, taking the kids to school or visiting friends. Driving longer distances is also not a problem on any of the major roads, not least because mobile phones tend to have good network coverage along the major road networks in the country.

There are some areas, as I have mentioned, that are not wise to visit alone, regardless of gender. And some areas where, especially at night, women are better off not going alone.

GETTING AROUND IN THE CITIES AND TOWNS

Public transport in South African towns and cities leaves a lot to be desired! Although the pros and cons of metros or mass rapid transport systems reach heightened debate now and again at local authority and even government levels, there is still not a single system in the country. The reason is that it is too costly to be viable. So the first option for most who can afford it is a car. There are also bus systems in most of the major cities and also a good network of minibus taxis.

At the moment, the Gauteng Provincial government is in the process of building a fast train that links Johannesburg to Pretoria since the highway linking these two large cities—and all their satellite suburbs and industrial areas—is just not coping with the dramatic increases in traffic as the economy grows faster than it has in decades. This is no doubt going to alleviate a lot of traffic congestion, but it does not solve the general problem of getting around quickly and easily that a metro-type transport system would.

Many people who live in the satellite cities (like Soweto is to Johannesburg, or KwaMashu is to Durban) and work in the major centres, leave home in the wee hours of the morning to catch the slow, erratic and very crowded public transport. It can take them many hours of commuting to reach their places of work, and on occasion, no matter how good their intentions, they may not get to work on time.

If such a situation arises with one of your employees, give them the benefit of the doubt, at least at first. Don't just chastise them as you would someone late for work in, say Germany where public transport is rarely the cause of a late arrival. You will soon find out the truth for their delay.

Driving

For an easy, spontaneous lifestyle a driver's licence and a car are the best route if you can afford it. Cars are fairly expensive and the price of petrol is high compared to, say, the United States and some other countries, but still generally less than you would pay in Europe.

A foreign driver's licence is valid in South Africa for a period of time, usually six months, provided the licence is written in English and has a picture of the driver on it. If your licence is not in English then you need to get a translation of it. If you are a permanent resident or applying for citizenship, you can exchange it for a South African licence within those six months, but if you let this slip beyond six months you will have to take the South African driver's test.

Another way around this, if you are sure of the length of your sojourn, is to get an international driver's licence in your home country as this will be valid for 12 months, or 18 months in some countries, and can usually be renewed, but only in your country of origin. You should check this up with your home authorities.

Your licence can be exchanged for a South African one, now the size of a credit card, if you have been given permanent residency or have become a citizen. Your licence must be valid on the day the exchange takes place and must be in English (or one of the country's other 10 official languages, but I doubt yours will be in one of them!) If it is not, then your application must be accompanied by a translation issued by a 'competent authority' such as your embassy or a legitimate translation service.

Remember we drive on the left hand side—like the United Kingdom or India, and not like North America, China or Europe! Wearing a seatbelt is compulsory for all sitting in the front of a vehicle and advisable for all in the vehicle. It is also compulsory to carry your driver's licence with you at all times you are behind a wheel! Fines for non-compliance are high. Drinking and driving is a no-no here and fines for this are also very high. Especially during the end of year festive season, but not only at this time, the police set up 'booze traps' where they are fully entitled to test your breath and if deemed necessary your blood for alcohol levels.

Converting Your Licence

To convert your foreign licence to a South African one you will need to take your passport with permanent residence permit as proof of identity and residency to any drivers' licence testing centre. Once there, you will need to complete an application form DL1 and hand it in with:

- a letter from a 'competent authority', such as your embassy, confirming the validity of your foreign driver's licence as well as defining the class of licence, that is the type of vehicle that it can be used for
- your foreign driver's licence
- four black-and-white ID photos
- the applicable fees.

You will then need to have an eye test at the centre before the exchange can be finalised, after which you will be given a temporary driver's licence valid for six months which is issued immediately free of cost. You will not need to do a driver's licence examination. Also remember that your foreign licence is only valid for one year after you have been given permanent residency or become a citizen, so don't leave the conversion to the last minute!!

Using Public Transport

If a car is out of your reach, it is possible to get around by public transport, at least in the major cities. It just requires a lot of tenacity to get used to the various types of transport available and patience too.

Sedan Taxis These regular taxis have operated in South Africa since the 1930s, but are expensive and have strange legislation governing their operation which forbids them from cruising. The easiest way to get one of them is to phone for one, or if you are lucky you may stumble on a taxi rank outside hotels or in central city streets. They should all operate proper meters, but check this before you board one. On the other hand, you may wish to try bargaining for a good deal if you know where you are going. This, of course, is not playing the game by the rules, but it's up to you. Generally taxis from the airport into town do not run on meters, and in my experience can be pretty bad at inflating the price, so be sure you and the driver are quite clear on the exact fare to your hotel or home before you even put your luggage in the car.

Taxis

As there are no national taxi telephone numbers, the best is to ask the hotel you are staying at or once living in South Africa just look in the phone book for your town or city. Here are a few to try in some of the major cities:

- **Johannesburg** Roses Taxi, Tel: (011) 403-9625, (011) 403-0000; Maxi Taxi, Tel: (011) 648-1212; Safe Cab Tel: (011) 245-1903 or 079 529-9136
- **Pretoria** Rixi Mini Cabs, Tel: (012) 362-6262
- **Cape Town** Centurion Taxis, Tel: (021) 934-8281

Or use www.infotaxi.org and click on the country for a fairly good list of taxi services in major centres.

The Combi-taxi The vast majority of South Africans who cannot afford a car or don't want one tend to use the combi-taxi, a minibus taxi. This form of semi-mass transport began here in the mid-1970s in the predominantly black communities where the lack of public transport was, and to a large extent still is, chronic.

Initially, the apartheid government tried to put a stop to it, as it was competition for the inadequate state-owned bus services. But the need was so great that the industry took off like a bush fire, informally at first but now it is a major industry.

A combi-taxi, or mini bus seats between eight and 15 people—and in extreme and rather unsafe illegal conditions, closer to 20! In the early days, the combi-taxis were sometime called 'Zola Budds', a reference to the world-record-breaking South African runner of the early 1980s. The implication therefore is that combi-taxis drive too fast! And often they do.

There is quite a complex culture to catching and using a combi-taxi, especially since they run specific routes although they may deviate a little depending on the will of the majority of the passengers. Using them can be great fun, but get a local to explain the hand and finger signals as well as the method of payment before you try. They are inexpensive, especially when compared to their relatives, the sedan taxis.

City Buses The quality and availability of municipal or city buses vary considerably from city to city and even from suburb to suburb. Relatively inexpensive, they run infrequently except during peak hours, and have few routes. Most cities have tried to run more buses in the less affluent areas, but in general there are not many bus routes nor do they run often or very late in the evening. Also, remember South African towns and cities are fairly spread-out so a paucity of routes may mean quite a long walk from the bus-stop to your destination. Bus timetables are not easy to get hold of, but once in your city of choice, if you need to use the buses, call the city bus operator and you should get some assistance. Some of the bus services are run by the private sector, others by the city itself.

Commuter Train Metrorail, a division of the state owned railway operator, Spoornet, runs commuter trains in greater Johannesburg, Cape Town, Durban, Tshwane (which includes Pretoria), East London and Port Elizabeth. This form of city transport is inexpensive but not easy to use unless you should live in the areas it serves. For example, it links Soweto to Johannesburg, but unless you live in either Soweto or downtown Johannesburg you are going to have to also take a bus or taxi from the train to your destination. The trains tend to run to and from the less affluent areas of the cities where many people cannot afford cars.

New Systems In Gauteng a rapid train transport system, the Gautrain (http://www.gautrain.co.za), is in the process of being installed between the airport, downtown Johannesburg, Sandton and on to Pretoria. At the time of going to press the airport to Sandton link is fully operational and the rest of the system should be completed in 2011.

A legacy of the Football World Cup in 2010 is the rapid bus transport system, Rea Vaya, which zips around downtown Johannesburg and also links you to Soweto. Expansion plans are also on the cards. See http://www.reavaya.org.za

GETTING AROUND FROM CITY TO CITY

South Africa's inter-city transport is generally very good, but certainly not cheap. All major centres are linked by fairly frequent flights, luxury buses and trains.

By Air

South African Airways or SAA, is the national carrier and operates both local and international routes. As the national carrier it does have the lion's share of the local trade, but it is certainly not without competitors. Although owned by the government, the organisation is operated along private sector lines, so in theory is not a monopoly and is run in a more customer friendly and business efficient way.

Its competitors and hence your alternative choices include SA Express, Airlink and Comair, all of which operate on some of the routes in South Africa and some of which operate all of the major routes. In addition, there are currently three low budget Internet-driven airlines: Kulula (Website: http://www.kulula.com), Mango (Website: http://ww5.flymango.com) and 1time (Website: http://www.1time.co.za). These no-frills operators are great for low fares if you know well in advance where and when you plan to travel, but all the local airlines offer some low fares. You or your travel agent just has to try and grab them when you can. Most standard fares are very high, especially when viewed against a normal local salary.

If you need to get to the more out-of-the-way places, there are sometimes operators doing these routes on an ad hoc basis. This more off-the-beaten-track information is best sourced from your travel agent once you are settled in South Africa and know where and how you need to travel.

On a practical note, you do not need documentation to travel around within South Africa as there are no borders to cross. But my advice is to always have some form of photo ID (most usefully a passport, or at least a legally certified copy of it), as you need very specific ID to book in for all airlines these days. South Africans have identity books which are used for this, so if you have such a document you could use that too.

Major Airports In South Africa

South Africa has a very high number of airports—over 700, if you count all the smaller and larger ones together, as well as the ones run by the military and some private ones. At present only one has a special name—OR Tambo International in Johannesburg, but in time I am sure all the major ones will be named after people or events important to the majority of the country.

By Train

Inter-city trains run on an almost daily basis, but remember the distances are so great that even an express trip from Johannesburg to Cape Town takes close to 24 hours, while a trip to Durban is usually an overnight affair. Train fares are divided into various classes offering degrees of privacy and comfort, including sleepers on some routes. They range from rides which are not much more than a seat, to one which offers comfortable sleepers with attached dining cars. Right at the top end of the luxury market is the Blue Train, which travels from Cape Town to Johannesburg and back, much in the fashion of the Orient Express.

For schedules and timetables it is advisable to call the train station when you need to do a booking as this sort of information can and does change frequently. It is also important to note that often trains run behind schedule, sometimes hours behind, especially on the longer routes, so don't expect to arrive spot on time. Leave your important meeting to the following day—or take a plane.

By Bus

If you are not used to driving long distances, a city to city bus may be a good idea. A number of operators link the major cities, so have a look at the likes of Greyhound, Intercape Mainliner, City to City and Translux, all of which offer a variety of national routes. You can even book these long distance bus tickets on Computicket (Website: http://www.computicket.com)—an automated phone or Internet booking service mostly used for sport, movie or theatre tickets.

The distances in rural South Africa are often far greater than you may realise so if you take a road trip be sure you have sufficient fuel in your car, a spare tyre that works and enough water to drink, especially during the hot summer months. The beauty and solitude makes the effort so worthwhile for outdoor enthusiasts.

As with the trains, it is wise to call ahead of your planned trip to find out the current bus schedules and the prices.

By Car

And then there is always the option to drive from city to city. The main arterial roads in South Africa are generally good and, other than at peak holiday periods, the traffic on the roads is not too heavy. But beware. The distances in South Africa are great so it may well take you longer to get to your destination than you ever expected.

A trip from Johannesburg to Durban takes some six hours, while Cape Town is about 1,400 km (870 miles) from the Johannesburg area, so it is wise to break the journey overnight unless you have someone to share the driving with.

I firmly advise you to stick to the speed limit of 120 km per hour (75 miles per hour) on the open roads, unless otherwise indicated, and 60 km per hour (37 miles per hour) in urban areas. Speeding fines are heavy and an unnecessary evil. Furthermore, it is not safe to drive fast here, even if some of the open roads and toll roads look like they are good for some low flying. Far too many drivers drive selfishly and dangerously, leading to us having one of the highest road death tolls in the world. Some of this high death rate is also the fault of pedestrians who don't think and just wander into and across roads or people who are inebriated. It is far better to be too cautious than to become a statistic.

Renting a Car

If you don't own a car or don't want to own one in South Africa, you certainly do have a big pool from which to rent vehicles. Most of the major international car hire companies operate here, such as Avis, Budget, Hertz, Eurocar and the likes, and all allow you to pick up and drop off your vehicle in various destinations, so you can usually drive one way and perhaps fly home should you need or want to. But there are also often city specific companies that rent out cars, and if you are not doing the long distance thing they can sometimes be a lot less expensive.

Both the international and local ones hire out a wide range of vehicles from the super top luxury types to small runabout vehicles. The cost of car rental here is fairly high, mostly due to the high cost of insurance.

To hire a car you will need a valid driver's licence, and to include on the rental agreement form the details of everyone who is going to drive the car and they must also show their licences. Only if you are over 18 may you drive legally in South Africa, but some rental companies refuse to rent to those under 25, or sometimes charge a high insurance premium if they do. This does not apply to all companies.

SHOP TILL YOU DROP
When to Shop

Most residential shops operate between about 9 or 10 am and 5 pm from Monday to Saturday. Closer to the inner cities, shops tend to open earlier, but still generally close at 5 pm, although some tend to close closer to 6 pm. Most major supermarkets have extended shopping hours, often to 7 or 8 pm. Some also open earlier towards the end of the week and close later, and almost all are open from late morning to early afternoon on Sundays. The home improvement shops also keep these extended hours as do some hardware stores, gardening shops, nurseries and selected pharmacies. Of course opening times can vary from city to city and neighbourhood to neighbourhood. But you will soon get to grips with the timing.

Remember, the above opening times apply in the cities and larger towns. In the smaller towns, the shopping hours seem to have remained more strictly 8 am to 5 pm, often with the 1 pm to 2 pm lunchtime closure, and they close on the dot at 1 pm on Saturdays as well. Seldom are they open on a Sunday at all in smaller towns, except for the convenience stores and supermarkets.

The Great South African Cafe

There is a strange and wonderful entity in South Africa called the cafe, or corner cafe. Not to be confused with a coffee bar *a la* the French! In South Africa, a cafe is more like a general provisions store carrying small amounts of almost anything that you are likely to run out of when the shops are shut. Mostly consumables like eggs, bread, milk, some vegetables and fruit, tinned foods, a wide range of sweets, cool drinks, newspapers and magazines are sold…and much, much more! Some also sell a range of fast foods, like fried chips, pies or sandwiches. Some cafes in the smaller towns, and especially those on the main arterial roads, have tables and chairs and offer a sit-down tea, coffee, snacks and light-meals service.

Cafes are open seven-days-a-week, usually on most public holidays too, and keep very long hours from around 7 am to 10 pm at night. Prices for provisions are higher generally than in supermarkets—but you are paying for the privilege of your forgetfulness and their long opening hours.

Sale Of Alcohol

Sale of alcohol in South Africa is governed by quite strict laws which limit the type of shop that can sell it and also the hours it can be sold. Mostly you buy your alcohol in 'bottle stores' which sell all forms of liquor, but not much else. You can now also buy wine, and sometimes beer, in most of the major supermarkets which have special liquor-trading licences. But do remember that no store is supposed to sell liquor of any sort on a Sunday, so the bottle stores are closed and the wine and beer sections in the supermarkets are closed off. This can be extremely irritating and sometimes even embarrassing, because often when impromptu dinner invitations are made, you could be asked to bring along some wine or beer, so it's wise to keep a few in stock.

The laws for selling liquor to children under the age of 18 have been tightened, and fines for bottle-store owners who transgress this are high and can include a jail sentence. The legal age for drinking and purchasing alcohol is 18 years old and this also applies to pubs and bars. Drinking alcohol in your home is of course a totally private affair.

Where You Least Expect it

Speaking from my personal experience of moving from South Africa to Europe and then to Southeast Asia, back to Africa and then much later to Canada for a while, I've learned that some household items are sold in different types of stores, in different countries. An example is a purple liquid called methylated spirits in South Africa which is used for cleaning windows or getting greasy marks off surfaces. It is freely available in all supermarkets and virtually every grocery store across the land. In England, you can only get it in a pharmacy, and then you may be asked exactly what you want it for!

You may even find that certain things you are accustomed to using at home are just not available in South Africa, or to make it even more complicated have a completely different name. There is a fine line between how much energy you spend looking for the right thing and how much you spend trying to use a different product or ingredient from the one you use back home. Whatever it is, don't get too stressed about it. What can seem so strange or unusual when you are new in country, becomes simply one of the many tiny little differences you will laugh about later on.

If there is some household application or even cooking ingredient you just can't seem to find, ask around—and don't be shy to ask in the most unlikely places. You are sure to establish a rapport with the shop owner who will want to know more about you, the newcomer to the land.

Hawkers selling traditional crafts and curios by the roadside offer good and unusual buys at attractive prices.

Making acquaintances at every turn is one of the quickest ways to integrate.

Roadside Shopping: Funky Craft and Even Some Home Basics

On many a street corner and even on the open roads sometimes, you may come across artists or crafts people selling a wide array of wonderful local handicrafts and occasionally even painting. My top favourites at the moment are ornaments or decorations made out of wire onto which beads have been threaded. Initially the scale of the trinkets was quite small—you may even have seen friends returning from South Africa with wire and beadwork key rings or small Christmas tree type decorations, but more recently some of the craftspeople have increased the scale to include wonderful beaded wire baskets ideal for fruit or just pure decoration on a table. And you can even buy life-sized sheep, goats, warthogs and slightly less than life-sized leopards, zebras and giraffes too. Bright, colourful, delightful!

Another choice, at least for those who decide to drive the route from Johannesburg to the eastern Cape are miniature windmills made with full working parts. You usually find them on the side of the road almost at the junction of the N1 and the N9 near Colesburg, just on the edge of the Karoo. Also made out of wire, tin and other found objects, and usually painted silver, they are very locally inspired as the area is dry cattle and sheep country where farmers use windmills to drive the boreholes to water their livestock.

Of course there is also a wide variety of craft markets and craft shops spread across most of the major or more tourist-oriented towns and cities. Some well-know markets include the Rosebank Craft Market held every Sunday in the parking lot of one of the larger suburban malls in Rosebank, Johannesburg; in Cape Town, Green Market Square and the pedestrianised St George's Mall which leads into it are both filled with art, craft as well as an array of clothes, often handmade and unique; in Durban there is a strip behind the beachfront esplanade where you can also buy a wide variety of unusual goodies. But don't limit yourself to these major markets. Just keep a look out whether its on city pavements or by the roadside. Often you will find something you just can't live without and it's an easy way to localise your home decoration too! Expect to bargain, but not too harshly.

At most major city intersections, there are also people selling a variety of basic domestic things: fruit, tissues, sunglasses, soft drinks, *biltong* (the local dried meat sticks like beef jerky)—the variety is endless.

Because the number of poor and very poor in South Africa is high (like many developing nations), you will also find a number of people begging at traffic lights. Some just have a hand out, or perhaps a cardboard sign asking for money and explaining why they need it; others are more creative and sell jokes written on a slip of paper, or ask you to drop the rubbish from your car—soft drink tins, bits of paper, read newspapers—into their large rubbish bag for a few Rands.

MEDIA MADNESS
The news industry in South Africa has always been intent on maintaining responsible press freedom. Make no mistake, this has not been easy. The earliest newspapers in the 1800s were often at loggerheads with the government of the time, and in the politically turbulent times leading up to the end of the apartheid era, the then government implemented a barrage of harsh press restrictions on both local and foreign press to curb reporting on the horrors of those violent times.

Now freedom of the media, freedom to give or receive information and ideas, freedom of artistic creativity, academic freedom and freedom of scientific research are all enshrined in our constitution. Add to this an information-hungry population and we support a volatile, broad ranging and fairly large media market. However, at the time of going to press the government is trying to curtail some of this hard-won freedom with a Bill before Parliament. It is hoped by many that they do not succeed.

The Printed Word
South Africa has a wide range of newspapers, ranging from the most conservative to the fairly liberal. There are both

morning and afternoon dailies, Sunday papers and weekly newspapers in which the debate is often quite lively, be it on politics or sport—probably the two most discussed subjects! There are really too many to list here, so my advice is that once you have chosen your home town, just buy a broad spectrum of papers and soon you will know which suites your taste. Some are excellent, some not so good, some more popular, others aimed at a narrower audience—you make the choice. (My top favourite is the national, weekly hard-hitting *Mail & Guardian*, which also has a good entertainment section.)

Foreign newspapers are available in the major centres, but they are expensive as most are flown in, although a few, such as the United Kingdom's Financial Times, are now printed locally. You can also subscribe to almost any overseas publication you wish to, either in hardcopy or of course online.

A recent phenomenon is the dramatic explosion in the magazine market which ranges from a few good business magazines, to a plethora of women's and home decor magazines, general interest magazines and of course a vast array of sport and outdoor lifestyle publications. Quite a large number of them are international franchises such as Oprah Winfrey's *O*, *Vogue*, *Runner's World*, *Sports Illustrated* and many more. Foreign magazines tend to be pretty expensive in Rand terms, but at least there is a fairly good selection of European and American publications to choose from.

What's a Couch Potato to Do?

The government-owned South African Broadcasting Corporation (SABC), controls most of the free-to-air television stations and some of the radio stations. At this stage there is one free privately-owned television channel, e-TV, which broadcasts news, sport and entertainment, mostly in English, and is a good competitive alternative to the state TV stations: SABC 3 which broadcasts in English, and SABC 1 and SABC 2 which tend to broadcast in a variety of the other 10 national languages.

A typical South African barbecue spread. Traditional *boerewors*, a type of sausage, are made from coarsely minced beef and spices and then formed into a continuous spiral. *Sosaties* are meat cooked on skewers.

Located between Robben Island and Table Mountain, the Victoria and Albert Waterfront in Cape Town is South Africa's most popular tourist attraction. Besides its shopping and dining options, visitors can also enjoy themselves at the Two Oceans Aquarium and Chavonnes Battery Museum.

Street vendors hawking vuvuzelas, which are plastic horns, and South African flags during the 2010 FIFA World Cup held in the country. Soccer is the most widely played sport in South Africa and a quick way to break the ice with locals is be able to discuss the game with them.

A street food stall in Cape Town selling popular snacks such as *biltong,* a kind of cured meat. Various types of meat are used to produce it and the texture is similar to beef jerky.

A dancer in a Tokolosh mask at the Lesedi Cultural Village, a tourist attraction near Johannesburg that celebrates the cultures of the various groups of people present in South Africa.

There is one major pay-TV group, Multichoice, which has dominated this market for a good few decades. It does have a very broad bouquet with some 60 channels (depending on your choice), including a variety of international 24-hour news channels, although its licence at this stage does not allow it to produce its own local news channel. Most of its programmes are in English and a large number are international, but there is also a degree of local content and a very wide range of sports channels.

For technical buffs, or anyone who wants to bring their telly with them and needs to know if it can be converted, the system used in South Africa is based on the C.C.I.R. 625-line system 1 standard, and is PAL. It is a toss up whether it is worth bringing a TV from a country where the system is not the same. I did (from Singapore) and had it converted and some 10 and more years later am still using it, but I am not an avid TV watcher. In addition, today's TVs are so much more complex that it is certainly worth asking someone with a good understanding of 'TV technicalities' for advice.

Radio used to be very much in the hands of the SABC too, but with democracy came the democratisation of the airwaves and although the SABC does operate a number of public and commercial radio stations, there are now a number of privately-operated stations too. Most are regional or even city-based, and vary from the Gauteng-based Classic FM to stations geared for the funky youth. Some stations have hard-hitting news and interviews, some host talk and phone-in shows, while others broadcast in various languages. There are also about 100 community stations for interests as varied as rural women and different religions.

For Bookworms

The bad news is that most books are fairly expensive in South Africa, and the very specialised ones are very expensive. Some of the blame is foisted on the fact that many are imported and our exchange rate is not as good as it could be. But even locally produced or locally printed books—of which there are many since many of the international publishers represented here also print here—are expensive by American, British or Singaporean standards.

The good news is that there are some pretty good bookstores: the big chains like Exclusive Books, and a fair few independents (sadly dwindling though) which carry a wide variety of both fiction and non-fiction. Books by South Africans and about South Africa—our past, present and our hoped-for future—are currently in great abundance. This is good news for anyone who needs to get to know the country and its foibles.

Library services are a bit patchy. In some areas they can be excellent and this is generally the rule in the more affluent parts of the bigger cities and also in certain smaller towns. In some areas, mobile libraries offer a periodic service.

KEEP COOL WITH A SWIMMING POOL

As you fly into Johannesburg's OR Tambo International Airport, or over any other major South African town, you will see thousands of tiny turquoise patches alongside the rows of suburban homes. They are private swimming pools and many homes in nearly all medium to affluent suburbs have one.

A lot of summertime socialising takes place around the pool, including the *braaivleis* or barbeque. And there is

Quite a few suburban homes have pools where a lot of summer entertaining takes place. They are also great playgrounds for children (supervised of course!)

no doubting the amount of pleasure the entire family, but especially the children, will get from a pool.

But don't be totally seduced by this cool, turquoise beauty. Pools require a fair amount of time-consuming maintenance and fairly costly chemicals to keep them looking cool, sparkling and turquoise. If maintenance is not kept up, the pool quickly turns a murky green from algae, and begins to resemble your suburban lawn!

In the past, you also had to scrub the walls and floor, and clean the leaves out. But now, thanks to a great South African invention, the 'Kreeply Krauly', with a flip of a switch this magical creature made up of weights and counterweights wiggles its way around your pool, sucking up leaves and dirt and spewing them into the filter system. It's worth its weight in gold!

A pool can also be dangerous. If you do have small children, you cannot be too safety-conscious and a good fence or pool net is essential. It is also essential to ensure your children learn to swim, especially if you come from a country where swimming is not as much a part of life as it is here.

There are a number of superb public pools in the larger urban centres—far too many to numerate, but I can vouch for one in particular: the Seapoint pool on the seafront in Cape Town. For the sum of R 10 per entry (you can also get very inexpensive season passes) you can choose from an Olympic size pool, a 28-m (92-ft) single depth pool, a diving pool with 1 m and 3 m boards and a kiddies' paddling pool—all filled with sparkling seawater!

Once you are in situ and want to find a public pool, the best route is to phone your local municipality or look up their website. In smaller towns if there is a pool you surely will know where it is, if only from the noises of rowdy happy children of a summer afternoon.

BE WEATHER WISE

The weather is very volatile in South Africa, with droughts, high or low pressure systems, hail storms and on a rare occasion even a snow storm or two, especially in the higher mountain areas. You may well experience the occasional totally unseasonable weather conditions. In November 1992, it snowed in parts of the Western Cape Province when normally at that time of the year temperatures there would be in the high 20s or even 30s (68°F–86°F).

Other than some amount of unpredictability, the South Africa climate is renowned for its warm to hot summers and mild winters. Even when a cold spell hits the country, it rarely lasts more than a week or so at a time. Snow seldom falls, except on the mountain tops, but when it does fall in or near the urban areas—every five or 10 years—it is cause for great excitement. Then you will quite likely see besuited businessmen building snowmen or throwing snow balls in the streets of downtown Johannesburg.

Winters are not long, between June and August mostly, but homes are not geared for the cold weather and you may find yourself a lot more uncomfortable than expected. Central heating is not common, nor is double glazing or well-fitted doors and windows, especially in older homes.

Because we are in the southern hemisphere, the sun is almost directly above us in summer, while in winter it is north of us and its angle is more oblique. This means that north-facing houses are best for light and warmth in winter. So get your bearings when house hunting.

Summers are generally pleasantly warm, but can become quite hot, especially in the northern parts of the country and in and around Durban, where the sub-tropical climate adds a good dose of humidity to the high temperatures. Although most office complexes are air-conditioned, other than in Durban, few homes are. So if you do feel the heat, try to find a home that has good ventilation, a big veranda (also called a *stoep* here) or a shady tree!

Dressing for the Season

Dressing for the weather is a big part of enjoying the climate here. In summer, light cotton or linen clothes, formal and informal, are the order of the day. Businessmen usually are expected to wear suits in the bigger city environments, so be sure to have a few light-weight ones. In the evenings, temperatures usually drop a few degrees, and a light jacket or wrap may be necessary, especially if you are outdoors.

In spring and autumn, you can usually get away with wearing your summer wardrobe and adding a light wool jacket or cardigan. Both seasons are very short and hardly worth a wardrobe of their own.

In winter, especially in the central part of the country (the Gauteng area) and also the southern Cape, you will certainly need winter wear. Woollen suits, sweaters, jackets, and even boots are quite appropriate attire. A coat will certainly come in handy, especially at night. But there really is no need for the ultra-cold weather gear needed to brave a northern hemisphere's cold, dark winter.

The day/night variation is less than most European or north American seasons, which means we have less of the long, dreamy, sunlit summer evenings, but it also means winters are not as long or dark!

DRESSED FOR SUCCESS

In general, the dress code in South Africa is becoming ever more relaxed as the various cultures mix and socialise together. But it is also gaining a style of its own. Young local designers are having the time of their lives creating wonderful clothing ranges that take from various cultures and mix and match to form some unique and stylish outfits for a variety of occasions. Dare I say this does apply far more (but not solely) to women! I am sure you have all seen photographs of ex-president Nelson Mandela in many formal and often international venues in his famous 'Madiba' shirts instead of the ubiquitous suit and tie!

But there is still some degree of dress code expected at times, sometimes quite different across the different cultures. It also varies quite a bit from one region to another. Your easiest option is to imitate your work colleagues and friends until you have a grasp of it. You are seldom likely to cause major offence to your hosts by inappropriate dress as they are sure to take into account your recent arrival in the country, but you may well feel ill at ease standing out like a sore thumb in your jeans at a function where everyone else is smart and fairly formal.

In big cities, like Johannesburg and Cape Town, people from all cultures dress fairly formally for your traditional office jobs. Businessmen are expected to wear suits or at least a jacket and tie, although this is easing a bit now as some people foresake the tie on occasion. Evening wear is sometimes less formal, but still smart, unless your hosts insist that it's very casual—which can mean jeans and open-neck shirts or T-shirts. In some of the seaside or resort towns and cities, dress is less formal as the beach culture permeates the business one.

In rural communities, the Boer or white farmers often wear khaki shirts, short knee-length socks and boots or shoes. However, being the conservative element of the population, their formal dress worn mostly to church is quite Old World.

Traditional or tribal Africans mostly wear Western style dress today, but for certain celebrations or special occasions they may don their traditional attire. This varies from group to group and often includes clothes and head dresses made of gloriously bright and colourful fabrics (take a look at the opening of parliament each year in February to get an eye-full of modern/traditional style). Some clothes and adornments can also be made from animal skins, while on occasion some men may carry spears, shields and fighting sticks as part of the full outfit.

CULINARY CROSSROADS

CHAPTER 6

'Ex Africa semper aliquid novi.'
(Out of Africa, always something new.)
—Pliny the Elder, Roman scholar

FOOD, FOOD, GLORIOUS FOOD....

Eating, whether at home or eating out, is most often a sociable and shared occasion. Among the Western and Westernised communities, who are mostly city dwellers, sharing a meal is done mostly in friendship, but it can also be in the interests of a good business relationship. However in the more traditional, rural, or tribal communities, the sharing of food characterises the spirit of the people and is a cultural tradition to be shared with strangers and possibly even enemies.

Because South African society as we know it now has grown through the centuries out of merging local cultures with those of various immigrant communities, the cuisine has grown out of a healthy and varied mixture of cultural ideas and flavours, tempered by what was locally available. The era of the 'global village' has also enabled an ever-widening array of foods to grace the tables of restaurants and the fast food joints across the country, making our cuisine as open to change and experimentation as is our new and progressing society.

Sometimes dishes or ingredients are not what they seem, not what you are accustomed to, but on many occasions they are simply hiding behind a different guise. You just have to dig a little deeper, or become accustomed to finding them with a different label or a different name. Some things will certainly be a totally new experience so try them with an open mind, or unbiased taste buds. You will certainly love some and no doubt you will loathe some too. It's all part of the excitement of being a newcomer.

Traditional Foods

Traditional South African food in its various guises, is becoming ever more popular as we learn to appreciate our own styles and tastes and not always hanker over foreign fare. This is a well-developed trade in the wine lands and farmlands around Cape Town where locals and tourists alike enjoy a wide array of traditional cuisine, savoured from little taverns to top-end restaurants, as they drive through some of the country's most idyllic rural scenery. Besides the Western Cape, top class restaurants and smaller bistros and pubs in all the major cities, and often some of the smaller villages, also offer a wide choice of local dishes.

Cape Malay Cuisine

Some of South Africa's greatest traditional dishes come from the Cape Malay cuisine. In the 15th century, the Dutch brought Malays to work for them at the Cape during their many voyages to the East in their quest for control of the Spice Trade. The Malay women, who were excellent cooks, brought a vast knowledge of both oriental and Indian spices with them, then developed a culinary tradition based on the ingredients available to them in the Cape at that time. Refined over the centuries, these dishes are now considered great delicacies in many homes and are served in many restaurants as well.

There are some excellent and unusual Cape Malay dishes to look out for. Try one of the *bredies* for example. They resemble a vegetable and meat stew, but it's the unusual additions that give them a mouth-watering edge. Some have a strong tomato base, others have quince, pumpkin or cabbage in them. And one of the most famous is called *Waterblommetjie*, a *bredie* made with the addition of a special water flower that grows wild in the ponds in rural areas in the Western Cape.

Bobotie is another hot favourite. Originally made from leftover mutton, it is a baked minced-meat dish that is deliciously spiced and usually also has some dried fruit added to it. Before being served, curled fresh bay or lemon leaves are poked into the top of the pie and then an unsweetened custard is poured into the holes made by the leaves, as well as over the rest of the surface.

Or you could try some of the more traditionally Malay fare: *Pinangkerrie*, a meat curry to which tamarind and fresh green leaves from an orange tree are added; or *Denningvleis*, meat flavoured with bay leaves and tamarind. Each dish has special accompaniments like sliced onion sprinkled with powdered chilli, fresh grated quince fruit mixed with chilli powder, a mixture of mint leaves, and powdered chilli moistened with vinegar. Sometimes a drink made of soured milk with a slice of orange is served with the curries. A variety of preserved fruits and other sweets may also be served.

Don't be at all surprised to find many of the traditional Cape Malay dishes served with bright yellow rice. This is a local speciality, coloured and delicately flavoured with saffron or turmeric, and often has sultanas added for that tiny touch of sweetness quite common in this style of cooking.

There is an excellent book, part cookbook, but mostly a cultural culinary history of the early days of South Africa, and especially early Afrikaner cookery. It is called *Leipoldt's Food and Wine* (Ed. T S Emslie and P L Murray. Cape Town, South Africa: Stonewall Books, 2004), and documents the culinary skills of C Louis Leipoldt who also wrote the old (and hence also part of our new) national anthem, as well as poetry, novels, prose and children's books. In fact, he is seen as one of the greatest South African creative minds of the late 1800s.

Sauces/Chutneys/Atchars

The Malays also gave South Africa the heritage of wonderfully pungent and well-spiced sauces, chutneys and *atchars* (pickles). The chutneys and *atchars* are made with vegetables and fruit boiled and preserved in strong and spicy chilli, vinegar and sugar mixtures. Tangerine peel and pickled peaches are other delicacies. These are frequently served as condiments or side dishes.

From the West

Much of the rest of the cuisine in South Africa is based on an amalgam of European influences: French, British, Flemish, German, Italian, Portuguese, Greek and others. Pasta dishes are a firm favourite in many homes. A large Portuguese immigrant population has meant that the likes of a '*prego* roll' (similar to a steak sandwich, but encased in a crispy Portuguese-style bread roll) is quite common fare, especially as a pub snack.

But today, with the global trend in fusion cuisine, it is often hard to pinpoint any specific cuisine in many restaurants. More often you will find a glorious mixture of tastes and styles blended to suite the climate, season and whim of the chef.

From the East

Indian and Chinese food, although they have not become as mixed into the local cuisine as European food has, are eaten with relish by all, especially in restaurants and also at home in those communities.

Many South Africans prepare curry dishes in their homes, with the assistance of some excellent local Indian cookbooks like *Indian Delights* edited by Zuleikha Mayat, and Ramola Parbhoo's *Indian Cookery for South Africa*. In the Indian markets—in Durban they are by far the best— there is an abundance of exotic spices and curry mixtures to buy for your home cooking. One of the most notable of these, at least by name, is 'Mother-in-law Exterminator' which gives an indication of the potency of much of the Indian food in South Africa. Nearly all the exotic spices and herbs are also available in speciality shops in the main centres. Quite a few are even found on supermarket shelves now.

Chinese food is more often eaten in restaurants, but this cuisine too is becoming more mainstream as some of the larger supermarkets carry a good range of ingredients—and even pre-packaged fast-food varieties too. Although the Chinese population is fairly small with its heart in Johannesburg—the city centre and the suburb of Sydenham—there is an enclave of supermarkets and shops that stock a wonderful array of dried or canned imported

Chinese delicacies: from dried shrimps to water chestnuts, umpteen varieties of soy sauce...and much, much more. An endless array of noodles is also stocked.

AFRICAN DISHES

Some of the very indigenous dishes may well be a touch out of your ambit, as they are for many Westernised South Africans. But the adventurous could do a trial run on *morog*, a local version of spinach and not totally unlike its European cousin; or sorghum porridge for breakfast, in place of cereal, which is quite delicious with milk and sugar. For the very adventurous, you could try mopani worms, which are dried and eaten as snacks (like *biltong*), or added to rural African type stews. But along with flying ants, they are not obligatory and very unlikely to crop up in your food circuit unless you purposefully seek them out!

Quite a delicious snack found at the end of the summer and in early winter is a fairly dry *mealie* on the cob, which is roasted over an open brazier. Fairly dry, chewy and crispy, this is one of my favourite snacks and is usually sold in the downtown city areas, near the bus and train stations and the taxi ranks.

WHERE TO GET...
That Soupçon From Home

In the main cities, the bigger and better supermarkets as well as the delicatessens and speciality food stores carry a fairly good array of foreign food. But you will have to curb your desires a little as anything imported usually carries a higher price-tag. This is partly because of the novelty value, but mainly because you are paying for the pleasure of it being transported all the way to South Africa.

But be consoled with the fact that because this is a culturally diverse community and has been for many years, there are a number of things made in South Africa, but modelled on foreign foods. Any number of neo-European cheeses, for example, are made here and many are of high quality, and a pretty good imitation too! If you are hooked on the Australian spread 'Vegemite', you will find a South

African substitute called 'Marmite' (vegetarian) and 'Bovril' (meat extract), both of which are just like their namesakes in England. A lot of the international food conglomerates manufacture in South Africa and you will probably be surprised at how many Western-style and Western brand-named ingredients are available here.

Many of the health food shops stock the unusual goodies you may need for your own special brand of home cooking: pine nuts (ensure they are fresh!), *carob* powder (cocoa substitute for chocolate flavouring), buckwheat, tofu, *tahini* paste and a wide variety of vegetarian foods are available. They may also stock unusual cheeses, goat's milk and natural yoghurts, as will some of the speciality food stores. In reality, there are very few ingredients you cannot get here, but it may take a while to source them.

The amount, variety and quality of organic produce is growing fast—and the more there is a demand for it, the more this sector will expand we hope! Most often you will find organic foods in health food stores, but certainly some of the larger supermarket chains, Woolworths in particular, carry a good range, especially of fresh produce.

A South African supermarket shopping quirk to remember is that we pay for plastic shopping bags. The reason for this is ecological: to try and prevent people littering the environment (plastic shopping bags are often referred to as our 'national flower'!) we are encouraged to reuse them as often as possible, or better still not use them at all, but rather take your own bags with you.

From the Oceans

There has always been an abundance of seafood in South Africa's coastal waters. Because of the icy west coast seas and the markedly warmer Mozambican current on the east coast, the variety of seafood is also extensive. Unfortunately today, like most parts of the world's oceans, many of our favourite fish species are dwindling so fast they are close to becoming endangered.

In the days of yore, due to the hot and sunny climate, preservation of fish was of prime importance. Pickling was popular, especially with pepper, chillies, ginger, coriander seeds, caraway, aniseed and cumin being favourite pickling spices. Today, the tradition of pickled fish is carefully followed to gourmet delight! And as a dead giveaway to my culinary abilities, I have to admit that some excellent canned varieties are found in most supermarkets!

Snoek, a type of cod found in the Cape seas, is very popular today and often sold smoked. It is great to eat cold on sandwiches and often served at picnics, or as an excellent side-dish at lunch or on a buffet spread.

Some of the other top deep-sea fish are really good, especially when served fresh (never having been frozen). Some local names to remember are Kabbeljou, Cape Salmon (no resemblance to Scottish Salmon), Yellow Tail and even hake. However, like in much of the rest of the world's oceans, fish stocks are being seriously depleted here too. For this reason the World Wildlife Fund for Nature (WWF) in South Africa has drawn up a list of which fish are 'no-no', 'maybe' or 'definitely okay' to eat from a sustainability perspective. (See http://www.wwf.org.za/sassi)

Shellfish is also easy to get here, although some of the frozen fare is certainly imported from across the globe, not that it detracts from its quality or flavour. Prawns, crayfish, mussels, oysters and clams are seafood favourites and descendants of the French Mauritians, now owners of some of the sugar cane plantations on the KwaZulu-Natal coast, have added their Creole touch to these dishes. The South African Portuguese with some input from their Mozambican relatives seemed to have made prawns their trademark, and you may often see dishes called 'LM prawns' or '*Piri-Piri* prawns' on the menu—delicious but beware of the fire in the *piri-piri* chilli.

Landlubbers Have Their Share

Although many of the major cities are not coastal, this does not prevent landlubbers from getting very high quality fresh and frozen fish. Demand is so high, especially in Johannesburg, that some of the coastal dwellers complain that inlanders probably get some of their best catches, popped on a plane and rushed to the restaurant tables and supermarket shelves, almost quicker than they do.

Meat—The Regular and Exotic Kind

Most South Africans like to eat meat and the country certainly does have a reputation for producing good quality beef, and the mutton or lamb from the Karoo region is also said to be extremely good. In fact, many people just do not consider a meal complete without a meat dish. Chicken, mutton, fish (more recently) and pork (to a much lesser extent), follow hot on the heels of beef on most shopping lists.

Venison, that is game meat from antelope and warthogs (similar to wild boar), is a winter favourite, probably because this is the hunting season. However, there are now also a number of commercial farmers farming these animals as well as game birds to supply the city markets throughout the year, so you certainly will be able to get venison out of season, but not quite as readily. Certain restaurants specialise in 'wild' cuisine and have some of the more exotic ones on offer most of the time—try a steak of crocodile, a slice of warthog, or guinea fowl stew if traditional venison is not exotic enough for you.

Ostrich meat which also falls into the 'wild' category is now more easily available, even from some supermarkets these days. The ostrich industry, which in the period leading up to the first World War was a major money spinner from feathers for women's high fashion, took a depressing dive as war broke out and fashion changed. But today, the ostrich farmers are smiling again as meat—very low fat so it's very healthy—from this large bird makes it on to ever more dining tables.

Biltong and Other Specialities

Biltong, this strange local delicacy, originated in the 1830s when the Trekboers (the forerunners of the Voortrekkers) decided to explore the interior of the country and needed to preserve as much meat as they could from the game they shot. This snack has endured ever since with some spicy updates. It is made from strips of meat, very often game, but now also frequently beef, which has been marinated in spices and salt and then dried in the wind and sun. It is often served as a snack with drinks, but more and more restaurants serving traditional fare are using it in salads and as a topping for some of their dishes. Try it—you may be surprised how easily you take to it. It is easily available from both speciality *biltong* stores as well as in supermarkets, and also frequently found in the convenience stores attached to roadside petrol stations.

Other specialities, born of necessity by the explorers, are rough breads and meat dishes which are baked in an outside clay oven, fairly similar to those used in some Arab countries to bake bread.

Cooked green maize, a local version of corn-on-the-cob, is still a favourite even among city-slickers. If in the mid- to late-summer you hear a high-pitched shriek as you quietly go about your business in your residential neighbourhood, don't be alarmed. It quite often is, what seems to me, the unintelligible call of the green *mealie* sellers. Their wares are worth investigating, as they are usually freshly picked in the rural areas and make a delicious easy addition to a meal. Just boil until tender and serve with butter, salt and pepper. A microwave oven shortcuts this process to a matter of three or four minutes!

Maize is called *mealie* in South Africa and refers to the cob and its pips, or to the plant actually growing in the fields. Maize meal is called *mealie* meal and is a coarse-ground maize flour. In its cooked form, called *putu* or *pap* locally, this is the staple starch of many Africans in this country, in fact much of the southern African region—like rice is in China—and is also a firm favourite with many others, especially at a barbecue or *braaivleis*. It is cooked either to be like a thick porridge, or often made a little more dry and served with meat or gravy dished rather as mashed potato is in some cuisines. Corn flour is a fine white powder made from ground dried *mealie* and used as a thickening agent in sauces, desserts and the likes.

Fruit and Vegetables

Very good quality fruit and vegetables are grown in South Africa and a large variety is available in the supermarkets and greengrocers, but prices can be quite high, especially when something is not in season. An increasing quantity of fresh produce is exported these days, sometimes leaving those of us who live here with second best. But you can always find what you need, it just means a harder search or a higher price tag at times.

Some of the more exotic Eastern fruits like starfruit or rambutans are quite new to these shores, but entrepreneurs are starting to grow them as certain areas in the country are well suited to sub-tropical fruit production. Mangoes, guavas, papayas, paw-paws (similar to a papaya), avocados and bananas have a long traditional on these shores, as do pineapples, watermelons and a wide variety of citrus fruits. Deciduous fruits are mostly grown in the Western Cape with apples, peaches, nectarines, plums, apricots and the like easily available and of high quality when in season. Lychees and Cape gooseberries are other more unusual favourites. The berry family—raspberries, blueberries, strawberries and blackberries—were a rare luxury some years back, but ever more are being grown here and some are now imported too. A large, fresh fruit-juice industry has grown up in South Africa, with many *au naturel* juices (with no added sugar, colour or preservatives) competing for your attention on the supermarket shelf.

The Small-Timer

In recent times, the small fruit and vegetable producers have become disenchanted with the monopolistic approach of many of the large chain stores and supermarkets. Consequently, a host of vegetable and fruit stalls and farmers' cooperatives have sprung up on the outskirts of the cities and bigger towns, as well as along some of the trunk roads. Although not quite as convenient as the store just down the road, prices are often much more reasonable as the middleman has been cut out and freshness is usually assured.

There are also a number of small farmers on the perimeters of the larger cities who grow fresh herbs of excellent quality. And if you are lucky enough to have a home with a garden, growing your own can be fun and very a rewarding addition to your dishes.

Typical Local Dishes and Delicacies

- Boerwors: local sausage
- Biltong: dried meat
- Butternut squash soup: made from a deep yellow butternut squash, very slightly sweet, thick and creamy
- Sosaties: skewers of meat often interspersed with dried fruit or vegetables
- Boboti: minced meat dish with Malay spices and egg topping
- Potjiekos: meat stew cooked with lots of vegetables and spices in a three-legged pot on an open fire
- Rooibos tea: indigenous plant used as an alternative to regular tea. Caffeine-free and has many alleged health properties
- Marula Jelly: made from the fruit of an indigenous tree, it is a sweet accompaniment for venison and sometimes game birds.
- Koeksisters: traditional Afrikaans fare made from plaited dough which is deep fried and immediately dropped into icy-cold sweet syrup. The dough absorbs vast amounts of the syrup and the result is a crunchy, very sticky dessert—ideal for the very sweet-toothed!

Fresh Produce Prices

Don't expect inexpensive food in South Africa just because of our sunny skies, an abundance of agricultural land and a strong farming tradition. Sadly, the cost of food—even of staples like bread, maize meal, milk, meat, fruit and vegetables—is fairly high, especially top quality produce which is only a little less expensive than in Europe. Strangely, eating in restaurants, which, although costly to most locals, is not anywhere near as high as, say, London or Paris.

EATING OUT: BE BOLD

Restaurant dining is certainly a large factor in the general socialising and entertaining process in South Africa, obviously more so in the larger towns and big cities. This is partly because more city slickers have a bigger disposable income, and partly because there are many and varied restaurants to choose from—but of course one feeds the other. Add a dose of high tourism potential like Cape Town and you have an even greater number of restaurants with a vast variety of cuisines.

For almost all restaurants in South Africa the etiquette is very dependent on the type of establishment. The more casual and easy going restaurants—and this does not necessarily mean a lower cuisine quality—require less formality in dress and style beyond the normal requirements of polite behaviour. Raucous children (or for that matter childish adults) are not particularly favoured in these middle- to upper-end places, although they would certainly not exempt children who are well behaved.

Where to Go
Fine Dining

- **Johannesburg**: Auberge Michel; Linger Longer; Restaurant La Belle Terrasse and Loggia
- **Cape Town**: Bosman's; Cape Colony; The Atlantic

Casually Excellent

- **Johannesburg**: Gramadoelas; Moyo; 74; Koi; Browns; La Cucina di Ciro; Thomas Maxwell Kitchen
- **Cape Town**: Wakame; Constantia Uitsig; Five Flies; The Africa Café; Aubergine
- **Durban**: Jam restaurant (in Quarters on Avondale); Wodka Restaurant

Easier On The Pocket, Easy On Style

- **Johannesburg**: Franco's Pizzeria and Trattoria; Lucky Bean
- **Cape Town**: Willoughby and Co; Olympia Café and Deli
- **Durban**: Nourish; Billy the Bums; Bean Bag Bohemia

CELEBRATE IN STYLE: GRAND STYLE

To celebrate a very special occasion, or to treat yourself to some of the finest dining around, South Africa has a fair number of excellent top-class restaurants to choose from. Cape Town and Johannesburg have the greatest number of good dining places simply because they both have a big cosmopolitan population, while Cape Town also attracts a high number of top-end tourists, and Johannesburg is host to most international business transactions.

Ambience, style and cuisine are very individual, but in general they follow a Western European tradition in terms of etiquette, dress code and general behaviour, and on occasion may even be slightly less formal in manner, although style and service is usually out of the top draw. No particular no-no's apply bar the normal need for low-key, quiet and refined behaviour, and of course small children

Tips on Eating Out

Remember

- Booking is always a good idea for any restaurant that you have been told is popular, or currently trendy, and booking is essential for Friday and Saturday nights;
- Some restaurants close on Mondays, some on Sundays and some are not always open for lunch. It is always good to check this out in advance if you have your heart set on a time and place since there is no regular rule of thumb. Of course, there are some open seven days a week for lunch and dinner;
- In most restaurants you can dine fairly early, from about 6:30 pm onwards, but mostly kitchens tend to close between 10 pm and 10:30 pm. This doesn't mean you have to be out by then, but that you need to have placed your order by then. Some kitchens are open later on Friday and Saturday nights, but don't bank on it! Lunch is generally served from about noon to 2:30 pm or 3 pm.

too young to appreciate either the good conversation or the highbrow cuisine of your dinner would probably not be very welcome.

Décor is generally traditional and conservative, if very tasteful, and in some establishments you can certainly expect the full gamut of silver cutlery, fine bone china and crystal glassware, with staff trained in the nuances of serving in a refined dining environment. Dress is always smart casual and you can dress up as much as you like, but anything less than smart trousers and a jacket for men and elegant evening wear for women—dress, or a skirt or pants paired with an elegant evening jacket—is not acceptable. Ties are not usually required these days and shorts of course are a no-no!

To experience this level of sophistication and service you can certainly try **Auberge Michel** in Sandton, Johannesburg. Established by Frenchman Michel Morand and top

Tiny Tots

- For those with boisterous tiny tots, there certainly are easy-to-manage places and some that really make a big effort to cater to little children. An example in Johannesburg is Mike's Kitchen, and nationwide, most of the chain eateries, such as Spur steakhouses or Nando's, are easy on the kids and on the pocket.

Tipping

- It is not obligatory in South Africa but almost all diners do tip at least 10 per cent, and more if the service and attitude of the staff is good or excellent. It is worth noting that the salaries of waiting staff are very low as restaurateurs tend to expect them to make much of their income from tips. I certainly always tip generously in restaurants and coffee bars, and should I have the misfortune of really bad service I will certainly not tip at all, but I will also make it quite clear why I am not doing so to ensure it is understood that bad service is not acceptable at all.

Johannesburg businessman Vusi Sithole, it serves superior French cuisine in a relaxed atmosphere with top quality service. It also has an extensive wine cellar. And if you are interested in local South African politics and business, there is every chance you will catch a glimpse of many a famous person too. Another Johannesburg stalwart in the top league is **Linger Longer**, also in Sandton, which has beautiful grounds and a long history of fine dining. Food is a combination of classic French fare with a touch of the East. The Westcliff Hotel has one of the most superb views in all of Johannesburg, which adds ambience to the top quality of its fine dining restaurant, **Restaurant La Belle Terrasse and Loggia**.

Cape Town and the surrounding wine lands also has its fair share of fine dining restaurants. One of the most impressive is **Bosman's Restaurant**, part of Le Grand Roche hotel in the Drakenstein valley at Paarl, some 45 minutes outside Cape Town. The setting is superb in the heart of the wine lands with dramatic views of the nearby mountains. The food is a fusion of imagination and innovation and the wine cellar is excellent. (It is Africa's only Relais Gourmand restaurant). You can dine on the patio in good weather, and for a table of eight or more they will help you choose a menu to suit your tastes. The Le Grand Roche heritage began in 1717, and the current buildings were restored to their original Cape Dutch splendour in the 1990s and have now been declared a national monument.

You can also try the **Cape Colony Restaurant** in the world-famous Mount Nelson Hotel which offers fine dining with impeccable service and a traditionally elegant décor. The menu on the other hand has the best of contemporary local cuisine with a touch of Asia to add spice. The wine list is also very good. Another fine dining restaurant to try is the **Atlantic Restaurant** in the Bay Hotel, which has superb views of Table Mountain and specialises in South African and Asian cuisine.

WHAT'S THERE TO DRINK?

Generally, you can get almost any regular alcoholic drink in a South African bottle store. There is a huge variety of local beers and wines, and a great many imported ones too. Almost any form of spirits is available—some of the more standard spirits are made locally, while the top end is generally imported from the country of origin. There is a big range of brandy, many of which are locally made and very good. Nearly all whiskies are imported; while the other usual spirits like gins, vodkas, rums and such are both imported and locally produced. Of course not all bottle stores stock all products, but with a bit of research your every choice is sure to be covered.

Local And Potent

There is also a local speciality called 'cane'—the name is derived from the fact that it is a sugar cane distillate—and frankly, it has very little taste. It is not the most sophisticated of drinks, but adds an alcoholic kick to any mixer. You'll hear people yell, "Ji'me (give me) a glass of cane an' coke!", which means, "May I have a glass of cane spirits and Coca Cola".

A number of other weird and wonderful local concoctions are also available, which are based on a simple alcohol like cane mixed with flavours like the marula tree fruit, or pineapple perhaps, or even strawberry or mango. These drinks are definitely for less sophisticated palates, but quite good fun. Beware of the morning-after headaches, though!

Talking of headaches and hangovers, beware if you are offered *mampoer* or *witblitz*, the latter meaning 'white lightning'! These are home brews, similar to European schnapps, and are famed in some of the rural farming areas. Illegally brewed, they contain very high levels of alcohol and need to be drunk with caution by the uninitiated. Locals seem to be able to quaff them with great abandon and love nothing better than for you to join them at it. You will fall over long before they do. You have been warned!

Beer—The National Drink

Indigenous African beer, made from sorghum and called *maheu* (pronounced 'ma-he-oo'), is a fairly thick drink, sometimes even like very runny porridge, quite sour, and very much an acquired taste. However if you do learn to like it, it has a fairly high nutritional value and a low alcohol content.

Farm workers enjoying some traditional beer, *maheu*, after a hard day's work.

The real home-brewed thing is most often found in the African rural areas and drunk in great quantities at special feasts and traditional ceremonies. Beer consumption often forms part of the ritual at a ceremony like a tribal marriage, a courtship or a funeral.

Sorghum beer is also made commercially for consumption in the urban areas. They are packaged in glazed cardboard cartons, rather like milk cartons, and are sold almost solely in the townships. In the 1976 riots that flared across South Africa's black urban areas, angry students burned the state-owned beer halls in protest, not against the beer, but against the fact that so many people spent so much money there and it was all for the state's coffers.

Drinking 'clear beer'—the kind most of you will know as normal beer—is a national pastime among almost all South Africans. No social function—*braaivleis*, sports match (live or on TV), or party—is thought complete without the consumption of vast quantities of Lion or Castle, Hansa or Millers. South African Breweries (SAB) is the producer of the whole toot, and until recently, they have been a very successful near monopoly.

However, with the quest for a little more individualism, a few small breweries have sprung up around the country,

sometimes selling their beer only in their own locality. Many of these beers are of excellent quality and often worth the extra cost. But do a taste test yourself across the board. If nothing else, you will have a lot of fun and endear yourself to local drinkers with your superficial knowledge of the brews which can be shared during those endless discussions about sport—any sport.

Wines and Vineyards

Although the early Dutch settlers may have brought the first vines to the Cape, the French Huguenots brought viticulture to the southern shores of South Africa, and an extensive and internationally acclaimed wine industry developed and flourished over the years. Some stalwart brand names to help you negotiate the copious racks in the bottle stores until you have a handle on the subject are: Boschendal, L'Ormarins, Nederberg, Backsberg, Thelema, Hamilton Russel, Meerlust and Groot Constantia. Of course there are many, many more, but these will be a good guide to begin with.

In the wine-growing area of the south-western Cape, not far into the hinterland from Cape Town, you can visit a number of the country's best wine estates on what is called the 'Wine Route'. You can drive from one to another

Some South African wine labels, showing the diversity available.

tasting the wares and, when you find what you like, you can buy it directly from the estate. Although you won't effect a huge price saving compared to some of the larger bottle stores, you certainly will have a wonderful time. You may even discover a small hidden-away estate that suites your taste buds and your pocket, and does not sell its products through the larger retail outlets.

Many of the estates are hundreds of years old and the traditional Cape Dutch architecture is unique and often set against idyllic, mountainous backdrops. Some estates offer wonderful lunchtime spreads which gives you a chance to sample the local cuisine with the fruits of the vine. For the more popular ones, like Boschendal, it is advisable to book ahead of time. As the day wears on, beware, the wallet gets progressively lighter along with your head, while the crates of wine weigh heavily on the axles of your car.

Check the Cape Town tourist information outlets or website (http://www.capetown.gov.za) for information on the Wine Route: which estates are open to the public, the opening times, what is on offer, and the likes. There are also some excellent pocket books written by wine buffs to help guide your choice of wines without you having to make too many costly mistakes. My favourite is the highly informative *South African Wines* by John Platter, which is updated each year with information on all the new vintages and is ideal for anyone who wants to make the most of South Africa's long wine tradition and especially the small, new and not commonly known boutique wineries. There is also one called *The Plonk Drinkers Guide*, which rates the cheaper wines by price as well as quality. These books will also explain the meaning of the blue, red and/or green bands around the neck of the bottle.

The Biodiversity & Wine Initiative (BWI), found at website: http://www.bwi.co.za, is an organisation which promotes organic and eco-friendly wine farming. They can alert you to which wines are farmed and produced in this manner.

Drinking in Restaurants

It is good to remember that some restaurants have a full liquor licence which means they can sell any alcohol, while others only have a wine and malt licence which means you are restricted to beer, wine and the odd liqueur only. There are still a few restaurants that do not have a licence at all, so you bring your own drinks. This lack of licence does not necessarily denote a lack of quality in a restaurant, it just means they have not been able to get a liquor licence or do not want one. For the customer, as long as you are familiar with this quirk, it means you can drink exactly what you choose because you bring it along, and at half the price! As with restaurants the world over, drinks, especially wine, have a pretty high mark-up.

Although many licensed restaurants will frown rather long and hard at you, you are allowed to take your own alcohol into any restaurant you like. They are, however, allowed to charge you a corkage fee, for letting you drink it there. It is not an unforgivable thing to do, but it honestly doesn't win the friendship of the proprietor. I think the most appropriate time to bring your own wine to a licensed restaurant is when you have been there before and have found the wine list inadequate or of bad quality.

ENTERTAINING AT HOME

A lot of entertaining is done at home and most of it is pretty casual—in fact, South Africans are not very formal people in general. It is quite common to have people round for dinner or even a casual supper during the week, but it is most often done over the weekends. It is also fairly standard to offer to bring something: either a dish of food, or a salad, or (less complicated for a newcomer) some beer and/or wine. Often your host will tell you not to worry about bringing anything. It is then up to you to gauge the situation, to see if it is really meant or not. Except in the most pretentious homes, a bottle of wine or a box of chocolates is always welcome.

Dress for home entertaining is usually casual too. Men will be fine in decent jeans, chinos or other casual trousers and an open-neck shirt. Much the same goes for women. There is no harm at all in asking your host how you should dress, rather than arrive in a dress suit and find everyone else around the pool in swimsuits!

Don't be too casual in manner, however. Slouching on someone's lounge suite (unless you are really good friends) or prying into the private rooms will not be welcomed, unless you are invited to view a new possession or to have a look around the house, in which case your host will no doubt show you around. And don't take your pets to visit your friends! Most people have pets: and animals rarely get on with your friends' four-legged friends.

The Braaivleis or Barbecue

The *braaivleis*, literally meaning 'roasted meat', is a barbecue—a distinct cultural occurrence, which has spread from being mostly part of white South African culture to being pretty ubiquitous in one form or another. Usually shortened to the word *braai,* it is one of the most favoured ways of outdoor entertaining, and is also one of the easiest and most relaxed. And it's very much a family affair—kids are always welcome.

If you are invited for a *braai*, here's the ritual: it's always outdoors, and around the pool if your host has one. It could be for lunch which means you arrive at about noon and expect to eat an hour or so later. Then the afternoon is usually spent chatting. If it is a dinnertime *braai,* you arrive in the early evening for a night-time affair. Of course when a *braai* is going well, lunchtime can stretch right through to suppertime and beyond. Vast quantities of beer are usually consumed, wine too.

The spread includes a variety of meat, fish (on occasion), a range of salads, bread rolls and special sauces. *Sosaties*, a traditional favourite, consists of little blocks of marinated meat sometimes interspersed with pieces of onion, green peppers (capsicum) and other vegetables on a skewer, similar to a kebab. Another favourite is *boerewors* or 'farmers' sausage', which is a South African-style sausage, not too refined and often spiced with many 'secret' ingredients. Sometimes home-made *boerewors* is served, but often they are bought from good butcheries and supermarkets.

If it's a very traditional *braai*, you will have *mieliepap* or *stywepap*, also called *putu* (described earlier), which is a type of stiff, fairly dry porridge made out of maize (a little like Italian *polenta*). *Mieliepap* is often an acquired taste for newcomers. Often, guests chip in by bringing a salad or a dessert, or perhaps some beer or wine. When you are invited, ask your host what you should bring along.

Early on at a *braai*, you may find all the men in a huddle and the women forming their own social group. It's the men's role to cook the meat to perfection—probably the only time many South African men can be persuaded to do anything remotely domestic, so leave them to stand around the fire, always with a can of beer in their hand, discussing both the merits of cooking methods and the day's sporting events. Once the meat is ready everyone tucks in and a grand time is had by all.

'Without the arts we run the risk of becoming
a nation of housing and taps.'
—Thabo Mbeki, past South African president

ONE OF THE MOST SUCCESSFUL WAYS of getting to know a country quickly and learning the quirks and foibles of its culture is to immerse yourself in its leisure time activities: outdoor activities, formal sport, informal gym and leisure centre activities, theatre, music, fine art, anything and everything that takes your interest. In this way, you will soon meet a host of people from a very varied sector of the community, and often they are people you may not come into contact with in your home or work environment. Fortunately, most South Africans are easy going, sociable and chatty, so whether you are at the gym, at an art exhibition opening, or having a drink at an interval at the theatre, it is very easy to just strike up a conversation. Friendships so often grow from the most unlikely of meetings!

LEISURE—IT'S AN OUTDOOR WORLD

South Africans love being outdoors. Whether it is socialising, relaxing, watching or playing a game—if they are out-of-doors under the sunny blue skies, they tend to be happy.

Weekends are a particularly special time for outdoor living, which is why so many South Africans are reluctant to work on Saturdays. This is not good for the work ethic nor the country's productivity, but certainly good for the soul, or so they feel. What people do depends a lot on the city they live in.

In Johannesburg, especially in the more affluent areas, a great deal of entertaining is done at home, in the garden.

South Africa's long west coast beaches, often deserted, are ideal to get away from it all, but beware the icy water!

Otherwise, a Sunday drive out into the Magaliesberg mountains north-west of the city, or a picnic at one of the parks, or the zoo, is quite common.

In Durban, with its mellow climate, even in the winter people flock to the beach to soak up the sun and enjoy the sea. For a longer outing, a drive to the southern end of the Drakensberg mountains takes not much more than an hour.

Cape Town also has a beach culture, especially during the summer months. In winter, the sea is far too cold to swim in and so beaches are best for long walks. An added bonus for the outdoor enthusiasts is Table Mountain, which offers some of the most beautiful, if sometimes strenuous, hikes. It is also possible to walk a short distance up one of its slopes and then settle down with a bottle of wine as you watch the sun set over the sea. A drive around the peninsula is a firm favourite, as is a wine-tasting trip into the hinterland.

On weekend nights, the city centres tend not to be the bustling metropolises they are during the workday week as South Africans generally live in the suburbs. Part of the reason is that many of us prefer living in houses with gardens, and partly it is because there has been very little residential space in city centres. Durban has tried to integrate its lively after-hours life into its city centre and to some extent it has succeeded. And now, especially in downtown Johannesburg and Cape Town's inner city bowl, big old office blocks are being converted into luxury apartments and attracting a young and hip clientele.

Dress Codes?

Leisure-time dress code is fairly casual, but it's as well to know just how casual to be. For starters, there are still a few places, mostly elegant bars and some restaurants, that may deny you entry if you are wearing jeans—no matter how prominent the designer label is! To be truthful, I recently tested this rule in a top hotel bar that had a well displayed sign saying: 'No Jeans Allowed'. Donned with a smart silk shirt, formal jacket and a pair of designer blue jeans, accented with a touch of jewellery, I marched right in. Not a word was said. Knowing the management well, I later asked why the sign was up if I had been admitted. The answer was obvious: being a top-rate hotel, they insist on a degree of formality in their formal bar. If dressed in a T-shirt paired with jeans or shorts, I would have been asked politely to use the casual pubs that are aplenty in the seaside resort.

For casual outdoor functions, and especially sports matches, jeans or shorts with T-shirts, sweatshirts or open-neck shirts are perfectly alright for both sexes. Sundresses and skirts, too, are ideal for women in the hot summer months. South Africans are quite accustomed to women baring their arms and backs, so sleeveless tops and dresses or halter-neck tops are just fine, even in a more formal situation, except in the more conservative churches. Men, on the other hand, may need to wear a jacket for more formal functions. Of course style has changed dramatically with independence, and African style collar-less shirts (like those ex-President Nelson Mandela always wears) are seen as suitable for almost any occasion. Many formal invitations which used to stipulate 'black tie' now add 'or traditional' which encompasses the many forms of formal dress worn across our rainbow nation. It makes for much more interesting dress too! And, like much of the rest of the world, formal dress has eased into a far less restrictive style.

In summer, most people wear sandals or sneakers to any very casual event. Going barefoot in your own home or in a friends', if they suggest it, is fine too; but in public places, it is not often done. Of course if you are being entertained around a pool, then bare feet is the norm. Mostly children can get away with bending any of these norms.

Generally, Johannesburg is a tad more formal in its casualness. In Durban, a much more laid-back seaside city, an ensemble of flip-flops (rubber thong sandals), shorts and a T-shirt is quite often the dress of the holidaymakers. Cape Town is a strange mixture of the two. More formal and proper in manner, it also has a great beachwear culture. However, in the city centre, people are more formally dressed.

The Sun Factor

Remember that in South Africa the sun shines almost every day of the year. Sounds great in theory, but it takes its toll on your skin. The fairer your skin and the less accustomed you are to harsh sunshine, the greater the toll. So be wary and make use of the umpteen different sunscreens and suntan lotions available on the market. They are worth every cent you spend as the incidence of skin cancer here is very high. Children are often outdoors for much longer hours than you are, so try to ensure they are smothered in lotion and preferably wear a hat too. It is so easy to forget the time or the intensity of the sun when you are sitting absorbed in a game of cricket. Your scarlet face, neck, shoulders and ankles will remind you of your folly for days afterwards! In Africa, sunstroke can be a reality—spending too long in the sun when you are not accustomed to it —or even when you are—can make you really ill. It's not worth it.

NIGHTLIFE
Pub Culture

Pubs, bars and shebeens form a large part of city nightlife, especially over weekends. Pub culture is generally similar to pubs anywhere—often, rounds of drinks are bought by one person for the group. This can get a bit tricky if you don't want to spend all night there, but have to wait your turn to buy a round! If you want to leave early, try to buy an early round, so that when you leave, no one will call you miserly for not having paid your share. Not all pubs work like this and in many, probably what I would call a bar, you will go along with specific friends, order a few drinks and split the bill. In fact this is ever more the norm now.

Because, in the past, the state would not grant pub licences to Africans in the townships, the small backyard illegal shebeens developed. Usually a room in a home was set aside where home-brewed beer could be bought and consumed in a congenial, if spartan, atmosphere. Most often they were owned and run by women, and as the trade was quite lucrative, the more successful women became known as the Shebeen Queens. As the years passed, a greater variety of alcohol was served in shebeens, especially beer. Many shebeen queens (and kings) began to openly flout the law with big successful, music-filled establishments. Today of course anyone with the correct credentials can apply for a liquor licence. Do remember that you have to be over 18 years old to be served alcohol, even in a restaurant, and generally under-18s are not allowed into pubs and bars.

The Night's Bright City Lights

Night life in South Africa is limited almost entirely to the cities where, with a bit of help from friends and the *Mail & Guardian* newspaper guide, you will find the kind of entertainment that suits your fancy. Clubs, pubs, discos, jazz bars and a wide variety of traditional and local theatre are available. There are also many movie complexes with loads of different cinemas screening most of the mainstream international movies, and there are also a few movie complexes, really only in the bigger cities, that specialise in art house films.

Remember one thing about nightlife in South Africa, and this applies to restaurants too—it often begins and ends earlier than, say, in Europe. There are not many restaurants that will seat you much after 10 pm, so be sure to check when the kitchen closes if you are planning a meal after a show! There are of course exceptions.

Where Can You Have a Flutter?

Gambling was legalised in the new South Africa, but is strictly controlled by a special licence and of course it is totally off-limits to anyone under 18 years old. In the recent past, a number of large casino complexes have been built on the outskirts of all the major cities and even in some more obscure parts of the country. So if you feel the need to have a go at the tables or on the slot machines, just hive off to any of these plastic worlds where all is fantasy and night-time. The most famous of these is of course Sun City which, although it developed around the gaming business, is now a huge entertainment complex with swimming pools, a fake ocean with waves, water rides and one of the world's top golf courses. It also has a range of hotels from top-end 5-star luxury to more affordable family fun.

Horse-racing is quite legal and there is a lot of it in all the major centres. Most races are run on Saturdays, but there are also weekday races. The most famous, moulded on the Epsom Derby, is the Durban July. Always run on the first Saturday in July in Durban, it attracts huge crowds and attention is always focused on celebrities and outrageous dress sense. The Cape Met, Cape Town's equivalent, is not quite as famous but a lot more stylish.

SPORT

Most South Africans are sports mad. It is the one thing that unites the country more than anything else. It crosses racial, language, political and, yes, gender barriers. If you are as sports mad as we are, you may remember the first Rugby World Cup played in the new South Africa in 1995. The Springboks, as our international rugby team is called, won and then president Nelson Mandela put on the No. 6 shirt of the captain, Francios Pienaar, a white Afrikaner. The two embraced and the barriers of hundreds of years of racial segregation seemed to melt, as did the hearts of most South Africans. But remember it wasn't always like this. During the latter years of apartheid, international sanctions prevailed and our sports teams were not allowed to compete in any international competitions. The main reason for this of course is that all sports, bar football, and cricket to a small degree, were racially segregated.

For most of us, if we are not playing sport, then we are watching it—either live or on TV. You may even find sports-mad colleagues taking a day off work to watch cricket live, or even some international competition on the television that is scheduled on a weekday. If they are not watching the games, they are talking about it. Strangely though, there seem to be very few homegrown sports, but almost every major international sport is played here. Some international competitions are hosted here on occasion: Rugby World Cup in 1995, Cricket World Cup in 2003 and the football World Cup in 2010. Many of the major international sports competitions are screened on local television.

Football, or soccer as it is called here, rugby and cricket are seen as *the* top sports played and watched here, and in all three we have players who make it big on the world stage. The respective national teams also compete internationally each season, and both rugby and cricket have been fairly successful on that front in the last few years. Our national soccer team, called Bafana Bafana, is having a fall period, but no doubt it too will take its place nearer the top of the international log one of these days.

All of the three major sports—football, cricket and rugby—are also hotly contested at club and provincial levels, and, in the case of rugby, also at international 'provincial' level in the highly popular Super 14 series. This competition pits 14 provincial teams from the three major southern hemisphere rugby playing nations—South Africa, Australia and New Zealand—against each other with the games being played in each of those countries. It is hugely popular as a spectator sport!

Springboks, Proteas and Painted Faces

Officially our national sporting emblem is a protea flower—it is our national flower too. So when a sportsperson is awarded their national colours for excellence in their sport, such as competing at an international level or doing exceptionally well at home, they will wear what is called 'the green and gold'—our national colours. The badge on their formal sports blazer and any of the team clothes they wear has an image of the protea flower. And generally the sports team will be referred to as The Proteas. Our international cricket side is always called by that name, the soccer team is, however, called Bafana Bafana and their women counterparts are called Banyana Banyana—but they still officially are Proteas too!

Now to complicate the matter even further the national rugby team has always been called the Springboks—and still is. If you look closely at their logo or badge on all their team gear, it is an amalgamation of both a protea and a springbok. This is because our national rugby team has been known as the Springboks since 1906 and the sport administrators felt, even with all the changes in the country, the name Springbok was bound to the game, just like the All Blacks is to the New Zealand rugby team, for example. And just to stir it up even more, some people still refer to anyone who has their national 'colours' for sport as a Springbok, since that was how it was in the past and so the word has become synonymous with South African international sporting success. But slowly I am sure the Protea will become the lingua franca instead.

But whatever the emblem and what ever the sport, you can rest assured that fans generally push aside all the complexities and paint their faces to match our joyful, colourful, national flag instead!

Who Gets Down and Dirty in Sport

A lot of outdoor activity and socialising has always revolved around the non-professional side of most sports like cycling, jogging, swimming, sailing, tennis, and generally being activie in the sun. So when the health-and-fitness wave swept the world, many South Africans were and still are being taken along for a good, healthy ride.

Generally, South African women have participated less in sport than their men. Often men will rush off to play soccer, rugby, squash and more; women, on the other hand, either stay at home, sit on the sidelines watching, or perhaps organise the social activities of the event. However this is changing fairly fast and now a large number of women do play almost every form of sport, both socially and competitively—we have a women's national soccer team called Banyana Banyana which competes internationally. At one stage, a young woman soccer player, who had played in a women's soccer team for a number of years, was incorporated in a regular men's club competition and she proved her salt immediately.

The world famous ultra-marathon, Comrades, which attracts top athletes but also tens of thousands of ordinary runners, is currently experiencing a big growth in the number of women entrants as more and more women realise they are just as able to tackle such a taxing event as their male counterparts. At international competition level, women have held their own in some sports more than others—athletics and tennis being the notables.

The Bicycle Buzz

Like the trend in other parts of the world in recent years, cycling—particularly mountain biking—has increased in popularity by leaps and bounds. Over weekends, and especially on Sundays, people jump on their bikes and either pedal down the sweeping trunk roads in the city suburbs (never cycle on a freeway or motorway as it is against the law!), or they go mountain biking on any rugged terrain close by, or at the many new venues outside the cities with specially built trails dedicated to mountain biking.

Two of the most famous and the most fun bicycle races in South Africa are the Pick 'n Pay Cape Argus Cycle Tour, a 109-km (68-mile) tour around the Cape Peninsula and back to Cape Town, and its sister race in Johannesburg, the Pick 'n Pay 94.7 Cycle Challenge, of similar distance. Both are very hilly courses, so you do need a reasonable level of fitness to enjoy—along with more than 30,000 others! I can attest to the fact that it really is good, if strenuous fun. Racing rules and etiquette apply as it is a serious race for the serious racers, but for the rest of us it is a wonderful way of testing our stamina, enjoying the camaraderie of other cyclists, and especially in Cape Town, enjoying some beautiful, scenic views too (if you have any energy left for that!).

> ## Just for Cyclists
>
> If you are a cyclist or would like to start cycling, you may contact the following sources for assistance:
>
> - Cycling South Africa. Tel: (021) 557-1212; email: info@ cyclingsa.com; website: http://www.cyclingsa.com
>   The national cycling body, they will be able to put you in touch with any of the vast array of clubs and organisations spread across the country.
> - Cresta Wheelers. Email: info@crestawheelers.co.za; website: http://www.crestawheelers.co.za
>   If you are in Johannesburg, Cresta Wheelers is a very helpful club for professionals, competitive types and weekend warriors alike.
> - Pedal Power Association. Tel: (021) 689-8420; website: http://www.pedalpower.org.za
>   If you are in Cape Town, Pedal Power Association will give you information mostly about Western Cape.
>
> Or you could buy a copy of one of the two main cycling magazines *Bicycling South Africa* or *Ride Magazine*, both of which are packed with information.

Joining any form of sports club or group is a great way to meet a wide variety of new friends, people that you would perhaps not meet while going about your day-to-day life.

Pavement Pounders

Jogging has always been a favourite way of exercising for many South Africans. At first light on a summer's morning, or in the evenings after work, you will see people of all shapes and sizes pounding the pavements or running round sports fields; or if you are in the rural areas, you may see someone taking off down a dusty track. On the mines, running has become somewhat of a cult, and many of those mineworkers who started running for pleasure have become some of South Africa's world-class marathoners.

A lot of joggers draw their inspiration from the competitors of the ultra-distance Comrades Marathon, an event which is run uphill and down dale for some 87 km (54 miles) each year between Durban and Pietermaritzburg. Over 30,000 people

Only an hour's drive outside hectic Johannesburg there is a great nature reserve, Suikerbosrand, where you can hike in the hills and valleys, bird-watch or just have a great outdoor picnic. You can also cycle or drive the 60km paved road around the reserve and are sure to see a big variety of antelope, zebra and other (harmless) wild animals.

enter this race each year, which has some of the greatest spectator support of any road race in the world, according to international athletes who compete in it.

The camaraderie it engenders is quite special. Of course, you will have the world's top ultra-distance runners out to snap up the gold medals and the prize money; but even among them, the spirit of friendship is always of first importance. In the field, you will find every shape and size of person imaginable. There are blind runners helped every step of the way (and every step of the year-long training sessions leading up to the race) by fellow runners; veterans, some well into their seventies; and a number of women, whose membership is rapidly increasing. Recently, a woman who suffered from multiple sclerosis completed the gruelling course to huge applause from the crowd lining almost the entire route from start to finish.

Just for Runners

To get in touch with a running club near your home, contact:

- **Run SA.** Website: http://www.runsa.co.za

  It is the national organisation responsible for social and competitive running, and from its website you can choose a club near you.

Almost all running clubs are geared for good social running, even if they also have some very serious competitive athletes. You can try the Hash House Harriers, an international organisation with branches in almost every country—very sociable with a bit of running thrown in too.

- **Africa Hash.** Website: http://www.africahash.co.za

  It provides a list of Hash Houses within the country.

Golfers' Paradise

Because space is not really at a premium in South Africa, there are a number of golf clubs scattered across all the major cities, and there is hardly a small town that doesn't have at least a 'nine hole'. By Western and Japanese standards, most club memberships are not too expensive and playing the game does not usually cost an arm and a leg either. Many of the golf courses are owned by clubs and admittance of casual members is allowed only by some.

In the recent past there has been a huge growth of golfing estates where a whole lot of homes, sometimes even holiday homes, are clustered around a golf course. In theory this is quite a fine idea as it gives you lots of open green space, but in reality there are far too many being built, and since they gobble up gallons of water to keep the courses lush and perfect, they are particularly bad for a country that is fast becoming very short on water for the basic needs of its population.

Anyone for Tennis?

Tennis has certainly been the preserve of the more affluent in South Africa. Saturday afternoons and Sundays see almost every tennis court in the urban areas in full use. Most tennis courts belong to clubs, but there are some that are owned by the city or town municipalities where anybody is allowed to play. Because properties tend to be quite large in some of the affluent residential suburbs, there are quite a number of private tennis courts. Consequently, tennis parties can be a feature of weekend social life. You may well be invited to play a few games on a Saturday afternoon and then stay on for a casual dinner.

For competitive players, all the local tennis clubs take part in the various levels of league tennis. Sometimes, this becomes very serious stuff as inter-club rivalry is intense. There are also a number of tennis tournaments and competitions held across the country. Most clubs insist tennis players dress in standard tennis clothing, and even on private courts, most people wear standard tennis gear.

Football is Serious Stuff

Football, or soccer to South Africans, is one of the most widely followed and played games in the country, with its traditional support base in the black community, but like all things, this is broadening out quickly. The overall controlling body is the South African Football Association (SAFA), a body representing all football organisations in the country, and it is a member of the Confederation of African Football (CAF) which locks it into the international football organisation, FIFA. The Premier Soccer League (PSL) is the top local league competition here and is hotly contested each year between August and May. There are lower leagues and age-group leagues, and of course amateur leagues, so there is ample opportunity for a social football player to have a lot of fun too.

If you are a keen amateur player, there is a host of clubs you can join. Football has been the most multiracial game in the country for many years. If you are a player, joining a club is an ideal way to meet and mix with a wide cross-section of the population. Matches are most often played on a Sunday morning and, quite often, the whole family turns up in support.

As a football fan, you really should choose a team to support and join the camaraderie of endless conversations, arguments, views and opinions about the many games played each week. Attending matches is a far cry from some of the hooligan-infested nations. Rowdy the supporters in

South Africa are, with many supporters blowing the raucous *vuvusela* horn to stir up the fans, but it is rare to see thugs brutalising each other at football games—and long may our fans remain above that sort of horror.

To find out more about the clubs in your area, or anything else about South African soccer, contact SAFA at (011) 494-3522 or through their website: http://www.safa.net.

2010 Fifa World Cup South Africa

In 2010 the football World Cup came to South Africa, in fact it came to the African continent for the first time ever. And despite a last minute frenzy to get some stadiums ready, new transport infrastructure completed and the negative voices of a few nay-sayers, it turned into one of the most successful events ever hosted by our country and, vicariously, the entire continent. It was surely the best four week party Africa has ever held. Slick, efficient, fun and wildly colourful.

Matches were held in 10 different stadiums across the country, giving avid fans from almost every point on the compass the chance to sample the Rainbow Nation's many facets while following their teams with gusto. With the rhythms of the closing party still in their heads, they headed for home, heaping praise on South Africans for their joyous, friendly and spirited hospitality.

We certainly lived up to our World Cup slogan: *Ke Nako!* Africa's time is now. (And remember South Africans almost always refer to football as soccer!)

Sports Gear: It's Here

Almost all sports equipment and clothing is easily available here from specialist stores or the major sports equipment and clothing chains. Quite a lot of the top end goods are imported, so you tend to pay the same price for them as you would say in Europe—give or take a bit for the import costs. Some sporting goods are locally made too, which does reduce the price a bit.

I recently needed new running shoes and when I commented on the astronomical price of a good pair, the sales assistant quipped, "Well, take a second mortgage on your house. That should do it." To be honest, when I checked the prices on the Internet they were really similar across the world!.

General Sporting Helplines

Whether you have a competitive bent or just want to play sport for fun, Sport and Recreation South African (SRSA) should be able to put you in touch with an organisation in your field since their aim is to encourage South Africans to play sport regardless their abilities—and hopefully create some international stars in the process. Contact them in Pretoria at (012) 304-5137 or check out their website at http://www.srsa.gov.za. But you can also always ask people around you for recommendations of where to get involved in your favourite outdoor activity.

The Politics of Sports

The segregation in sport, and the fact that white communities had the most access to good sports facilities and proper training during the apartheid era, did a lot of damage to the development of almost all types of sport across the country. And sporting sanctions meant few South Africans knew what real international competition was all about. But that is all in the past now.

The first major step back into the great sporting world was South Africa's participation in the 1992 Olympic Games in Barcelona, after being excluded since the early 1960s. The effects of international isolation had certainly taken their toll. As in most sports, South African athletes were far outclassed. But the nation's joy of being back with the rest of the world was encapsulated in the touching gesture of African solidarity when the white South African Elana Meyer, silver medallist in the women's athletics 10 000m, embraced fellow African and gold medal winner, Derartu Tulu, from Ethiopia, and ran with her as she was doing her lap of honour. They are firm friends to this day.

The country then hosted and won the Rugby World Cup in 1995 and a year later the African Cup of Nations soccer tournament. Now of course South Africa's participation in all international sporting competitions is normal and depends only on the abilities of the contestants.

Some Major Sporting Events To Watch Out For

I've placed the names of sponsors before the name of the sporting event, but in brackets because the sponsors change often.

- **(ABSA) Currie Cup** is an annual rugby championship played during the winter months between 14 teams loosely based on the nine provinces, with the more populous ones having more than one team. The top eight teams play in the Premier Division and the other six in the First Division.
- **Comrades Marathon**, the annual ultra-distance run between Durban and Pietermaritzburg which usually attracts over 30,000 competitors.
- **(Hansa Powerade) Dusi Canoe Marathon** is a three-day race down the Umsinduzi River, from near Pietermaritzburg to the ocean in Durban.
- **(Spec-Savers) Ironman South Africa** is an ultra-triathlon, part of the international circuit.
- **(J & B) Met** is a horse race in Cape Town.
- **(Vodacom) July** is a horse-race that is always run on the first Saturday in July in Durban.
- **(Yellow Pages) Ultimate Athletics Competition** or the South African Senior Track and Field Championships, as it was previously called, is the annual national athletics championships, while the **South African Youth and Junior Championships** is for 15 to 18 year olds,
- **(SAA) Provincial** is a premiere league inter-provincial three day and one day cricket competition played throughout the summer each year. There is also a **(Standard Bank) Pro20** one-day tournament.
- **(Castle) Premiership Soccer League** is the major professional soccer league, teams also have individual sponsorship.
- **(South African Airways) Open** is one of the major internationally acknowledged golf tournaments that attract international players.
- **(ABSA) Cape Epic** is a gruelling 8-day international mountain bike race.

SOME OF OUR SPORTING HEROES...

...in alphabetical order lest I be accused of bias!

- Brian Mitchell A former junior lightweight world-champion boxer, he is now a boxing trainer.

- Bruce Fordyce An ultra distance marathoner, he has won the gruelling Comrades Marathon nine times and also dominated the world ultra distance circuit in the 1980s.

- Chester Williams He played wing for the Springbok rugby team from 1993 to 2000 and is best known for his role in the Springbok squad that won the 1995 Rugby World Cup. He played 27 international games, scoring 14 tries, and also played provincial rugby for the Western Province. In 2001, he began coaching the national seven-a-side team and since 2003 has been coaching various provincial and similar sides.

- Elana Meyer A diminutive middle-distance athlete, particularly good at 10,000m and 5,000m. She won a silver medal at the 1992 Barcelona Olympics for 10,000m and also held a number of records in Africa.

- Francois Pienaar One of South Africa's most famous rugby players and charismatic Springbok captains, he led the national team to World Cup victory on home turf in 1995, as the country re-entered the international sporting world after anti-apartheid sanctions. He made his first-class rugby debut in 1989 and retired in 2000 after playing club rugby in England.

- Gary Player South Africa's most famous world-class golfer has won 163 international tournaments and played the world circuit for decades. Player has also made a name for himself internationally by building world-class golf courses.

- Graeme Pollock A Springbok cricketer and a left-hand batsman, who, at 16 years old, was the youngest player ever to make a first class century. He is retired and is now a cricket selector.

- Jomo Sono One of the country's best ever soccer stars, he played in the United States alongside world great, Pele. Retired from soccer, he is now a wealthy businessman who owns the Jomo Cosmos football team and is the longest-serving coach in the South African Premier League.

- Kaizer Motaung A retired soccer great who is also the founder, chairman and managing director of Kaizer Chiefs, one of the top teams in the country.
- Karen Muir As a 12-year-old, she was South Africa's greatest swimmer. By the time she was 16 years old, she held 15 world records. Today she is a medical doctor.
- Lucas Radebe An international soccer star who earned 70 caps for South Africa and was the national team captain. He also played for Leeds United from 1994 onwards, before retiring from professional football at the end of the 2005 season. He is currently living in South Africa and is a goodwill ambassador for South African football.
- Makhaya Ntini A cricket player—a fast bowler—of note, he made his test début in the South Africa national team in 1998, and at the beginning of 2007 took his 300th test wicket, in his 74th test match.
- Naas Botha A Springbok rugby player with great kicking skills, he captained the Springbok side at times, but was not the world's greatest diplomat. Retired now, he is a well-known TV commentator.
- Oscar Pistorius Dubbed "the fastest thing on no legs", since he is a world record holder at 100 m, 200 m, and 400 m for amputees. In 2007, he became the first amputee to break the 11-second barrier for the 100 m when he flew to victory in 10.91 seconds. He is a double-amputee, having had both legs amputated when he was just 11 months old, because he was born without shin bones.
- Roland Schoeman He is a world record breaker and swimming hero who struck gold in the 2004 Olympics. He declined a multimillion dollar package from Qatar to switch nationalities, preferring to commit himself to help in making South Africa a "haven to all its people".
- Shaun Thomson A world-class surfer, and a world champion at times, who is now retired and in the surfing/beach clothing business.
- Terence Parkin An excellent swimmer, he won a silver medal in the Sydney Olympics, competed again in the 2004 Olympics, holds African and South African swimming records, won the country's biggest open water

race, the Midmar Mile—and is totally deaf. He has also won medals in the swimming championships for the deaf, and in 2006 won the 120-km (75 miles) cycle race in the World Deaf Cycling Championships.

- Willie Mtolo An international name of international fame, he is a world-class marathon runner who has won the New York City Marathon and has a host of other trophies under his belt. He takes an active role in helping the poor rural community he came from when he is not on the world circuit.

- Zola Budd A barefoot-wonder child who broke a host of South African middle-distance records and, for a while, held a world record too. After all the fuss of getting a rushed British citizenship to be able to overcome the sports boycott and compete in the Los Angeles Olympics, she collided with Mary Decker in the race which put her out of the running.

TRAVELLING IN SOUTH AFRICA

Travelling around South Africa is almost a must for a newcomer. There is a great deal to experience in almost every part of the country and it really will just depend on your tastes as to where you go and what you do. Of course the game and wildlife reserves are top of most visitors' list, as is Cape Town and its environs, but there is a great deal more to see and experience if you have the time and energy.

If you enjoy driving, or even if you just don't mind driving, it is often the only way to really experience the great variety and cultural wonders of this country. Public transport— planes, trains and inter-city buses—tend only to get you to the major centres. It is beyond the scope of this book to give you details of things to see and do, so please do your own homework and remember that unless you have immigrated, the day will come when you have to leave these shores, so get out there and do it!

If you are travelling with children, especially small children, do remember that distances are great here and trips can be hours-, if not days-long. And on the same note, remember to fill up your car with petrol more often than you would in a smaller environment as there are sometimes very long gaps between filling stations. If you leave your car to view a site or even to have a roadside meal or coffee break, make sure you lock it and don't leave valuables in the car, or at least not obviously so as it is inviting theft. Of course if your car is parked right near you this is not relevant. It is also important to remember that South Africa has a very high road-death toll, both from car accidents (there are some very bad drivers here!) and also from pedestrians wandering onto roads both in rural and urban areas, so do take extreme care.

Things to See and Do

Just to get you started I have listed a few of the tried and trusted, and a few of the slightly less known ones too.
Some tried and tested sites…

- Cape Town: Robben Island; Table Mountain; the Houses of Parliament and De Tuynhuis; Cape Point Nature Reserve; the Waterfront; Hout Bay; the Waterfront.
- Durban: The old City Hall, library and adjacent Victorian building; the beach front promenade; the Hindu temples; the Indian Market; the Bat Centre; the new harbour-side Point Waterfront development.
- Johannesburg: Constitution Hill and the Old Fort Prison complex; Melville Koppies; mine dumps (the few that are left); Soweto; Gold Reef City; Walter Sisulu National Botanical Garden (you may see Black eagles nesting there); the Cradle of Mankind; The Origins Centre; Johannesburg Art Gallery.

And now for some of the less known experiences…

- South African Astronomical Observatory in Sutherland, Western Cape, where you can observe the stars in crystal clear air through two dedicated visitor telescopes. (You cannot visit any of the research telescopes at night, not even SALT, the largest single optical telescope in the southern hemisphere—but you can do this during the day.)
- The Northern Province government building in Kimberley is a new structure, designed to be appropriate to its environment through a mix of modern African architecture and design.

- The Owl House in Nieu Bethesda is a fantastical, some say mystical, world of sculptural creatures created in the home and yard of Helen Martins. In the Eastern Cape near Graaf Reinet.
- Rock art from the ancient San/Bushmen found in the Drakensberg and other mountains in the heart of the country in KwaZulu-Natal and elsewhere.
- Namaqualand flowers carpet a region in the arid West Coast north of Cape Town in iridescent colour IF the rains are right. They can be seen some time in August or September and only last a few weeks. In the Western Province.
- The Swartberg Pass is a steep, narrow, winding mountain pass (not for the faint hearted!). Scenic views and rock formations of note. En route you can turn off to Die Hel, a tiny village where life has changed little for a century or more. In the Karoo, Western Cape.
- Mapungubwe, which existed between about AD 900 and AD 1300, was one of the largest and most sophisticated kingdoms on the continent, and is now a World Heritage site. It is located north-west of Musina in Limpopo Province and is surrounded by a game park.

Game Reserves: A Walk on the Wild Side

South Africa is renowned for its game parks and well it should be. Many are state-owned and controlled by the South African National Parks, called SANParks, which generally does a sterling job in running the parks for the benefit of the public and the game alike.

The most famous is the Kruger National Park which stretches down the full length of South Africa's border with Mozambique in the east of the country.

It is home to the country's Big Five: lion, elephant, leopard, cheetah, rhino and buffalo, as well as thousands of other species of African wildlife, birds, and of course, a huge array of plants and trees. It is very well stocked so it is highly unlikely that a trip to this game reserve (as they are usually called here) will go unrewarded. SANParks runs most of the state-owned parks in the country. They have a good website at http://www.sanparks.org.

A giraffe with her youngster in Lapalala Wilderness, a 36,000 ha nature reserve where visitors can rent self-catering accommodation right in the heart of the bush: you just can't get any closer to nature than that!

An exception is the province of KwaZulu-Natal which, under the auspices of Ezemvelo KZN Wildlife runs all the provinces state-owned parks and is also responsible for all wildlife and environmental management in the province. It has some superb game parks and wilderness areas in its control that are certainly worth visiting, both in the lowlands and in the Drakensberg mountains. Check out their website at http://www.kznwildlife.com.

There is also a huge number and variety of private game lodges across the country, an industry that has grown substantially now that South Africa is again part of the international tourism community. They range from the ultimate in luxury and style, worth hundreds of US dollars a night, to those that offer much more rustic accommodation and can also be self-catering. Often a lot more fun, especially for children. Many are now equipped to cater for business conferences too.

A privately-funded organisation, the Endangered Wildlife Trust, commonly called EWT, specialises both in the protection

A lioness crosses the road, apparently oblivious to tourists watching her in the Welgevonden Game Reserve in Limpopo province.

of endangered species and in running special-education programmes for youths at the game reserves. Membership is not expensive and the benefits are tremendous.

Because of the extreme popularity of the game reserves, bookings may need to be made months in advance, particularly during the school holidays and over public holiday weekends.

SURVIVAL SENSE

To enjoy the wilder side of South Africa's great outdoors—and that of our neighbours—you must be well prepared. There are a few things that are seriously dangerous in the bush, but you will be quite safe as long as you play the game by the rules, and if you are not sure, err on the side of caution. Below are a few tips that will certainly go a long way to making your experience a pleasant one. Since many South Africans have grown up with the wilds being part of their experience, they may forget to prepare you sufficiently regarding the clothes to wear, or what to take along with you. Remember, in the wilderness there are no shops just down the road!

Organisations like the Endangered Wildlife Trust, the SANParks Board, Ezemvelo KZN Wildlife and others offer huge amounts of information and help, and some even run courses and outdoor programmes like hikes and trails for enthusiasts, which are a combination of education and pleasure. They also focus strongly on educating the youth to environmental matters, as many schools do.

Some Practical Tips
Snakes

South Africa has a great variety of snakes, many of which are poisonous. There are anti-venom preparations for most species, but there are one or two that are deadly and have no antidote. Don't be alarmed by this as very few people get bitten by snakes. Take precautions and you should be fine.

DO NOT pick up or provoke any snake you may see, unless you are with an expert! And even then let them deal with it. The chances of doing this are slim as almost all snakes slither away instantly upon feeling the vibrations of your approach.

If you are bitten, which is highly unlikely, do not do the trick you probably have seen in the movies of tying a tourniquet between the bite and your heart—this does more damage than the snake bite. Act quickly. Apply firm pressure with a crepe bandage, a piece of shirt or nylon stocking wound extensively around the bitten area. This limits the blood supply but does not cut it off. Keep as calm as possible. Get to a doctor or hospital as soon as possible. You can take snakebite serum with you; but many people react very violently to the serum, so it is far wiser to have a doctor administer it in the highly unlikely event of you getting bitten.

If you do disturb a snake unwittingly, this will give it a huge fright and may cause it to be aggressive—the closest thing to it will most often be your feet, so when you are out in the bush always wear closed shoes or hiking boots.

Ticks

Ticks are common in most rural areas in South Africa. They are parasites that latch onto a host animal—wild, domestic or you—and feed on the blood. They carry a wide variety of animal diseases, especially something commonly called 'Billiary' which affects dogs and can be deadly. So if you do take your dog to a farm (which is not really recommended), be sure to watch it once you're home for any signs of lethargy or being off its food. Go straight to a vet if that happens.

There are two types of human illnesses caused by ticks. You can get tick-bite fever. But that is not to say that every tick bite gives you the illness. Symptoms include a severe headache, fever, and hot and cold sweats. It is not a dangerous disease, but you can feel really bad for quite a while. If you are feeling ill and have been in the bush, tell your doctor.

On occasion, when walking in the bush it is possible you may walk into a nest of ticks. Often they are so tiny at first that you may not even see them. People have landed up with hundreds of tick bites on their body, and the collective poison from so many of them can make you ill. One or two bites are unlikely to do much damage other than itch and be a nuisance.

Wearing long trousers, shoes and socks when in the bush will help keep them off you, as will any of the anti-mosquito preparations like Peaceful Sleep or Tabbard. If you do find a tick on your body DO NOT pull it off. Often the head remains in your flesh and can cause a septic sore. The easiest way to kill it is to cover it with oil, after which it will just drop off your skin. Something simple like bath oil or even cooking oil is fine.

Getting Lost

If you are out walking in a wilderness area, remember that it is very easy to get lost. Land marks may be unfamiliar to you and your sense of direction may get a little confused. If you are adept with a compass or a GPS, it is useful; otherwise, just don't wander too far from your campsite at first and familiarise yourself with the terrain slowly.

Fire

Bush or *veld* fires are one of the greatest hazards in rural and wilderness South Africa, especially in the dry months of the year: winter, for most of the country; but in the southern Cape, it is summer.

If you do make a fire to cook over, be sure that every last spark is dead before you leave it or go to bed. Also, if you are a smoker, DO NOT drop your match or cigarette butt. The *veld* can be so dry that it ignites better than tinder and a fire could break out in seconds. If you do notice a *veld* fire, alert the nearest authority you can. If it is caught early, it can be curtailed and eventually put out; but once it has become a runaway blaze, it can do enormous amounts of damage.

If you do stumble upon a *veld* fire, move away as fast as possible. These fires burn very quickly and are often fanned by the wind. If the wind changes, the fire can change direction which might put you in danger. With the very dry grass and scrub, fires fanned by even a small wind can run a great deal faster than you can!

Some Do's and Don'ts

- If you are going on a walk for an hour or two, be sure to take a flask or bottle of water. Summers are hot and you may easily get dehydrated. You may even get lost or take a little longer getting home than intended. Be prepared, rather than thirsty. Many people like to take along cool drinks, but when you are really parched the most effective thirst quencher is water!

- Try not to wear very brightly coloured clothes when in the bush. It makes you very conspicuous and far less likely to blend in with nature. Also keep your voice down, so as not to disturb or scare away any wild animals like antelope or birds that you may come upon.

- Do not litter at all. And if possible, take all your rubbish home with you. If this is not possible, at least bury it deep in the earth so that wild animals cannot easily dig it up—it will eventually decompose. To save you the trouble of disposing the rubbish yourself, many of the wilderness areas have good rubbish cans that are cleared frequently

- Almost all property is private in South Africa, so don't just wander into any bush area you may come across. Most often it is farmland, and the farmer could become exceedingly angry and may even prosecute you for trespassing.

There are other do's and don'ts which may be relevant in a specific situation. The best way to find out is to ask a local who may be with you. It is far easier to take your cue from them, than to do something that is a little silly or dangerous because you are unfamiliar with the situation. But most of all, enjoy one of the great privileges of Africa—wide open spaces!

WILDLIFE AND ENVIRONMENTAL MANAGEMENT

The early settlers in South Africa hunted game for the pot, but they also hunted for pleasure, until the vast herds of wildlife that roamed much of the country had all but been wiped out. Once it was realised how detrimental this was, conservation policies in keeping with global thinking of the time were put into place. To sustain the wildlife available, the national policy until recently focused more on wildlife management than on care of the whole environment. Admittedly, this holistic thought process was new to most parts of the world at the time, but it did at least lead to South Africa having some of the best wildlife management programmes in the world with up-to-date theories based on good research.

Now the broader issue of environmental management, as opposed to wildlife conservation, is at the forefront of national environmental conservation policies. In the past, the vast majority of the population had no vested interest in the country; but now everyone has a stake in the bounty. The United Nations believes that increasing people's standard of living is the best, and probably the only, way of increasing their care of the world around them. This holistic approach has been adopted by the government, since the greatest environmental problem in the country is poverty.

Conservation Versus Development

As in most developing countries, the South African wilderness areas have been threatened by urban development, but the concerned public has fought back frequently, and most often won it case. Some decades ago, a long, hard and bitter battle finally stopped the then government from allowing mining in the Kruger National Park, our largest natural treasure!

Conservation versus development is an emotive issue, but it is important for South Africans to realise that this is a developing country, so the balance must be determined relative to our level of development. Since democracy in South Africa—and hence an upsurge in tourism—there has been a far broader approach to conservation, and this has included looking for innovative ways of empowering local communities to benefit from the tourist dollar, but simultaneously keeping a very tight rein on any development to ensure it does not in any way damage the long-term sustainability of our wildlife and wilderness areas.

Sustainable development is not just a catchy phrase in South Africa, but a concept taken very seriously (some say still not seriously enough) by the government through the Department of Environmental Affairs and Tourism (website: http://www.environment.gov.za) to ensure our natural treasures remain pristine for future generations—and also for future generation of tourism income.

AND TRY OUR NEIGHBOURS' FARE

And if you've got that travel bug, South Africa's neighbours are also great countries to visit. Mozambique, a long narrow country, has an incredibly beautiful coast line, with thousands of miles of gleaming white sandy beaches and a tropical climate to match! Botswana, directly north of South Africa, has some of the most wonderful game parks, many of which are centred around the Okavango Delta, a wetland, which at the end of the rainy season is like a shallow lake, attracting huge varieties of wildlife and birds.

North-west of South Africa is the very arid country of Namibia. Its attractions are vastly different to its neighbours since most of it is desert and semi-desert, but its scenery is some of the most dramatic on the continent, and ranges from Saharan-like desert sand dunes, some of the highest in the world, to a wild coastline named the Skeleton Coast for good reason since its hinterland is a waterless desert. In the centre of this huge but scantly populated country lies Etosha Pan and the vast game reserve surrounding it.

It is impossible to do justice to these vast and wonderful neighbouring countries here, but to whet your appetite, I will list a few of the must-see sights and once you are 'just across the border' in South Africa I am sure you will do some research of your own.

Namibia

The easiest and quickest way to get to Namibia is to fly to Windhoek, the capital, which is also fairly centrally located. From there you can take a tour or rent a car and follow your heart—and a very good map! It is also quite possible to drive from South Africa, although this would be a long trip and would take at least a day or two just to reach the South Africa/Namibia border either travelling from Cape Town or Johannesburg. The main roads in both countries are generally very good, but the distances are vast!

If you are not taking an organised trip, it is essential to plan well as it takes time to get from one major attraction to another. It is also a very sparsely populated country, so distances between towns, villages and sites (and petrol stations!) can be many hundreds of kilometres, but frankly this is what makes it such a special experience. You could also take a number of trips focusing on different regions each time. Because most of the country is desert or semi-desert remember that temperatures can be extreme, especially in summer when daytime temperatures can soar way above 40°C (104°F), while at night in some areas, especially along the coast, it can be very chilly. It is best to visit from about April to October.

The Skeleton Coast which runs north from Walvis Bay to the country's northern boarder is one of the most desolate coastal regions on the continent, but utterly beautiful in its remoteness. Dramatic and icy cold oceans pound long, deserted beaches for many hundreds of kilometres. You can safely visit the southern part of this coastline, stopping at Henties Bay from where you can drive eastwards to the Etosha National Park, one of the largest game parks in Africa. It has an excellent variety and volume of game and is centred around the Etosha Pan, a lake until a few thousand years ago, but now mostly a dry, dusty salt pan. During a good rainy season it becomes a very shallow lake attracting an even greater variety of birds and animals.

In the south of the country, you can plan a trip to the rugged, craggy and harshly hot Fish River Canyon, which is easy to view from either the lookout point at Hobas at the northern end, or the village of Ais-Ais near the southern end. South-west of Windhoek at Sossusvlei in the Namib-Nauklift Park are some of the world's highest and oldest sand dunes. They really should be viewed at sunrise or sunset for dramatic and constantly changing colours and moods that you will never forget! And don't forget your camera either.

Botswana

The Kgalagadi Transfrontier Park is a good springboard into Botswana from South Africa since it straddles the border and was formed by amalgamating two adjacent national parks. Part semi-desert and part savannah, it is the particular home of black-maned Kalahari lions, gemsbok (majestic desert antelope), the pygmy falcon, Africa's smallest bird of prey and of course a host of other game.

Botswana is most famous for its safaris to the Okavango Delta region in the far north, and the Central Kalahari Game Reserve plumb in the heart of the country, also home to the *San* or Bushmen for many centuries. The inland delta is the largest in the world, and its permanent water is a magnet for wildlife in an otherwise desperately dry region. Its spider's web of lagoons and waterways are best explored by boat, or even on foot. And accommodation in rustic, but top-notch lodges is mostly idyllic, if a touch on the costly side. It deserves it reputation as one of the world's most famous safari options.

Travelling to Botswana is of course easiest by plane. From Johannesburg you can fly to Maun, the centre for most tourist safaris, including the delta. There is little need to fly to the capital, Gaborone, other than to visit it per se as it is in the south of the country—and it is almost quicker to drive there from Johannesburg than to fly. Of course once more familiar with the region, a 4x4 safari is a lot of fun, but it also requires a lot more time, planning and outdoor skills! (And do try and read the delightful novel, *The No. 1 Ladies' Detective Agency,* by Alexander McCall Smith, which is set in Botswana.)

Mozambique

In some ways Mozambique is one of my favourite neighbours. Perhaps because the country has emerged from a devastating civil war that tore it apart—both its infrastructure and its people—with its dignity and its love for life still intact; perhaps because it has a glorious tropical climate, warm, crystal clear water and some of the whitest, softest beach sands I have ever seen.

Maputo is also one of my favourite African cities. Its centre has wide boulevards—designed in its Portuguese colonial days—which still boast a host of pavement cafes and coffee bars. Not stuffy colonial ones, but joyous, boisterous African ones. Sheer chill. It also has the Polana Hotel which is one of the great hotels on the continent, lovingly restored after the war to colonial splendour, but run with 21st-century African aplomb. For a great weekend treat, there is usually a special package deal which includes the return flight from Johannesburg to Maputo and a weekend in the Polana.

The islands are also magical. Although Inhaca Island is close to Maputo and is worth a trip, I think it is well worth the effort of getting to Vilanculos. It is a quaint little town on the coast and the springboard for the Bazaruto Archipelago, where there is a variety of lodges from 5-star luxury (and prices) to more moderate options, and a number of islands, many uninhabited. A large area of the ocean around the archipelago is a marine reserve where the water is so clear you barely need goggles to explore the coral reefs and the iridescent tropical fish.

If you want to go even further north, you will need a lot of time if you plan to drive and it is not really recommended until you are more *au fait* with the country. But you can of course fly to some of the northern coastal towns such as Pemba, where they are just beginning to develop top-end tourist accommodation.

And please remember that Mozambique still has some unexploded landmines, so don't wander off the beaten track, especially the further north you go.

THE ARTS

The old image of South African culture being summed up in words like *braaivleis*, sport and beer drinking is not quite fair. There has always been a small but vibrant arts world encompassing both the performing and fine arts. In fact, one of the first records of Western-style theatre in South Africa is found in a sailor's diary entry—in 1607. He was working on board one of the vessels calling at the refreshment station of the Cape at that time. The sailor mentions that they performed a play by Shakespeare on board the ship anchored in the harbour.

There is no doubt that a great deal of the earlier art forms in the country were largely Eurocentric. Because of apartheid, however, artists in every discipline have played their role in commenting on and condemning the ubiquitous atrocities of that system. The arts has always been one of the most successful mediums of bringing people of all races and cultures together in a spirit of mutual trust and understanding.

Generally sponsorship of the arts has not been vast, but the state and the private sector over the years have made some funds available to further the creative spirit. It is a hard call for both government and private funding as there are many worthy causes in need of financial help in any developing country, so the resources are often spread much more thinly than in developed countries. But this rarely curtails real creative talent!

So What is Art Anyway?

You certainly will still come across South Africans who are proud to announce things like: "Who me? Go to the theatre/ballet? No ways, that's for sissies", or "That's a painting? My kid could do better." These are stereotyped responses and probably internationally similar. But there are many, many more who enjoy and participate in the great variety of cultural experiences that arise from our newly forged and vibrant rainbow nation.

The variety of art and entertainment is so diverse that you are sure to find a variety of cultural experiences to dip into, no matter your taste. There is the traditional Eurocentric theatre that a number of people still feel most comfortable with, and which ranges from Shakespearian plays to British-type comedy and farce. Then there are local interpretations of some of the major European works too—theatre, opera, dance—and in my view, these are often far more interesting productions since they highlight the issues right here at home.

The public access to more traditional art forms is also expanding. One can often see very traditional tribal dance performed in less formal venues like open-air public places or at the weekend flea markets. Alternative theatre, rich in South Africa's cultural and political history, has also continued to develop and expand in its content and variety. No longer does apartheid and the struggle against it dominate the arts to the extent it has in the past.

The spectrum of painting and sculpture, of fine arts in general, is equally varied, ranging from the internationally renowned and highly sophisticated pieces to works by young artists who are just starting out on their chosen path. There is also work by amateurs that is sold in the flea markets and outdoor art markets, and even on the streets. Many of my foreign friends have bought loads of local work not only for their homes here, but have taken most of it on to their next posting, or back home with them. Collecting such vibrant work is infectious!

And Who is Paying?

From the artists' point of view there is never enough state and private funding available. Their point is quite valid if it is seen in relation to the levels and nature of arts sponsorship in the developed world. However, in a developing country where there are major and basic demands made on the state coffers for social services, education and housing, the arts tends to get short-changed.

Fortunately, the South African government since 1994 has taken a more long-sighted view and has allocated pretty reasonable funds to the cultural environment—in 2007, it allocated R 1.6 billion, R 2 billion in 2008 and R 2.4 billion in 2009—both through the Department of Arts and Culture (website: http://www.dac.gov.za) and the National Arts Council. In general, government policy favours funding the infrastructure, leaving the theatre, dance, music and other arts companies or individuals to source funding for themselves. However, the Department of Art and Culture does sometimes help fund travel for artists.

But many feel the manner in which funds are allocated and/or spent is not always as good as it could be. There are two fundamental problems: some projects receive way too much money for their level of national importance, while others that serve wider audiences are seeing constant cuts in funding, such as some of the national museums; and the management of the national lottery funds distribution is not up to scratch, so although it has the money and the good intention of allocating it, it does not have the managerial capacity to deal with the funding requests. This has on occasion led to 18-month delays in fund distribution, which means some organisations have had to close their doors before they have even begun! One can only hope that these problems can be ironed out so that the good intentions of the state carry through to the benefit of the arts world—and ultimately of the nation!

In the past, most funding was aimed at a white Eurocentric audience and although this was a totally unacceptable format, its lasting benefit was the construction of a number of high quality theatre complexes in some of the major cities, which now attract a far wider variety of entertainment and hence wider spectrum of South African audiences.

In reality, there is a vibrant arts and cultural environment in the country—but like in most places in the world, there is always room for improvement.

The Role of Big Businesses

The other major sponsor of the arts is big business. There has always been ad hoc sponsorship from large corporations and the bigger high street banks. But in 1997, Business & Art South Africa (BASA) was formed as a formal joint initiative between government and the business sector.

BASA's main aim is to ensure continued development of the arts through sponsorship by business, a process that must—and will—benefit the greater community in the longer term. To do this, it has to encourage mutually beneficial and sustainable business-arts partnerships based on sound business principles. Once these relationships are in place, BASA believes firmly a sponsor will see the value in the partnership to its company—in business-speak, it will see sponsorship as a strategic opportunity which in turn should ensure a longer term mutually beneficial relationship—and fabulous art for the people of South Africa!

South Africa hosts a number of art competitions, dance festivals and general cultural festivals—again usually sponsored by big business. This certainly gives creative people a chance to show off their talents to a much wider audience than they would normally reach through commercial galleries or traditional theatre and dance companies. In addition some of the larger corporate companies have local art collections which means they buy new works on an ongoing basis. Mostly they tend to buy from better known or more established artists, but nevertheless it helps establish a market. Sadly, much of this work is not on public view, but on occasion you can get to enjoy it. Standard Bank has a great gallery in their downtown Johannesburg head office where they host a fair number of very good art exhibitions each year; the bank also collects and promotes African art.

How Seriously Do We Take Our Artists?

Unfortunately, in the grand scheme of things, South African art in general is not accorded great importance by the nation. Perhaps some of the fault lies in the fact that our outdoor climate encourages more earthy, sporty pursuits. But there are groups and individuals who work hard to bring art to the public and the public to art.

A few art competitions are held mostly annually, and these are financed by corporate sponsorships that has mostly taken the place of government funding, or top up state sponsorship. In a country with such huge distances between major centres, this fairly generous funding sometimes enables the exhibitions or performances to travel within the country and people to see the work of artists who do not live in their area.

An example is The Standard Bank Young Artist of the Year award, which popularises the winner locally by taking their work round the country; to some degree, international acclaim is conjured up too. This award is rotated annually between all the artistic disciplines: fine art, music, dance and drama. An exhibition of the artist's work or performance is taken to the major cities where the winners are given the opportunity to interact with their peers, colleagues and students on an academic as well as a practical level. Viewers and buyers of works include the major corporations like Anglo American, Rembrandt and the banks; private collectors; and state and private galleries.

The Spier Contemporary—an award given every second year—searches nationwide for artistic talent in both the urban and rural environments. In this way, it is also embracing traditional art. This programme also helps facilitate an art outreach programme.

The Need To Support The Arts

At the launch of Business & Arts South Africa, past President Thabo Mbeki expressed the importance of the arts to humanity:

"The arts are part of the phenomenon of human existence described as culture, which constitutes the barrier that blocks your path and mine towards regress to the ways of the beastly world. Their practice is not a luxury reserved for the idle rich, but an affirmation that our humanity presents a call to individuals and societies to a form of behaviour which must respect the individuality of each person and the humanity of all".

ANNUAL ARTS FESTIVALS—NOT TO BE MISSED

The National Arts Festival is an annual happening in the university town of Grahamstown during the winter months of June or July. It covers all the arts and is certainly worth attending. The arts festival has become ever more popular, which I am sure has a lot to do with the very wide variety of performing, dramatic and visual art that is represented there. The programme includes a lively mix of imported and indigenous productions, both fringe and mainstream. Based in some measure on the Edinburgh festival, it offers everything from traditional theatre to the zaniest fringe productions, fine art and flea market-type craft. It is tremendous fun and certainly not to be missed by anyone who has a love of the arts, or just wants to see a very broad spectrum of the country's artistic culture in one fell swoop!

If you have mastered Afrikaans a little, or are willing to just go with the flow, you can also try the Klein Karoo Nasionale Kunstfees (translated from Afrikaans, it is the Little Karoo National Arts Festival) or KKNK which is held in the rural town of Oudtshoorn in late March or early April. It started off small in 1994—the year of independence—and has become somewhat of a 'new South Africa' happening. Despite its Afrikaans name, it is a showcase for the new-look South African artistic culture. Well worth a visit. Both past presidents Mandela and Mbeki have done so!

THEATRE
The Alternative Route

Theatre complexes like the Market Theatre (Johannesburg), the Playhouse (Durban), and the Baxter (near the University of Cape Town) played important roles, especially in the past, in offering an alternative vision of the local performing arts, to the traditional Eurocentric one. They also began the fight, as far back as 1971, for multiracial audiences. Some of these theatres defied the apartheid laws—again and again—and opened their doors to all races. By 1978, the government had bowed to pressure and 26 theatres were officially declared multiracial. At this time, apartheid was still firmly entrenched and not even sport facilities, hotels or restaurants were open to people of all races.

Now these theatre complexes are a hive of creative talent and one of the best ways to experience the full complexities of South Africa's multiculturalism. The Market Theatre complex (website: http://www.markettheatre.co.za), which opened in 1976, a poignant date in South African political history, was fashioned out of Johannesburg's Indian Fruit Market—built in 1913. It still retains some of original signage! The theatre went on to become internationally renowned as South Africa's "Theatre of the Struggle". It is now the centre point of a major cultural precinct in downtown Johannesburg and one of the must-do experiences for any newcomer to the country. Some of South Africa's most controversial and exciting theatre has been staged at this highly experimental venue, often to the extreme ire of the apartheid government. Some productions that were first seen at The Market, like *Master Harold and The Boys*, *Poppie Nongema* or *Sarafina*, have become world famous.

Apart from continuing its long tradition of innovative and

socially challenging theatre, the Market Theatre complex and its surrounds is a hive of multicultural entertainment, music venues, restaurants and more. The whole area has been revitalised over the years, with a big boost given when the beautiful Nelson Mandela Bridge was opened, feeding traffic straight into this vibrant area. As must be evident, it is one of my favourite spots and I highly recommend it to anyone who wants to get a great taste of real life in Jozi—that's the hip name for Johannesburg.

The Playhouse Company (website: http://www. playhousecompany.com) is one of the country's top theatre organisations, and like the Market Theatre, is right in the heart of the buzzing downtown. Apart from a wide variety of productions—drama, dance, music and more—it has various excellent festivals throughout the year.

ARTscape Theatre Centre (website: http://www.artscape. co.za) is one of two major performing art centres in Cape Town. The other is the Baxter Theatre Centre (website: http://www.baxter.co.za) at the University of Cape Town. ARTscape which has an opera house, a main theatre and a studio theatre, is run pretty innovatively as it does not actually produce work. It runs the complex as a business, and hosts productions put together by outside organisations which include ballet, opera, music and of course theatre.

The Baxter, being near the university campus, is a vibrant and living venue where a wide variety of work is staged. It has a large main theatre, a concert hall, an intimate Studio Theatre, as well as foyers and galleries in which it hosts a range of programmes that reflect well the multi-cultural society that is now South Africa.

The Civic Theatre complex in Johannesburg started off life much like the ARTscape in Cape Town: large, grey and somewhat imposing. But it too had to change its tune and now hosts a wide range of impressive local and international productions—traditional and avant garde. It received a huge dose of creative energy when Janice Honeyman, was appointed to lead it into a new era. She is one of the country's most highly regarded actors, producers and directors, particularly famous for her outstandingly innovative productions originally staged at the alternative theatres. Her annual year-end pantomime is an absolute hit as it is laced with exotic, colourful costumes and sets, and filled with childish delights and delightful adult innuendo.

Academia Plays its Role Too

The more liberal universities have always played an important role in developing local theatre by staging active, experimental productions. The focus is broad and a lot of indigenous productions have been staged, especially in recent years, as the universities have an increasing number of black students.

Very often the standard of the productions is excellent—and to prove it is not my own bias, I took a friend and long-time resident of Paris to a production at the local university. She was so impressed with the standard of the production, and the ingenuity of the locally-written play, that she trotted off to confirm from a stranger (in case I was having her on) that all the actors were undergraduate students. She felt some were of international calibre.

In spite of the talent available, funding always seems insufficient for the dramatic arts departments at universities, probably because of the strain of increasing costs on limited education budgets. However, students always seem to manage something innovative enough to get their show on the road regardless of finances.

Some Actors Make it Big

Some South African actors and playwrights have been very successful overseas. It is always a dangerous thing to single out a few of the famous, for there will certainly be many more who will be left out. But I'll risk it and mention a few examples. Anthony Sher, famous on the London stages for Shakespearian drama, was born, trained and began his early career in South Africa, as was the late Yvonne Bryceland—who later split her acting career between South Africa and London. She was famous for, among many other things, her roles in the internationally acclaimed Athol Fugard plays.

> **How to Access the Theatre**
>
> Most of the major newspapers carry a good arts and entertainment listings section, so scan them well. One of the most comprehensive listings is to be found in the 'Friday' pull-out section in the weekly newspaper, *Mail & Guardian*. This section is specifically customised for the different major urban regions in the country, and also has excellent critiques to help you make choices—a boon when you are new to the country and really don't know much about the culture.
>
> Reservations—Internet (website: http://www.computicket.com) or call (083) 909-0909 or (083) 915-8000 from anywhere in the country—can be made through a national centralised booking office called Computicket, which does charge a fee for the service. You can almost always also book directly at the theatre by phone and often online as well.

In fact, Fugard's plays like *Master Harold and The Boys*, *Boesman and Lena* and *The Island* have launched a number of careers, such as that of performer, John Kani, who is famous for his deeply moving roles in Fugard's later plays. He is also highly regarded as a local Shakespearian actor. Now a well-known director, Kani plays an important creative role in the Market Theatre productions. Janet Suzman, also well-known on the London stage, is another South African export.

Actress Nomsa Nene really made her fame in the dramatised novel based on the tragic life story of a domestic worker, written by Elsa Joubert, an Afrikaans author. Both Elsa and Nomsa became household words abroad as this quasi-factual story hit the international arena. Nomsa travelled overseas playing the lead role, and upon her return has made a great contribution to dramatic art.

Another well-known South African personality is Sibongile Khumalo, one of South Africa's globally known, home-grown divas. A Sowetan through and through, she started her musical training at the age of eight under the guidance of her music professor father, Khabi Mngoma. She then shot to fame when in 1993 she won the Standard

Bank Young Artist Award. She has a very wide repertoire of musical genres and moves fluently from one to the other, even within a single performance: classical and opera renditions, traditional African choral work, standard jazz ballads—she is also known for her vibey African jazz interpretations.

She has performed with well-known groups and artists around the country and has also been chosen for solo roles at diverse, if historic, occasions in South Africa's recent history: she sang at President Nelson Mandela's inauguration in 1994 after the first ever democratic elections; she led the national anthem at the Rugby World Cup in 1995 (which South Africa won); and also entertained Madiba, as ex-president Mandela is affectionately known, at his massive 75th birthday celebrations.

That Modern Day Fairytale: Charlize Theron

The story of Charlize Theron, an extraordinary woman and the first South African (and African) actor ever to win an Oscar, is as fantastical a fairytale-come-true as most Hollywood movies would have us believe is possible.

After a tragic upbringing—she witnessed her mother shoot her father dead in self-defence—in an ordinary little town east of Johannesburg, she trained as a ballet dancer before moving first to Europe and then the United States, where she was accepted at the Joffery Ballet in New York. She was also working as a photographic model at the time. Soon after her ballet breakthrough, a knee injury put an end to her dance career. Strangely undaunted she moved to Los Angeles, where she is still based, and began an acting career. She was only 18 years old.

She first garnered serious attention in the Tom Hank's film, *That Thing You Do* in 1996 and then again in Woody Allen's *Celebrity* in 1998. In 1999, the art-house hit *Cider House Rules* shot her to fame, but she also found that her next few roles really typecast her as 'a beautiful young woman', something that could have been rather career limiting in the longer term. But she soon put paid to this image with her extraordinary portrayal of American serial killer Aileen Wuornos in the film, *Monster*. Respected film critic, Roger Ebert wrote in his review of *Monster* that hers "was one of the greatest performances in the history of film".

The rest is certainly a true fairytale: for this role, she won the Oscar for Best Actress at the 76th Academy Awards in February 2004, as well as the SAG Award (Screen Actors Guild Award) and the Golden Globe Award.

FINE ART

Because the government policy across the cultural environment favours funding infrastructure more than the actual artists, fine artists tend to have a more difficult time than those in the dramatic arts do in making ends meet. Simply put, there is very little infrastructure to fund other than galleries, most of which are privately owned anyway.

But it's not all doom and gloom as the three major funding institutions: Department of Arts and Culture, its sister organisation, the National Arts Council and Business & Art South Africa, are all open to approaches from artists. They predominantly tend to help artists with the cost of having an art exhibition—things like rental on the gallery, printing costs for catalogues, and the likes. They also on occasion make small grants to artists for materials, but in truth most fine artists tend to have to find private funding or support themselves through other jobs so that they can afford to make art as well.

An interesting perspective from one of the country's leading painters is that he feels the effects of not being subsidised has had some positive spin. He said artists were mostly forced to make their own way, to act independently. It may not have done great wonders for their bank balances, but it made them find a vocabulary and subject matter that was independent.

Then: Very Anti-Apartheid

Like theatre, much South African art of the recent past reflected the urgent issues of the time and place—the socio-politics of the country, and played a major role in criticising the apartheid structures, especially over the last few decades. This work has been well supported by the major national galleries and it's well worth a look at the exploratory and innovative ways artists have approached the subject. Some of the more common visual imagery of the time showed chaos and destruction, with burning and fractured landscapes that depict the horrors wrought by apartheid and those that erupted in its overthrow.

Now: Vibrant and Varied

Now that fine artists are free, emotionally and in reality, from the constraints of apartheid, there is far more vibrancy, diversity and excitement in a lot of the work being created and shown around the country. In addition, local fine artists are much more in tune with international trends, not least because the end of apartheid also meant the end of the cultural boycott. The result is that work from some of our artists is as sophisticated as their international peers. This is borne out by the fact that major international art museums like the Tate Modern and New York's Museum of Modern Art (MOMA) have in their collections art by top South African artists.

Young fine artists outside gordart Gallery in Melville, Johannesburg, one of the venues that gives young artists a chance to show their work, and wily art lovers the chance to buy art works ahead of the pack

There is an added and very positive dimension to much of contemporary South African art: it is born out of the enormous differences of cultural backgrounds and economic discrepancies, the great differences between rural and urban experience. Add to this already exciting fusion the plethora of new mediums artists can work in, due to contemporary and changing digital technologies, and you get a new variety and vibrancy that is hard to match.

A Trip to the Galleries and Museums

To experience at first hand some of the art produced in this country—anything from traditional beadwork of extraordinary beauty and quality, to avant garde multimedia/new media work—it is really worth visiting the public museums and galleries, as well as some of the good commercial galleries.

In the public galleries, you can often see a good spread of work done over the years, giving you an interesting overview of the development of South African art, while the commercial galleries mostly tend to have specific exhibitions of an individual artist or group of artists whose work they are selling. There is of course no obligation to buy work when you visit commercial galleries—but I can vouch for the fact that the temptation is often irresistible!

Although our local galleries have never been able to afford a huge number of works from the world-famous greats, like, say, those in the United States have, there is a sufficient number of international masters to still your longings until you tune into the local scene.

The mixing of traditions, or cultural osmosis as the experts call it, caused by the interaction between Eurocentric and Afrocentric traditions can often result in work of a unique calibre. A small, but interesting example is the work of African artist Tito Zungu that depicts skyscrapers, aeroplanes and other icons of our contemporary culture, but presented in a mode that is very reminiscent of African beadwork. You will certainly see some of his work in the major galleries.

Other names to look out for when you do make a trip to any of the major galleries are Clive van den Berg, William Kentridge, Penny Siopis, Tommy Motswai, Willie Bester,

Derrick Nxumalo, Joni Brenner and Bronwen Findlay. You should also look out for sculptures by Cecil Skotnes, Andries Botha, Jackson Hlungwane, Bonny Ntshalintshali, Jochim Schonfeldt and David Brown. Again, this list is light years away from being exhaustive, but it will help direct your experience of South African art initially.

There are also some superb collections of African art from across the continent. One of the most splendid is that housed in the Gertrude Posel gallery at the University of the Witwatersrand in Johannesburg—an absolute must for anyone interested in African art!

Some Galleries To Visits

Here is an ad hoc and 'tip-of-the-iceberg' list of some of the art museums and galleries, both public and commercial, that may well be worth visiting, but remember that as interest in South African art grows, so new galleries are springing up across the country. Please do check the media and with your friends so you don't miss out!

Johannesburg: Johannesburg Art Gallery; Standard Bank Gallery; University of Johannesburg Art Gallery; Gertrude Posel Gallery; Goodman Gallery; Everard Read Gallery; Artist Proof Studio; Gallery on the Square, Sandton; Brodie/Stevenson.

Pretoria: Pretoria Art Museum; University of Pretoria Art Collection; Association of Arts.

Cape Town: South African National Gallery; Association for Visual Arts; Sanlam Art Gallery; Michaelis Galleries; Art.b; Irma Stern Museum.

Durban/Pietermaritzburg: Durban Art Gallery; Tatham Art Gallery, Pietermaritzburg; Durban Institute of Technology Art Gallery; ArtSpace Durban; BAT Centre, Durban; KZNSA Gallery, Durban.

CRAFT

As South Africans become far more sensitive to the importance of artists working in the traditional, indigenous forms, so the boundaries between art and craft become far less defined. Many of the artists and crafts people are now

Handcraft in South Africa is abundant, beautiful and often very unusual. It makes great inexpensive ornaments in your new home, or lovely gifts.

able to see their work in galleries and museums alongside those of more traditional fine artists. This re-evaluation of indigenous work has also helped to drive the groundswell of interest in local craft. Some rural communities produce—and use—artefacts and objects of great beauty like beadwork and baskets, embroidery, ritual sculptures, food and drink serving vessels, and other containers.

Old Skills, New Uses

More common to city dweller and much easier to find and buy is contemporary craft. A lot of this work is made with traditional craft skills, but with new materials. And they serve new functions in urban societies. It has become quite trendy to use these urbanised artefacts in urban homes as they serve a great visual and functional effect—I speak from personal experience!

Examples of such works are very finely woven baskets made out of telephone cable wires; beadwork where beads are strung on thin wire and fashioned into a variety of decorative and functional works from baskets and other containers to replicas of animals, flowers and birds; or candle sticks, wastepaper baskets and picture frames fashioned out of flattened food and drink cans.

Much of this craft can be bought in the outdoor markets that are springing up all over the major cities and towns across the country, or simply on the side of the road from independent seller, or even at some of the larger traffic intersections in the cities. The prices are good and the crafts are fun and often functional too. The museum shops and galleries sell good quality craft, but they are more pricey. Besides these, a variety of small shops and boutiques also stock good craft. One of my top favourites is Art Africa in Parkview, Johannesburg. Their goods are always of extremely high quality and they also have an excellent variety, unusual and funky. The also sell work from other African countries.

MUSIC

If music is the food of love, there shouldn't be an unloved South African in the country! Because of our cultural diversity, there is a plethora of different music styles and tastes, and as with fine arts, there is also a lot of mixing of local music with various music styles imported from across the world. This has given rise to a vibrant South African sound.

The Classics

The Eurocentricity of the past meant that Western classical music and opera played a prominent role, and received reasonable levels of state sponsorship in a similar way to the performing arts of the time. Local classical orchestras, and there are quite a few, are generally quite good and since the lifting of the cultural boycott and sanctions in the early 1990s, we now often see, or rather hear, some of the world's greats on our stages again. There are also some classically trained musicians who have used the platform and added their own spicy South African energy to deliver a unique experience—Rocco de Villiers is a great example.

All That Jazz

Jazz has always had a prominent role in the country's musical tenets with greats like trumpeter Hugh Masekela, the legendary pianist Dollar Brand (now Abdullah Ibrahim) and singer Miriam Makeba being some of our most well-known international players. But there is also an extensive array of excellent jazz musicians worth catching at any venue you can. Or on CD. They include groups like The African Jazz Pioneers and Ladysmith Black Mambazo, stars who play with various bands like Zim Ngqawana, McCoy Mrubata, Marcus Wyatt, Louis Mhlanga or soulfull jazz singers like Gloria Bosman, Judith Sephuma, or Thandi Klaasen. There are many, many more to choose from! Although jazz has always been popular, especially in the townships, more venues are springing up all over the major centres. Johannesburg's most famous is Kippies. It has moved venue a couple of times in its long history, but currently is on the edge of Newtown in the downtown and is an absolute must!

Contemporary or Traditional

South Africa has developed a wide variety of local contemporary music: sometimes a wonderful fusion of Western and African sound. Johnny Clegg and his band, Savuka, have captured the soul of this amalgamation superbly. Paul Simon did the same when he came to South Africa to talent hunt for his 'Gracelands' album. But right here at home, the variety is endless: there is township 'bubblegum', kwaito music, or township jive music which is a fusion of rural music with city pop. Go try them out.

Or try some of the more traditional and utterly glorious African choral work which has long been a favourite among many of the African communities, where competitions are held from school level onwards. The mountainous region of KwaZulu-Natal houses the world-famous Drakensberg Boys Choir. There, school boys with talent pursue their academic work as well as a hearty amount of singing. This choir has travelled around the world and hosted foreign visiting choirs too.

It is quite unfair to try and list the many great contemporary musicians and bands that play at clubs, gigs, in coffee bars on a Sunday, in the open air—anywhere. But for those of you who really want to feel our rhythm, pick up a copy of the *Mail & Guardian* every Friday for a comprehensive list of the happenings on the music front. The opinions of their reviewers are reliable on most occasions.

ARCHITECTURE

Although there is a growing number of buildings that reflect a South African-ness about them, most urban architecture, and especially the older buildings, predominantly reflect both European and American style. Each major region or centre does have a look of its own, partly because of the nature of the different settlers and also because of the climate and commercial differences.

Characteristics of the Major Cities
Cape Town

Cape Town and its surrounds has some of the oldest buildings in the country, beautiful in their rural simplicity. The old Cape Dutch farm houses, now most easily seen in the homesteads on many of the wine estates, were built mostly with readily available materials. They have high ceilings and very thick walls. Timber was used for floors, doors, and window frames. The farm houses are usually painted white with thatched roofs and much of the woodwork is painted a traditional dark green. Many of the old homesteads are open for viewing as you take a trip through the wine country.

The South African Houses of Parliament (legislative) and De Tuynhuys, the office of the president, built in the late 1800s are also majestic buildings right in the city centre, accentuated by an oak-tree-lined avenue leading up to them.

Modern architecture, as in all cities in South Africa, varies greatly from a few sensitively designed gems to rather too many ordinary to mediocre building, topped by some utterly crass structures.

Durban

Durban has a more Victorian feel about its earlier architecture, with some of the country's most beautiful civic buildings still operative in its city centre. The city hall, the old post office, Playhouse Theatre, the old railway station and the national museum are all in close proximity. It is quite wonderful to walk around this tree-lined area in the early evening or on a Sunday, studying the buildings unhindered by the weekday city rush.

The city's beach front has developed into what many feel is a bit of a concrete jungle, but it has made this area accessible to many more people. In leisure hours it is a buzz of Durban's cross-cultural lifestyle as people run and cycle, walk, swim, or simply just stand and watch the sun rise over the sea or the surfers riding the pounding waves.

As the country's major port, Durban has a functional relationship with its harbour. I always get a great kick from being able to look down some of the city streets and, at the end of them, see major ocean-going vessels loading their cargo. There is also a lot of modern development and rehabilitation of the area around the harbour for both residential and recreational use.

Johannesburg

Johannesburg is the new kid on the block. Although founded during the gold rush of 1886, architecturally it is a hard and modern city. There are some wonderful old buildings, which are mostly in the downtown area. The original Rand Lords, the entrepreneurs who made their millions early in the city's history, built homes of magnificent opulence on the hills just north of the old city centre. Today, many of these old mansions still exist mostly as corporate headquarters, company training centres and the likes, which with a bit or organisation you can usually arrange to visit. Well worth the effort.

But Johannesburg is really a fast track, regenerating city. Old buildings frequently give way to newer ones with glass skyscrapers being very prominent on its skyline, reminiscent of modern American cities. This is not surprising since some of the most overt glass buildings were designed by the famous American Helmut Jahn. An example of one of his buildings is at No. 11 Diagonal Street, next to the old Stock Exchange in downtown Johannesburg.

A new monumental banking centre for First National Bank was built in the city centre. It has an interesting concept with an innovative approach to street level culture. In addition to the spaces for hawkers and small shops, paths and walkways interconnect for easy access across its two-block mass.

A lot of the Johannesburg city life has spilled into the residential suburbs in more recent decades and many people never come into the downtown area these days. They have their own office and shopping precincts surrounded by residential life. For example, Sandton, an affluent area north of the centre of the city, has attracted a lot of business development, and even the new Johannesburg Stock Exchange, now called the JSE Securities Exchange, moved from the city centre to Sandton.

At least some of this decentralisation can be blamed on the high crime rate in the past in the city centre, but these days the downtown has begun a regeneration campaign—and like many in the world, it is fast becoming a sought-after environment for the younger and more avant garde, as well as home to many much poorer communities. Indeed, I enjoy the fact the city centre is a hub of the real South Africa: a melting pot of race, culture, creed and class. It also has some of the greatest multicultural entertainment areas in Newtown near the new Mandela Bridge.

Some Style—Or Lack of it

South Africa offers an array of architectural styles to choose from—most of them cribbed from various European countries and then somewhat adapted to suit our sunny climate. You can have a mock Tudor home if you so choose or a rustic, white Greek-style home. Spanish architecture, or more often a poor imitation of the coastal Spanish one, is quite a favourite urban-style home, so is a local interpretation of Tuscan villas. Some of the southern European-style homes make a lot of sense in our sunny climate, as do roofed verandas that allow outdoor relaxation without being too frazzled by the sun.

More recently, there has been a post-modern splurge as well as a move towards a type of neo-classical design, especially for townhouses and cluster home developments. But it is unfair to brand all architecture with an imitative label. There is certainly a growing amount of architecture, especially in the domestic environment, that is innovative, appropriate to the climate, people, culture and available technology. The style of these homes is peculiar to the architect who designs them and are often a pleasure to live in.

ART, CULTURE AND POLITICS—THEN AND NOW

From the 1970s until independence, South Africa experienced a cultural boycott as part of international moves to end apartheid. Some artists felt it was not the right course of action to choose because it isolated the country even further, and prevented the spread of internationally accepted norms and worldwide changes. Others agreed with it, believing that anything that would hasten the end of the horrific regime was worth the sacrifice. Whatever the view, one of the effects was an abundance of politically inspired protest work in both the fine arts and performing arts environments.

Once apartheid fell, there was a brief hiatus in both quantity and quality in the arts environment, as the nation's creative talent adjusted to its newfound freedom. But today, I believe there is a far greater level of artistic talent and expression fed, not from the negative, but driven by the excitement and challenges of developing a new, multicultural identity. In fact, if you are a collector of art, or love performing arts, there is an abundance of fresh, innovative and often very local fare to choose from. Go out there and enjoy!

LEARNING THE LANGUAGE... ALL 11 OF THEM

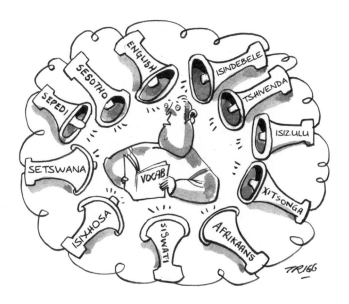

'...a language is a tool of which no nation in the world
can have a monopoly.'
—Modibo Keita, first president of Mali

ENGLISH IS CERTAINLY THE LINGUA FRANCA in South Africa. But don't for one minute think that means everyone can understand English, or that you will understand their English—well, not easily, anyway. We have 11 official languages and a host of others spoken by various groups in the country—other African languages, dialects, Indian languages, various European languages and Afrikaans (home-made by the early Boer settlers and one of the 11 official ones).

There are dialects within languages and lingoes of many sub-cultures, like *tsotsi taal* or 'jive talk'. Colourful expressions and vivacity are co-partners in South Africa's verbal communication, probably because people are often talking across a language and cultural divide.

It will be almost impossible for you to master all or even most of the vast array of languages, but you can certainly have fun trying—and you will so often endear yourself to so many people if you make the effort to learn at least something of their language.

LANGUAGES APLENTY—COLOURFUL AND DIVERSE

South Africa is certainly a land of linguistic diversity with some 25 living languages, many of which are 'home languages' or languages spoken solely or predominantly in the home. The majority of these languages are African, and some are specific to South Africa, thus, as a newcomer to this country, you are unlikely to have learned or even heard many of them. Don't feel alone because many white South Africans, particularly older ones, haven't either, thanks in most part to the stringency of apartheid, and the fact that African languages were almost solely taught in African schools. Now, since independence a number of them, especially the major ones, are taught in all schools.

But that does not mean we are a Tower of Babel. Not at all. Many South Africans speak many more than one or two languages. In fact, a lot of Africans speak many, even all, of the African languages. And many people, especially in urban areas and in government, can communicate in English and Afrikaans as well. However most South Africans have not learned languages from anywhere else in the world, except for a privileged few who may have studied foreign languages at school or university.

The Official Languages

The South African Constitution guarantees equal status to our 11 official languages as it was necessary to cater for the huge diversity of people and cultures. These are: Afrikaans, English, isiNdebele, isiXhosa, isiZulu, Sepedi, Sesotho, Setswana, siSwati, Tshivenda and Xitsonga. It is worth noting that the names of some of the languages have been slightly changed to include a prefix. This is the culturally and linguistically correct way of writing and saying them, even in English. You may well still hear the shorter pronunciation as many may still use it out of habit. But since you are most likely to be learning them for the first time, I suggest you do it the correct way from the start.

The Constitution mentions a few other languages, but these are not classed as official: San, Nama, Khoi, Arabic, German, Greek, Gujarati, Hebrew, Hindi, Portuguese, Sanskrit, Tamil, Telegu and Urdu, and even sign language.

The Constitution also ensures your right to be addressed in any of the official languages when dealing with government—and that includes all official documents too. A costly exercise for the state, but one that does ensure total equality.

Home Languages

Home languages are those spoken most often and by choice in homes. The users of the country's nine most commonly spoken African languages jointly make up nearly 80 per cent of the population. Of this group, most speak isiZulu as a first home language, which accounts for 23.8 per cent of the population. And the second most spoken home language is isiXhosa—17.6 per cent of the population speak it at home. Contrary to many foreigners' beliefs, a large number of Afrikaans speakers are not white. A high percentage of the Coloured population speaks Afrikaans as a first language, making it the third most spoken home language (13.3 per cent).

English Is The Lingua Franca Here

Although only the sixth most spoken language in the country, if you can speak English you will be just fine in South Africa. It is used a lot across the country because it is the language of business, of politics and of much of the media—and of course because it is the language that much of the world uses to communicate. All government departments should be able to communicate in English—one of the 11 official languages. This means that any dealings you may have with government can be conducted in English, and any forms you have to fill out will be in English too.

But please remember that not everyone speaks or understands English well, so be patient, especially when it is obvious that it is not the speaker's native tongue. Of course accents and even colloquial words may vary but they certainly add flavour, flair and no doubt a good dose of confusion and humour to your interaction with locals.

Early British Origins

With the British occupation of the Cape in 1795, the roots for an English-speaking community were put down and certainly hit fertile soil. Cape Town today still has a strong English, albeit South African English, flavour.

Then, with major depression and unemployment in England after the end of the Napoleonic Wars, and the reduction of the armed forces which put thousands out of work, it seemed an easy choice for some 5,000 English immigrants to sail towards the African sunset in 1820. They arrived in what is now called Port Elizabeth, on the eastern seaboard, and at that time these newcomers made up over 10 per cent of the English-speaking population.

As the English slowly spread into the interior of the country during the 19th century, establishing Port Natal (now the sprawling city of Durban) in 1825, annexing the Boer republic of the Transvaal in 1877 and then participating in the gold rush in 1886, they took the language with them. English became a major communicating force across the country.

In 1910, under British rule, English became the official language in this southern-most African country, making the Boers very angry. By 1925, the Boers had ensured the British made Afrikaans the second and equal official language. Strange that no one seemed to consider the vast bulk of the population who did not see either of those languages as their own. But such was the colonial era.

South African English: A Language of its Own

No language is static, and those in new and developing countries are often the most creative. South African English is no exception, being influenced by the many other languages spoken in the country. Many words were assimilated by the early English immigrants, especially for all new things that the English had certainly not encountered in their own land.

Today the compilers and publishers of the world-famous Oxford Dictionaries have collated a special dictionary on South African English. Even in the traditional *Oxford Dictionary* there are a number of South African English words that have become common usage by all English speakers. Examples are: 'kraal' (pronounced krahl), a noun meaning South African village of huts enclosed by fence, or enclosure for cattle and sheep; and 'trek' which is a verb of distinctly South African origin meaning to pull a load, travel by ox-wagon, migrate, proceed slowly—it originates from the early settlers who 'trekked' into the interior, ironically, to escape the English!

As the use of English spread in the sub-continent, words of even more diverse origins were assimilated from Arabic, French,

German, Malay, Portuguese and Persian. The distance in time and culture between South Africa and Britain isolated South African English from its source. It soon developed very regionalised characteristics, especially in vocabulary, pronunciation and idiom. The grammatical construction of the language, however, is still the same as traditional British English.

Not The Queen's English

Although written English in South Africa is the same as most other English-speaking countries, pronunciations and accents are quite a different matter. As a newcomer you could well be forgiven for not even knowing it was the Queen's tongue you were hearing. In large measure, the South African English accent is hard and fairly flat. A lot of its tone may well come from living in such close proximity to Afrikaans, but the different accent is also because the language has grown up in its own time and space—and at great distance from the motherland. There are also many words used by English-speaking South Africans which are certainly not English, but rather come from one of the other local languages, for example, *braai* (from Afrikaans), which means a barbecue, or *tsotsi* (from township slang), meaning thug or petty criminal.

Afrikaans —Born and Bred in South Africa

The basis for the beginnings of Afrikaans was set in 1652, when the Dutch East India Company established a halfway house at the Cape. Those Dutch settlers came into contact first with the language spoken by the indigenous Khoi people, and later also mixed in some of the languages of later settlers too—Malay, English, French, Portuguese. Linguistics boffins here think that by 1800, or at the latest, 1850, Afrikaans had developed in most part into the language it is today.

The majority of the Afrikaans vocabulary is derived from Dutch, but changed quite substantially, especially in pronunciation. Although there are strong grammatical similarities between Afrikaans and Dutch, it has a far less complex structure, making it a fairly easy language to learn.

Also, a great number of words were coined, especially for local plants and animals. Because of the mixed racial origins of the Afrikaner, the language has borrowed words from almost all the cultures which make up South Africa's diversity. There are words from African languages like *mampara*, which means 'an untrained or stupid person' and most often is used as a form of gentle rebuke; or *babelas* which means 'hangover'.

Words of English, French, German, Malay and Portuguese origin are also liberally sprinkled throughout Afrikaans. Because of their mixed backgrounds, the Coloured population had considerable influence in shaping the Afrikaans vocabulary as it is used today.

It's Not Only The Language of The Boers

In the early years of jockeying for power in South Africa, Afrikaans struggled against English and Dutch, the languages of the early colonial powers, for recognition as a medium of cultural expression. But by the beginning of the 20th century, it was generally recognised as a cultural language and vernacular. In 1933, the Bible was translated into Afrikaans, which did a lot not only to standardise the language but enhance its credibility among the many Boers, Coloureds and others who spoke it. Of course with the coming to power of the apartheid regime, it received extensive, and in the views of many, undue support from the state.

Afrikaans has now taken a more equitable place along all the other official languages in the country. There are several Afrikaans language newspapers as well as many famous Afrikaans authors—the most renowned being Andre Brink, who started writing solely in Afrikaans, but who now writes in English as well. In some parts of the Eastern Cape and Western Cape provinces, a very high percentage of the people speak Afrikaans as a home language. Apart from the white Afrikaners, this region has a large number of Coloured communities, where the language is spoken fluently too. In other parts of the country, the density of Afrikaans speakers is much lower, particularly in the urban areas. Of course a very large number of the rural white farmers speak Afrikaans since they originate from the early Voortrekkers.

Enforced Afrikaans: A Spark In Dry Tinder

Although racially discriminating policies were the underlying cause of the Soweto riots in 1976, the actual tinder that drove the students to rebellion was the insistence by the government that African students should study subjects such as maths or geography in Afrikaans, rather than in English or their native tongue. Not only was it more difficult for them, but Afrikaans was also seen as the language of the oppressor.

AFRICAN LANGUAGES—A COMPLEX MIXTURE

The subject of African languages is enormously complicated, especially in terms of the complexity of the different language groups, the relationships between some languages and the intermixing of the groups and languages. So here I will give a very simplified and potted account to whet your appetite, but if you are interested in more detail, the language studies faculty of any of the major universities is a good place to begin your research.

The four major African language groups in South Africa are: the Nguni (made up of Northern isiNdebele, Southern isiNdebele, siSiswati, isiXhosa and isiZulu), the Sotho (Northern Sesotho, Southern Sesotho and Setswana), the Tsonga and the Venda.

The linguistic differences between the four language groups are so great that they are mutually unintelligible from group to group, while the languages within a group are related closely enough for a speaker of one language to understand the other.

Within these major languages there are some 90 different dialects, and into this collection you can add the cross-cultural developments like 'Townie Sotho', an urban-mixed lingua franca, no doubt developed because people have been thrown together in the sprawling urban townships like Soweto.

But don't let this linguistic stuff fool you—the vast majority of African South Africans can communicate in many, if not all, of the prevalent African languages!

An Overview of the African Languages
Nguni

- **IsiNdebele** The Northern Ndebele people probably originated in Zimbabwe, mingled a bit with the Swazi from Swaziland, and then settled north of Pretoria. Some of their dialect is influenced by Sesotho, Afrikaans and English. The Southern Ndebele lived in the Pretoria area as early as 1650 and probably came from KwaZulu-Natal originally. The strong sense of Southern Ndebele identity is reinforced by their distinctive mural art and beadwork. As a written language it is still relatively new with only a few published books.

- **SiSwati** Not dissimilar to isiZulu, it is mostly spoken in the areas near Swaziland where the tribe is predominant. The first siSwati catechism and then the Bible appeared in 1846.

- **IsiXhosa** Sometime before the 16th century, the Xhosa people moved down from the regions along the east coast towards Cape Town. Along the way, they met the Khoi people and adopted some of the words and click sounds, made famous by singer Miriam Makeba. Some Khoi words in isiXhosa are *gush* (sheep), *inquire* (diviner) and *gei-xa* (magic)—a word with a click sound. IsiXhosa was also influenced by Dutch and English —*ijoni*, meaning 'soldier', is from Johnny, the British colloquial word for a man. Most written isiXhosa originates from 1857 and is somewhat different from the spoken word.

- **IsiZulu** Like the Xhosa people, the Zulus have inhabited regions of the east coast of South Africa since the 16th century. Now a very high percentage live in Durban and generally in KwaZulu-Natal province. IsiZulu, which has signs of Afrikaans influence and even greater English influence in vocabulary, is a fairly uniform language with few regional differences. It became a written language in the 1850s and is the most widely spoken African language in the land.

Sotho/Tswana

- Sepedi (also known as Sesotho sa Leboa) Sepedi is one of the two Sotho languages that are national languages in South Africa. The Pedi empire was founded over 300 years ago, although its people were later also called the Northern Sotho. By the mid-1800s Sepedi appeared in the written form and today is mostly spoken in Limpopo Province.
- Sesotho Sesotho, a language allied to Sepedi, is the language of the people sometimes called the Southern Sothos. It is spoken mostly in certain areas of the Free State and became a written language with the assistance of the French missionaries in the mid-1800s, and as a result there are a few French words on loan in Sesotho, as well as a fair few from both English and Afrikaans.
- Setswana Not only is Setswana spoken in South Africa, but it is also the official language of its northern neighbour, Botswana. The history of the Tswana people, from as early as the 17th century, has been one of fragmentation and amalgamation, of war and peace, of losing and regaining independence. The New Testament, translated in 1840, seems to be one of the earlier records of the written language.

Tshivenda

The Venda people crossed the Limpopo River from Zimbabwe into South Africa in about 1730, and have lived in the northern part of Limpopo province ever since. Tshivenda is a homogenous language with only slight dialect variations.

Xitsonga

This language is spoken by about 1.8 million Tsonga South Africans, most of whom live in parts of Mpumalanga and Limpopo provinces. Xitsonga was first used as a written language in 1883 and the first known creative work, a novel, was written in 1938. The language, in slightly different forms is also spoken in Mozambique (where the people are also sometimes called Shangaans), in Swaziland and by a few people in Zimbabwe too.

Immigrant Influence

Apart from the Dutch and the English, a number of other immigrants from Europe and the East impacted on South Africa's languages, cultures and creeds.

The most prolific early immigrants after the Dutch and English were the French Huguenots. They were Protestant refugees who landed at the Cape in 1688, adding their touch to the local languages, especially Afrikaans. Other European immigrants were the Germans, Greeks, Italians and Portuguese.

In 1860, the first Indians arrived in South Africa to work on the sugar plantations, importing a variety of indigenous languages which are still spoken by many at home. The Indian community has a near perfect command of the English language, which in many instances can be called a first language as well. Among the younger generations, quite often it is their first home language too.

The first Chinese arrived in South Africa after the Anglo-Boer War, and by 1906 some 50,000 were working here. Later they were all repatriated. A second small group arrived in the 1920s and settled down, and their native tongue was most often Hakka or Cantonese. Today, almost all South African-born Chinese speak excellent English, but sadly, among the younger generation, this has often been to the neglect of their mother tongue.

LITERACY: A LONG ROW TO HOE

The level of literacy in South Africa is lower than it should be! At the last census in 2001 17.9 per cent of the population over 20 years old had never attended school—that is some 4 million people. A further 16 per cent only had some primary education, and that is less than six years at school. And it gets worse: the percentage of unschooled population is much higher in the rural areas than in the urban ones, some say as high as 50 per cent or more in some rural areas.

Most of the blame for this can be laid at the feet of the apartheid regime which favoured whites with a privileged education over the rest of the population. In fact, white parents could be prosecuted if their children dropped out of school before they were 16 years old or had passed 10th grade! Not so for anyone else. In addition, the standard of education was not at all good in most other schools, so even those who did attend school usually received an inferior education. Although a long and difficult task, this is now being redressed by the democratic government. The statistics prove it, as the percentage of the population between ages five and 24 years who are in school is increasing steadily.

KALEIDOSCOPE OF COLOUR

Because of the cultural melting pot that is South Africa, there is a multitude of words that have grown up with this fairly young country. Sometimes they are bastardisations of words from other languages, and as such may mean something quite different from their original meaning in their original land. A classic example is the phrase 'just now', which in South Africa means at some stage in the not-too-distant future. "I'll see you just now" means they will meet you in a short while. It does NOT mean what is says, which is 'immediately'!

There are also many words that are typically South African, and although used in English conversation, may be words a native English speaker has never heard before. There are a few books and dictionaries to help you get a handle on the local lingo, but if in doubt, just ask the speaker to explain—there will be no hard feelings, they will not be offended at all by your asking the meaning of a word or phrase.

TOWNSHIP TALK

Ever since the heydays of Sophiatown in the 1950s, there has been a form of township talk or jive talk, a mixture of various languages, slang words with a lot of attitude thrown in for good measure and good vibe. But much of the vibe of Sophiatown was crushed—well at least temporarily—when the apartheid government forcibly moved the legitimate inhabitants of the area to what is now Soweto, and helped poorer whites get established in the suburb which they renamed Triomf (means triumph in Afrikaans). Today it is again called Sophiatown, but it is just one of many residential areas in western Johannesburg.

But the language lived on, and since independence in 1994 it has grown into a substantial communication tool, most especially for the urban youth to communicate across language and cultural divides. Called 'Scamto', it changes with the times, the fashions and the attitudes, but recently has been slightly more formalised by Lebo Motshegoa, first in his Scamto dictionary and then in his booklet, *Township Talk: The People, The Language, The Culture*, a hip introduction to township lingo which is now spoken fairly widely, at least by the youth, on most city streets.

In an interview, Lebo, a young entrepreneur working in the advertising industry, said that language and cultural differences are things that could divide South Africans, but Scamto breaks down barriers and is a tool young urban South Africans use for communicating and connection. He also said, "Language says a lot about who we are and how we live, this language is the essential us. It is about the new South Africa. It tells of diversity. It is not just political—it is bigger than that."

Here are a few words to get you going, but getting a copy of the booklet is worth the humour and the help you will get from it:

- G-string: BMW 3 series car because its front grill looks like one
- Jesus and his brothers: J&B whisky
- Bojwa: a trendy person
- Cherry: a girlfriend with whom one has a quick fling
- Regte: a steady partner
- CD: condom
- Jozi: Johannesburg
- Nine-nine: blunt or direct person

SOME WORDS AND EXPRESSIONS TO HELP YOU

- A couple of: as in 'Give me a couple of minutes', meaning wait a few minutes for me. Generally, it is used to mean 'a few' not 'two'. Even when buying fruit, a South African would say, "I'll have a couple of bananas, please."
- Ag shame: an expression of sympathy for someone or something as in "Ag shame, you have been ill."

- Babelas is a hangover and, although of Nguni origin, it is used and understood by all.
- Bakkie: a small truck or van, the farmers' most favoured form of transport
- Biscuit: the word used for what some would call a cookie. It's a perfectly ordinary English word, but the pronunciation might throw you.
- Biltong: a speciality snack of spiced and sun-dried meat, quite often venison. An acquired taste according to many immigrants!
- Bundu: used in English to mean in the middle of nowhere, or way out in the bush, it is derived from a Shona word meaning 'grasslands'.
- Chicken run: a local version of a chicken coop, but is also a colloquial and fairly new term for the action of emigrating because of the political instability.
- Cocopan: this is a fairly squat-shaped tipcart on rails used in the mining industry. It is a word of Nguni origin, perhaps coming from the word ghoekoe, which means 'hedgehog' whose shape is similar to this specialised rail truck.
- Eina: pronounced 'aynah', it means Ouch! It hurts, either literally or metaphorically.
- Eish! It doesn't really mean anything, but is used in the same way as 'wow' or 'hey' as part of generally cool jargon.
- Fundi: used in English to mean well-informed, or an expert on a particular subject. It comes from an abbreviation of the Zulu word umfundisi, which means teacher or minister.
- Girl/Boy: when not used in their normal sense, these words often refer to a domestic worker/gardener/office messenger. They are derogative and totally unacceptable. It is highly advisable not to use them at all, even if you hear some South Africans doing so.
- Green mamba: colloquially this means a peppermint liqueur and has been adopted from the Nguni word. Literally, mamba is a type of deadly snake.
- Isit? Pronounced 'izzit', it is a conversational word used in response to just about anything in place of "Really?".
- Ja: Afrikaans for yes, but is used by all to mean 'yes'.
- Ja nee: Although these are two Afrikaans words meaning

'yes' and 'no' respectively, as a phrase it is used in English to show ambiguity, and can be used to begin a reply. If you ask someone how they enjoyed the rugby match, they could reply "Ja nee it was good.", which means "It was good but...".

- Ja well, no fine: This is an opener or even a conversation closer. It doesn't really mean much but is seen as chatty.

- Joll or 'jawl': Refers to having a good time, usually at a social event.

- Larney usually refers to someone who appears affluent or smartly dressed, but can also be used to describe designer clothes as in 'a larney outfit'

- Mebos: probably of Arabic origins, mebos is minced, dried apricot formed into little cakes. It is a local delicacy.

- My China: meaning 'my friend' or 'good buddy'. As does okes (pronounced 'oaks', like the tree) and usually meaning 'the guys' (not women).

- Pampoen: a word of Dutch origin used in Afrikaans literally to mean 'pumpkin', but also used colloquially and humorously to mean 'blockhead' or 'bumpkin'.

- Putu: of Nguni and possibly Dutch origins, it means a fairly stiff porridge made from maize meal, which is also called mealie meal.

- Rondawel: a circular, thatched room or cottage. Of Dutch origin, this word is used in both South African English and in Afrikaans.

- Sharp or sharp-sharp: often accompanied with a thumbs-up sign, it is ubiquitous and is used in much the same as 'cool', or 'OK'.

- Shebeen is a township pub, and a 'shebeen queen', most often, is the woman who owns and runs it. Some shebeens are quite informal arrangements in the backroom of someone's home, but many have now gained liquor licences and are members of the Taverners' Association.

- So long: a colloquial way of saying 'goodbye' or 'cheers', and does have the connotation of "we will see you again soon". Also, the phrase means 'in the meantime' and can be used in "I'm going home, so long", indicating that the person is going home while you, in the meantime, will do something else.

- Spoor: the track of a person, animal or vehicle. This word is Afrikaans, but used in English too.
- Twak: this a contraction of the Dutch and Afrikaans word 'tabak' which means tobacco. It is also used colloquially in a dismissive manner to mean that you think something is nonsense.
- Voetsak: an impolite word and should not be used within earshot of polite company. It is a means of telling something to 'go away', especially dogs when they are chasing you while you are out jogging or cycling. Strangely, dogs everywhere in the world seem to understand this. The word is derived from an old Afrikaans/Dutch expression "Voort se ek", which literally means "I say go ahead/away".
- Sis: an expression of disgust and not to be used in very polite company. For example, "Sis, look at the dirt on the floor". It can be used to express dislike of food, but that is rude.
- Taxi: a seemingly universal word, but just remember it can refer to a normal taxi that you phone up and ask to collect you and drop you off at a given destination (strangely there are no cruising cabs in South Africa), but it often also refers to the mini-bus taxis that tend to be the mainstay of mass transportation here. These taxis run on semi-set routes and certainly can be hailed, but ensure you know where they are headed to or you could land up in a world very unfamiliar to you!
- Witblits: a potent, local and usually home-made brew. Rather like European schnapps, drink it at your peril! Literally, it means 'white lightning', and much more than a thimble-full could well strike you down without warning. The word has Dutch and Afrikaans origins, but is used colloquially by anyone who knows the drink.

WHEN WORDS FAIL YOU…

South Africans probably engage in various forms of non-verbal communication more often than they realise, not least because there are so many different languages, dialects, and varieties of slang that it is impossible for most people to know and understand many of them, let alone all of them. I think that for this reason people are perhaps more intuitive and also much more easy-going when verbal communications barriers break down. When you or the person you are addressing don't understand one another, my advice is don't lose your cool. Smile and laugh, and above all, don't try the colonial trick of talking or shouting ever louder—if someone didn't understand you the first time, it's rarely because they are deaf! Rather try rephrasing what you said, using a different word—and a bit of mime may also help.

Shaking hands is certainly an important way of greeting, both in the work place and in the social environment—and there is a very specific way in which a lot of South Africans shake hands (explained in Chapter 4 in *The African Handshake*) that does endear you to many. But it is equally acceptable and certainly not offensive at all to shake hands in the universal manner too. Women shake hands with men or women, mostly in a work environment and on first meeting. There after it is usual for women to verbalise greetings. Of course if you know someone well, some women tend to kiss, or at least hug, men or women when greeting or saying goodbye. But there is no standard and it is really about what you and they feel comfortable with.

Eye contact is normal between most people and both genders in South Africa, but in some rural traditions it is a mark of respect for women to lower their gaze when being addressed by elders, particularly men, and in some instances it is also done by younger men to their elders, or to those whom they respect. Also, some cultures believe it is polite to receive something with both hands: for example, should you pay your gardener his wage in cash, he may put out both hands, one resting on the other, palms up, to receive it. However, it is rarely expected that you, as an outsider, do the same. In the same manner it is possible that someone handing something to you will not just pass it to you, but hand it over much more deferentially, again possibly with both hands, than you would experience in most busy cities. Acknowledge their added effort with thanks and a smile.

ABOUT BUSINESS

CHAPTER 9

WELCOME TO THE COMPANY YOU'RE IN CHARGE OF THE HIPPOS

'We have also witnessed a remarkable transformation in the structure of the economy. A largely natural resource-based economy has given way to a more modern, dynamic and resilient economy in which higher value-added manufacturing and service are thriving.'
—Trevor Manuel, Finance Minister of South Africa

SOUTH AFRICA IS STILL A LAND OF GREAT OPPORTUNITY. It is a developing nation with an abundance of natural wealth, a large and youthful population, and a wide variety of cultures that all contribute to its economic opportunities. That you can be successful in business in this volatile and changing land is a belief that holds as true now as it ever did; but it does require a good understanding of the socio-political issues of a newly developing economy, coupled with those of a nation emerging from decades, if not centuries, of racial inequality. It takes a lot of energy, innovation, patience and dedication to make a go of it. But most people feel the rewards—both financial and social—are worth the effort.

In relation to the rest of Africa, South Africa's economy is doing extremely well, with a gross domestic product (GDP) that makes up about a quarter of that of the entire continent. Despite not being in the same league as the Asian Tigers in industrial efficiency, it nevertheless leads the continent in industrial output, making up 40 per cent of the total, 45 per cent of the mineral production and more than 50 per cent of electricity production.

THE WEALTH ETHIC

Most South Africans believe that life is about earning a living and preferably having a good life. The wealth ethic here is very similar to that in many countries, where people who are financially successful are looked up to. In fact, the nation's interest in the more prominent entrepreneurs and money magnates is seen in the dozens of magazine and newspaper articles written about them. There are often articles about their lifestyles, business deals and, should it happen, their fall from grace as well.

The policies of Black Economic Empowerment (mentioned on page 143 under *Business: The Toughest Barriers*) has seen the creation of a number of new super-rich business people, many of whom started out life on the bottom rung of the ladder. Some names to throw about include Cyril Ramaphosa, a former trade union leader and lawyer who is now a top businessman; Patrice Motsepe, who has massive holdings in the mining environment, as well as in the life insurance industry; Wendy Luhabe, who is an entrepreneur of note, especially in the financial sector; Saki Macozoma; Marcel Golding, and many, many more!

But making a fortune in and from South Africa is not a new phenomenon: it stretches far back into history when in the late-1800s, the mining magnates made mega-millions and formed companies that have developed into the present-day corporations like Anglo American. This company was the brain-child of Sir Ernest Oppenheimer, whose son Harry then developed it into one of the largest business entities in the world. Although no longer still strictly in the family's control, it is one of South Africa's largest corporations.

Not Everyone is Super Rich

For every super-rich person in this country, there are many thousands, in fact many hundreds of thousands who are still very poor. The general adulation of successful business people is tempered by the resentment of those who have not been able to get a foot on the economic-success ladder, due in large measure to the legacy of apartheid, but also to the complexities of an emerging market economy.

After independence, there was a hiatus when the workers of South Africa, through their trade unions, generally lent support to the new government—particularly through their role in the Tripartite Alliance (the grouping of the African

National Congress, the South African Communist Party, and the trade union umbrella, the Congress of South African Trade Unions or COSATU).

More recently, however, there have been rumblings that this community feels somewhat let down, as many of the socio-economic improvements promised by government have failed to materialise, or are very slow in reaching the poorer parts of society. I believe expectations were raised far too high, perhaps unfairly, for any government to realistically deliver in a developing country. The onus is now on each successive new government to ensure that it makes its priority that of alleviating poverty, and at least try to decrease the substantial gap between rich and poor.

MAKING YOUR OWN WAY

Opting for self-employment has not always been part of the South African business culture, as those lucky enough to have jobs in the past, especially with larger companies, often saw it as a job for life. I don't think this was so very different to many countries world wide a few decades ago. But in South Africa, especially from the 1980s onwards, the economy became ever weaker as sanctions bit hard. When this was added to a rising population growth rate, it meant more and more people had to attempt to create their own income.

But after apartheid was abandoned, sanctions lifted and the democratic government had put its pragmatic economic and monetary policy in place, the country began to experience reasonable to good levels of economic growth. They averaged about 4.5 per cent in the early part of the 21st century—a far cry from the minus 2–3 per cent in the early 1990s! Nevertheless, this has not yet been sufficient to make much of a difference to the very high levels of unemployment in South Africa.

One of the worst legacies of apartheid is the low level of skills in the workforce, due to the fact that most of the population received a very paltry education. Of course this is being addressed by the new government, but it takes years, even decades, to develop skills and professions.

At the moment, it is felt that this could be one of the brakes that may slow the economic growth in the near future. Many good businesses feel the frustration of being part of an economy that has finally begun to fly, and yet having to battle to find skilled staff to help them grow with the flow.

Tripartite Alliance of a Different Kind

To address the lack of skills in a large section of the workforce, the government has set in place a three-pronged approach. The Skills Development Act, the National Qualifications Framework, and the Skills Development Levies Act work in combination to help fast-track the nation's skills levels.

The Skills Development Act ensures increased investment in education and training, encourages employers to use their workplaces as active learning environments and encourages partnerships between the public and private sectors to provide education and training in and for the workplace.

In the past, many South African workers gained skills through years of on-the-job experience, despite the fact they had little or no formal education or training, and certainly no certification. Now under the National Qualification Framework (NQF), they gain recognition for their experience and abilities in a formalised, certified way which can be equated with more formal institutional training. In other words, accumulated experiences, as well as academic qualifications, are included in all skill profiles. The NQF also encourages ongoing skills training and development so that workers can be employable all their working lives.

The Skills Development Levies Act requires employers to pay into skills development funds. This compulsory levy of 1 per cent of the employer's payroll is paid monthly, and helps fund the education and training necessary to help the workforce catch up to the level of competitor nations. Under the Act, the employers and employees in each industry have to establish a Sector Education and Training Authority (SETA) to administer their training programmes. The SETAs are responsible for defining the needs of their sector and ensuring the relevant levels of education and skills training are being undertaken.

Grassroots: A Plethora of Informal Traders

Not many years ago, Granny Harriet Moyo died at age of 101. She hawked fruit and vegetables for 58 years to earn an honest living. But for nearly all of that time it was illegal for her to do this: illegal to try and earn herself a meagre living. She was forced under ridiculous apartheid laws to pay fines, and even spent time in jail simply because she wanted to hold her head up high by paying her own way through life. But she would not give up, she continued to work.

Today, of course all those laws have been scrapped and informal trading in various forms is the mainstay of many people across the country. They sell clothes and trinkets, craft and cosmetics, small consumables, fruit, vegetables— anything that can be easily carried away by the shopper and quickly packed away at the end of the day by the seller. These traders are often a fixture on many city and suburban pavements. Some may find this a little inconvenient as they block the thoroughfare a bit, but the benefit is lower prices and the knowledge that people have the right to try to earn a living. This right is enshrined in the constitution too!

Another favourite place to sell almost anything is at the traffic lights. Of course the captive audience makes it a lot easier too. And even if you really don't want or need what is being offered, it is often a pleasant distraction from the gridlocked traffic to have a cheerful conversation with the sellers, some of whom are likely to be foreigners too! Certainly some of these hawkers, from other African countries north of here, are plying a skill that has been honed over centuries on the great African trade routes.

The Logical Progression

A logical progression from the informal traders is the 'spaza' shops. Almost solely found in the sprawling African townships, these small backyard businesses do a roaring trade. As capital is almost non-existent and unobtainable among the poor, it is left to the would-be entrepreneur to buy a few goods with cash that is usually borrowed from mates or from a *stokvel* (see next section under *Alternative Financing*).

A spaza shop set-up in a seafreight container donated by a local shipping line, Safemarine, to the Khayelitsha township community. Photo courtesy of Safmarine.

With the profit, a few more items are bought the next time around and, in a remarkably short time, a thriving business is on the go. A lot of the credit for the success of spaza shops must go to the township residents who support them. Spazas are usually open from about 6 am to 9 pm every day of the week, while others may even open as and when you need them.

A quaint spaza shop story comes from South Africa's major shipping line, Safmarine. Faced with a number of old shipping containers that would normally have been sold for scrap metal, they decided to see if they could put them to better use among the poorer communities. Now many of them are used to house spaza shops.

ALTERNATIVE FINANCING

South Africa is not as lucky as Bangladesh to have Nobel Peace Prize laureate Muhammad Yunus and his Grameen Bank to help those with limited or no access to banking facilities, especially credit. But as they say here, people make their own plans.

The historical lack of easily accessible banking facilities in some regions, coupled at times with economic impoverishment, led to the people developing their own unique financial organisation. Called *Stokvels* (pronounced 'stockfells') or *mohodisano* (pronounced 'moe-dis-sa-no'), which means 'we pay each other back', these informal loan schemes are found often in the townships and mostly among the poorer and more traditional, middle aged people.

They are usually formed and run by women, although men sometimes participate too. The whole group, usually about 30 people, all pool a sum of money each month with one person taking all the money once in rotation. This allows each family to have a lump sum of cash once in a while to buy their large purchases. Monthly meetings, held at a different member's home each time, are also social occasions where food and drinks may be served and the participants can get together to discuss the problems of the day, or their personal problems. Great emphasis is placed on moral and social support, a far cry from the standard attitude of a traditional bank manager!

But according to the banks, today's youth is less likely to participate in a stokvel, so they have designed some fairly novel entry-level banking schemes. At the behest of the Financial Sector Charter, which encourages major high street banks to make financial services available to those who have never banked formally before, they have all set up the entry level product, the Mzansi. It is aimed at offering more affordable banking services to the unbanked millions—estimated at more than 13 million people. According to Standard Bank, one of the five participants, the cost of operating the account is low, fees are charged on a pay-as-you-go basis and you get an ATM card too for a opening deposit of R 20.

Another local way of buying something beyond your daily financial reach is the 'lay-buy'—and it is just that. If you cannot afford an expensive item, you pay a deposit and the shop will hold it for you. Every month, you pay a pre-arranged amount against the purchase price until you have paid the whole cost. Then the goods are yours to take home. Many of South Africa's lower paid workers opt to buy high quality purchases, especially clothes, and this is one of the few ways that makes them affordable. It is an arrangement between the shop owner and the purchaser alone.

The system of hire-purchase, used across all communities to purchase expensive goods, is arranged by traditional finance organisations like banks and other lending institutions. But finance charges are very high, which usually means you pay way over 100 per cent more for the item than its original cost. Many people use this means of financing to purchase cars and big-ticket household items.

GATEWAY TO AFRICA

South Africa plays an important role as the gateway to the rest of sub-Saharan Africa, especially for a number of multinational businesses, but also as a supplier of plant and equipment, domestic goods and food. It is also expected to be the engine that drives the rest of the region to greater economic success. In many ways a daunting prospect, but a hopeful one too.

The country has a web of well-developed infrastructure: top level financial services, fairly efficient commercial transport operators which includes road hauliers, freight forwarders, shipping and air transport companies and a good number of sea ports. It also has an extensive network of roads linking all major centres across the country. Many of the big centres are linked by high quality freeways, others by wide well-tarred roads. In recent times, some of the freeways and good trunk roads have had toll systems installed to cover the huge costs of road building. At present, these tolls are not unreasonably high, considering the comfort they provide when driving over long, long distances.

The deeper you travel into the rural areas, the less sophisticated the roads become; but even in the farming areas, many of the smaller roads are tarred or good quality sand roads. The railway network in the country is also fairly extensive, with passenger and goods trains offering fairly frequent services between major centres. Unfortunately, many of the sub-economic passenger services to the rural areas have been terminated, so long-distance taxis or bus services are the only options in some rural regions.

Regional Transport Web

South Africa has always had fairly good rail links with its northern neighbours, making cross-border rail transportation of commercial goods a distinct option, but only if speed is not of the essence. For time-sensitive delivery most organisations resort to road haulage and for smaller or vital goods, airfreight is usually the best option.

South Africa's harbours and shipping industry are both well developed. Durban is the busiest port but Richards Bay, further up the KwaZulu-Natal coast, moves the most cargo by volume, as almost all its cargo is bulk. Cape Town harbour handles a lot of the fruit exports and general container cargo, while Coega, near Port Elizabeth, is a new deep-water port that is expected to take some of the strain off the other ports as the economy powers ahead. Although the ports are run fairly efficiently and attempts are constantly being made to upgrade them, they are certainly not of the calibre of developed world facilities.

HIGH COSTS OF HIGH-TECH

To some, Africa conjures up images of tropical jungles, or weird and wonderful wild animals. South Africa has all that, but also large, modern, technically sophisticated cities—the concrete jungles of the 21st century.

Computerisation, electronic data transmission, and all the other high-tech contemporary business tools are as much a part of commerce here as they are in other developed nations in Europe, North America or parts of Asia. However, the biggest constraint in this environment at the moment is the lack of sufficient high-speed Internet access to fill the fast-growing demand for both business and domestic use. Of course every form of access is available here, but the costs are still prohibitive for many individuals and smaller organisations, and the speed of delivery of facilitative infrastructure is seen by many to be one of the potential brakes on an otherwise flourishing economy. The predominant reason is that the national telecommunications company, Telkom, has been a state-owned monopoly that only got its first taste of competition at the end of 2006, despite business crying out for the sector to be fully privatised.

That said, there is a fast-growing number of service providers across all the Internet delivery options—standard telephone lines, ADSL, wi-fi, 3G for cellular phone networks, satellite and high capacity leased lines, called Diginet here, used mostly by big companies. Most of them are fairly competent and the quality of service provision ranges from pretty good to pretty mediocre, but again, I think most of the bottlenecks and problems arise from the lack of infrastructural development. Simultaneously, the high consumer demand and use puts excessive pressure on what limited infrastructure already exists. I am sure that within a short period of time there will be sufficient competition forcing the entire industry to offer more realistic prices.

WHAT FUELS OUR ECONOMIC ENGINE?

Ever since independence in 1994, the South African economy has been growing and strengthening, slowly at first and now a great deal more robustly. The factors driving it are diverse—of course the lifting of sanctions, a truly democratic government and bringing the entire country 'into the country', so to speak, has done a lot to normalise a very abnormal economic situation. But a great deal of credit needs to be given to the government's sound economic policies, its desire to see them enforced regardless of how unpopular they may be to some, and the strict control maintained over the monetary policies by the nation's central bank, the Reserve Bank.

Once the GDP had reached reasonable growth rate levels by the late-1990s, consumer spending became one of the major economic drivers. At least part of the reason for this was that many thousands of newly-empowered South Africans were working in good jobs, earning good salaries and, for the first time in their lives, able to afford the normal trappings of urban existence—new homes, new cars, new clothes. In the coming years, infrastructural investment is expected to become the main economic driver, as the government attempts to upgrade and keep pace with new infrastructural demands, as well as keep to at least some of its promises to improve the lot of the poor in terms of low-cost housing, and more and better education and healthcare.

But emerging economies, always more fragile than developed ones, can be more at the mercy of uncontrollable factors like the value of the local currency, higher oil prices (South Africa has virtually no oil of its own), global economic slowdowns and higher food prices, often dictated by inclement weather patterns and drought. In addition, there is always the chance that current government policies could be put under severe pressure if more radical socialist elements in the country get voted into power.

INFLATION AND HOW WE CONTROL IT

South Africa currently holds a firm belief that controlling the rate of inflation is one of the reasons for its economic success. A stable, and generally low, rate of inflation has been one of the prime aims of the ANC since it came to power and it has succeeded in this by using 'inflation targeting'. We measure our inflation rate through the traditional consumer price index (CPI) although the Reserve Bank, our central bank, does take into account the wide differences in cost of living between big cities and rural areas when making the final calculation.

Inflation targeting was first introduced in February 2000 as inflation had again begun an upward trend. (During the last years of apartheid the country had been plagued by very high and volatile inflation which put added strain on an already weak economy.) The target levels are set by government after consultation with the Treasury and the Reserve Bank and initially were set at 3 to 6 per cent. Inflation hit an annual peak in 2002 of 9.3per cent but has mostly been on a downward trend ever since. Currently in 2010 it has moved upward slightly from about 3.2 to 3.6 per cent and, while the Reserve Bank is doing its utmost to contain it, external factors like the price of oil and the global recession make its task a lot more complex.

Where All The Money Comes From

Traditionally, the South African economy has always been broken up into five major sectors for purposes of evaluating the contribution to GDP. Although the table below indicates the 2006 approximate Rand values, the proportions remain pretty constant from year to year. Although some sectors way outstrip others in GDP contribution, certain sectors are vitally important to the economy, as they are mass employers in a country where levels of unemployment are unacceptably high and wealth discrepancy levels are on the increase with the concomitant political rumblings.

GDP Contribution By Sector in Rands Per Annum (2009 figures)	
■ Mining	R 95,185 million
■ Manufacturing	R 266,932 million
■ Agriculture	R 40,891 million
■ Trade (wholesale and retail)	R 213,939 million
■ Transport, storage, communication	R 162,722 million
■ Finance	R 378,421 million
■ General government services	R 243,144 million

What's Under Our Earth—The Mining Industry

The mining industry has played a dominant role in the economic development of the country ever since the first diamond was picked up in 1867 near Hopetown in the Cape Colony; and the first gold-bearing rock was discovered in 1886 near what is now Jozi or Johannesburg—or Egoli, the City of Gold.

For many years, the South African economy rode on the back of the nation's mineral wealth. In fact, because of it, the government was able to spend vast sums of money on the implementation of apartheid—the formation of the myriad governments for the separate homelands and so-called independent states, and the duplication of most government departments and services for the different groups and races. One can only dream about the economic well-being of the whole population that might have been, had those vast sums of wealth not been squandered over so many years!

Currently contributing some R 70 billion per annum to the GDP, the mining sector is also one of the largest employers in the land. In the past, most of the industry was in the hands of a few large and powerful mining companies, with huge barriers to entry, especially as mineral rights could—and were—purchased outright. This meant that the large companies sat on the mineral rights, exploiting them when they needed to. But it also meant that there was not much newcomers could do to gain access to mineral rights, start exploring and finally build mines, which would always create employment. It was a racially discriminating and monopolistic situation.

Democratic changes in South Africa led to the new government endorsing the principles of private enterprise, but on a level playing field! The government states its influence in the mineral industry is "confined to orderly regulation and the promotion of equal opportunity for all citizens". It also totally rewrote the Minerals and Petroleum Resources Development Act, which in essence puts all mineral rights in the hands of the state. Mining companies now apply for specific mineral rights on a 'use it or lose it' basis—a similar process to those in most other mineral rich countries in the world, such as Australia, and many others in Africa. The Act also facilitates Black Economic Empowerment (BEE) initiatives within companies and new BEE ventures such as African Rainbow Minerals, Mvelaphanda Resources,or Kumba. Strong focus is placed on environmental sustainability in the industry and on promoting not only the exploration and mining of minerals, but the beneficiation too.

And What We Grow On Top Of It—Agriculture

Agriculture accounts for less than 4 per cent of the country's economic activity—about R 25,000 million out of the annual GDP of well over R 800 billion (in 2006)—while not much more than a century ago, the country had an almost exclusively agrarian economy. Although its input to the country's bottom line is dwindling, farming is still seen as one of the larger and more important sectors, because it creates employment in the rural areas and is responsible for South Africa's self-sufficiency in food production. In fact, South Africa is usually a net exporter of food, particularly maize, to our northern neighbours. Very rarely do we need to import basic foodstuffs, as we did during the devastating drought that struck the entire sub-Saharan region in 1991–1992.

The agricultural sector is split in two. One is a well-developed commercial farming sector which is fairly well mechanised, but still supports a high number of jobs. Most of these farms are larger concerns that have economies of scale that help to withstand the vagaries of bad weather, droughts and the likes which can wipe out an entire season's production (and profit). The other is a subsistence-based sector, mostly deep in the rural areas, which, although sustaining the immediate population of the area, rarely contributes large amounts to the overall production volumes. But the government is working to improve farming skills and develop small-scale farming further in an effort to create more jobs.

Historically, much of the land in South Africa has been in the hands of whites and to redress this, a process of land restitution is currently underway. However, unlike Zimbabwe, it is an orderly, fair, legal process and is not restricted to farmland, but to all land. In some instances, the dispossessed community receives a monetary settlement rather than the actual land, while others have their land returned to them.

Expanding Local Production

The manufacturing sector is the country's biggest single contributor to the GDP, and despite economic up- and downturns, generally remains pretty stable because of its wide diversification. Some of its sub-sectors include agri-processing; the automotive industry, chemical manufacturing, information and communication technology, processing of metals, especially iron and steel, and the clothing, textile and footwear industry.

Manufacturing has made some headway in the global market in recent years, but it is sometimes eclipsed by certain other developing nations where wages are lower and skills and efficiencies higher. The country has a small core of scientific, academic and business excellence, but there is a large proportion who have little or no education or skills, although they are generally very willing to acquire them.

In July 2005, the government launched the Accelerated and Shared Growth Initiative South Africa (ASGISA), with its major objective that of halving unemployment and poverty and raising economic growth to as close to 6 per cent as possible, but not at any cost. It is determined that the growth must be sustainable and must be shared across a far wider section of the population than has happened to date. Under this programme, the government is obliged to address national challenges such as infrastructure development, education and skills shortages, public administration deficiencies and the challenges faced by small-, medium- and micro-sized businesses among others.

The government under President Jacob Zuma is as intent as it ever was under past presidents to continue the drive to create new businesses and expand existing ones in every way possible. Job creation is one of the most important ways of raising people out of poverty.

That Foreign Buck: Do We Really Need It?

Foreign direct investment (FDI) is a slightly tricky issue in South Africa. Not because it is not welcome—it is very welcome!—but because there is constant debate as to how necessary it is for the local economy. The answers vary from fairly unimportant to very important. What is more relevant is that the government and the law makes it very easy for investment to flow into South Africa.

Simply put, there are virtually no restrictions in investing in the country—either in the growing economy or in the stock market. No government approval is needed and there are almost no restrictions on the form or the investment or the amount. And there are some pretty good incentives too.

INVESTING AND INCENTIVES

For details on government incentives, and also on the exact procedures you need to follow if you bring money into the country, it is well worth having a discussion with your nearest South African embassy or the Department of Trade and Industry. But here are some guidelines:

- Investors in strategic industrial projects may get tax allowances of either 50 per cent or 100 per cent of an approved investment. The process is managed by the Strategic Industrial Project (SIP) programme, but will only be in place for as long as it is needed, so take advantage while you can!
- Foreign companies are now allowed to list on the Johannesburg Stock Exchange (and Bond Exchange of South Africa)
- The tariff reform programme helps lower input costs for producers
- Import controls have been normalised and reduced since South Africa is a signatory to the General Agreement on Tariffs and Trade (GATT) and the World Trade Organisation (WTO).
- Exporter incentives include marketing assistance, no value added tax (VAT) on exports and exemption from some customs duties.

Many investors are very bullish about South Africa as an investment destination. Some of the reasons include: a good economic growth rate of averaging about 5 per cent over the last decade (although currently at 3.7 per cent at the end of 2009 due to the global economic crisis); the stock market has done well over the last few years and this seems to be based on factors like a strong commodity sector that is broad-based and not just reliant on gold anymore; earnings growth for South African companies is good.

Of course, there are also some quite serious problems in South Africa as there are in most emerging markets. Even though the crime rate is dropping, it is still very high and needs constant attention; corruption is an issue as it is in many emerging markets (but it is good to remember that it takes both a giver and a receiver to create a bribe!); poverty level is high and often very visible, due in large measure to high levels of unemployment; the telecommunications industry is seriously cramped by the lack of good competition; the prevalence of HIV/AIDS puts an additional strain on the cost of doing business. But most of these issues are being addressed one way or another and there is strong hope that they will improve over the years.

That Pariah Status

Sanctions as a means of forcing an end to apartheid in South Africa first began as early as the 1960s in the General Assembly at the United Nations.

Trade sanctions were gradually more stringently enforced and by the 1980s were quite firmly in place by most of the world. However, as is always the case with sanctions, it did not mean South Africa could not sell her goods abroad, but merely that it became progressively more expensive to do so. All the intermediaries had to do was hide the country of origin—such is the hypocrisy of trade. Sanctions hindered trade, but did not stop it. However, the ability of the country to maintain economic growth was affected because it had to be self-sufficient, which strained its resources.

The Comprehensive Anti-Apartheid Act passed in the United States in the mid-1980s forbade trade relations with South Africa. Thus all American companies in South Africa either pulled out or sold the businesses off to local management. Some felt this move did not force the government's hand, but rather the reverse. It led to the perpetrators of apartheid drawing into their shells and pretending the rest of the world did not exist. Others, including me, felt that it at least gave the

Continue on next page

Continue from previous page

local non-voting majority the moral support they needed to force the hand of government.

There is little doubt that the effects of sanctions have been great. Money that should have been used for new business development was, in some cases, used to buy up existing businesses as the foreigners pulled out. Thus, with very little new business development, there was very little job creation. This is one of the many causes of the country's major unemployment problem.

The financial sanctions, also imposed in the mid-1980s caused the country major problems. Medium and long term non-trade related credit to South Africa was closed off, resulting in a serious balance of payment problem and a debt standstill.

In my view, one of the most severe effects of sanctions was the isolation of much of the business community from the international world, at a time when business trends were changing and moving ahead at a great pace. South Africa was left behind, and it has taken a number of years and a great deal of effort to catch up with the rest of the world.

FORMS OF BUSINESS ENTITIES

The laws governing commercial entities in South Africa stretch back to our early history and are based on Roman-Dutch law, like almost all of our laws. But as a result of the British influence, particularly on commerce and industry, we have quite an English flavour to our mercantile, company and insolvency laws.

Current law provides for a number of business entities, most of which are universal in nature. An additional entity, a way of encouraging small business development, called the Close Corporation was formed. It affords the small business person the personal protection that a company would, without the major expenses of a full company structure such as full audit and registration costs.

For foreigners, the advantage of setting up a South African branch of your corporation depends very much on the tax structure in your home country.

Regulations For The Various Business Entities

Here follows a general description of the regulations for the various businesses, but it is essential to get expert advice at the time you make this sort of decision as rules, regulations and even laws do change. In fact, the entire Companies Act is currently up for review and a host of significant changes can be expected that could also affect rules governing close corporations. For this reason, it is essential to get a good accountancy and auditing firm to advise you on which is most suitable for your needs at the time.

- Public Companies have limited liability and no restrictions on shareholders exist. But very comprehensive reporting and disclosure rules are applied, including a mandatory full-scope audit. (Audit and other governance related issues are expected to change with the amendments to the Companies Act, depending on whether the company is listed or not.)
- Private (Proprietary) Companies have limited liability and the number of shareholders is limited to 50. Comprehensive reporting is necessary, but disclosure is less onerous and a mandatory full-scope audit is needed.
- Close Corporations give you limited liability and you may not have more than 10 members who must be 'natural persons', meaning people and not other entities. Limited reporting and disclosure (to curtail costs) are needed, but no mandatory auditing is required.
- Branches of foreign companies have limited liability and do not need a local board. However they have the same strict reporting, disclosure and audit rules.
- General Partnerships have a limited number of partners, but no registration is necessary. No detailed reporting, disclosure or auditing is needed either and every partner is liable for ALL the debts.
- Limited partnerships have a restricted number of partners. They must be registered and at least one (it can be more) partner is liable for all debts. Liability

of anonymous partners is restricted and no detailed reporting, disclosure or audit is required.

■ Sole proprietorship has no statutory regulations.

BUSINESS ETIQUETTE AND PRACTICE

South African business is like a rough diamond. Some facets may appear quite clear to you because they are quite Western or international, like the workings of the banks and other financial institutions. Others will be strangely confusing, perhaps very parochial, such as the tax laws, or the complex manner in which Black Economic Empowerment (BEE) is applied to business and hence how it may affect yours. Then there are matters like the labour laws, dispute resolution through the Commission for Conciliation, Mediation and Arbitration of South Africa, always called the CCMA (which is also very helpful in explaining the labour laws and processes), and the trade unions, which have developed a very South African flavour cultivated by the issues particular to this country

Many people working or running companies here say it is an exciting place to do business. Red tape and some infrastructure limitations can be very frustrating, but the enthusiasm and innovative ways of many local employees can make it a very inviting challenge.

The South African Business Executive

Some top South African executives tend to be in demand almost anywhere in the world, as their high level of skills and quality training in the fast lane holds them in very good stead. Much of their experience is gained quickly and under less-than-easy circumstances. It is the result of a brain drain of skilled people prior to and just after independence to more settled lands. This has meant more hard work for those left behind, but it has also allowed them to advance more quickly.

Although South Africa is catching up very fast, there are, for historical reasons, still quite a few people in business who are relatively new to the environment, and not necessarily as skilled or dexterous as their counterparts in some of the more developed countries.

Office Etiquette

In some ways office etiquette is not too onerous in South Africa, as most people have a more open and casual manner and, although politeness is always an essential as it is anywhere in the world, hierarchy and pecking order do not play as big a role as in some countries. Nor are senior people particularly precious about their status. But my advice is always start off much more careful and cautious and formal in your approach and tone, and what you say to whom, until you really know the environment of your specific place of work. I would recommend you call people Mr Gumede or Mrs Walker if they are senior in your organisation, and on occasion it is not a bad idea to address people who appear a good deal older than you in that way too. In almost all cases you will immediately be asked to call them by their first name should this be their style—and it almost always is, but don't risk offence for the sake of familiarity or being too 'matey' until you know your ground.

Getting to work on time can be a touchy issue here as some people are sensitive to the fact that Africa in general has an image—sometimes quite unfairly—that people are always late for work or meetings. When public transport is someone's only way of getting to work, they are often at the mercy of a pretty inefficient bus/mini-bus taxi system. Many urban workers use cars, but it is worth noting that traffic congestion is getting ever worse as the number of cars on the road skyrockets! If you are genuinely delayed make a big effort to call your office and advise them. It will be appreciated. Also remember South Africans start work early, so you will just have to learn to get up that bit earlier to cope with the rush-hour traffic. Much the same rules apply to getting to an out-of-the-office meeting or appointment on time: it can be quite tricky as traffic congestion, outside of rush hour, is often intermittent, so you should always give yourself adequate time. Better be a bit early than stressed and flustered!

Although dress code has been discussed in Chapter 5, my general advice is that slightly too conservative and formal is a much easier way to start until you know the nature of the office environment you are working in. Some are much more casual than others. Some men are expected to wear suits and ties or at least jackets and ties to the office, while in other environments it is less formal. Women in the workplace, in my view, should always look smart and professional unless your office or industry is known to be casual and low key. My reason: there is still far more male chauvinism in South Africa than is acceptable and, frankly, looking less than formal opens the door to both being treated like a 'mere woman' and also to drawing attention to yourself for the wrong reasons! Rather stand out because you are good at your job.

Taking a break at lunch time is of course the norm here as it is anywhere else. What you do during that time depends as much on your job as where your offices are, as some are right in the heart of city life while others could be a fair distance from shops and restaurants. Some companies have office canteens, some people bring a packed lunch and some just take their chances with whatever there is to eat near the office. More often than not, work colleagues socialise together at lunch time, but of course there are also many who eat at their desk. It depends on your plans and the nature of your work. Since you tend to make most of your friends, at least in the beginning stages, at work, it is quite likely that you will be invited to join colleagues at the pub or for some other form of social get-together after work, mostly at the week's end. It is not obligatory, but it is a great opportunity to get to know people and to find out a variety of weird and wonderful things about life in South Africa.

Entertaining clients is also often part of your job, so you may be required to entertain them to drinks after work or to take them out to lunch or dinner. Almost all business-related meals are conducted in a restaurant and it is not expected of you to entertain clients at home. Some people, once they know their clients well, do arrange the occasional business dinner at home, but this is certainly not the norm.

DO'S AND DON'TS AT THE OFFICE

One of the most important things to smooth your way initially in the work environment is to remember that South Africa is a very multicultural environment, thus there are so many little things that could differ from person to person. Watch what others do and if necessary quietly ask someone if there are some things you think you just don't get. More generally here are some pointers:

DO'S

- Do ensure you take the time to greet people when you arrive at work, especially should they greet you first. And remember the service staff too—in a bigger office someone may bring you a cup of tea, deliver your mail, or clean the offices. Then get down to work.
- Do call the office early should you not be going to work due to illness or some other domestic emergency.
- Do call the office if you are going to be more than a few minutes late. This is even more important should you be expected at a meeting, briefing and the likes.
- Do dress appropriately for the office, erring on the side of conservative or formal. Men: suits or jackets, ties, trousers (not jeans); women: smart skirts, dresses or trousers, low-key jewellery. Even if your office is fairly casual, dress more formally if you are visiting clients or going out of the office for meetings.

DON'TS

- Do not use bad language. Swearing in front of anyone in the office is a no-no as most people find it offensive.
- Don't ever make any form of racial comment or joke.
- Don't raise your voice or shout at people if you can avoid it, and don't call them by animal names (e.g. silly monkey) even if it is meant humorously.
- Don't boast about your wealth, high level of education, or skills as it may be seen as a way of putting down locals who have had a lot less opportunities than you have.
- Don't refer to your seniors or people who appear much older than you are by their first name until, or unless, they tell you to do so.

DON'TS (continued)

- Don't complain ceaselessly about the South African infrastructure (telecommunications, traffic congestion, power outages) as compared to your developed world home. It is humiliating to your local colleagues since they are not personally responsible for the problems—and are also negatively affected by them.
- Don't use the email or Internet for personal surfing or communications until you know the office policy on this. And certainly don't use it for personal matters during office hours.
- Don't berate local staff if they are late for work; it could be that they have to take two, three or more taxi buses or buses to get to work, on top of the vagaries of the morning rush hour.

Graft—That Dirty Word

Graft is not a behaviour trend that is acceptable or encouraged in South Africa. Although there is a lot of talk about bribery and corruption, fortunately there is less actual occurrence of the scourge, but sadly that does not mean that there is none. The government, since coming to power, has been pro-active on this count, not least by ensuring that our constitution commits South Africa to implementing an ethical, accountable and democratic system of governance. It has also taken steps to see that this is implemented.

The Public Services Commission leads the national anti-corruption effort in general, and an ever vigilant press—newspapers and television—is hot on the heels of major stories. In addition, Business Against Crime, a joint government-business organisation, is a major facilitator of crime prevention in the country. It has a specific division solely responsible for white-collar crime and has facilitated a number of initiatives, including specialised commercial crime courts in all the major centres—which have had an excellent success rate because they have specifically trained personnel.

Doing Business

Certainly in a multicultural country there can be slight cultural differences in the approach to doing business, so don't expect total uniformity, but at the same time remember that South Africa, although an emerging market country, also has a higher than average level of first world economic, financial and structural infrastructure than most other developing nations. In this respect, it is fairly far ahead of the other countries on the continent.

The legal system in South Africa is first-rate, modern and progressive. The independence of the judiciary is protected under the Constitution while laws pertaining to business, such as those involving labour or transport are well developed. Laws regulating copyright, trademarks, competition policy and the financial services sector conform to international norms, and since many have been rewritten in the recent past, they tend to be modern, forward-looking and in line with best-business practice. Contracts are binding and are protected under common law. Financial institutions, accountancy firms and legal firms certainly follow a steel-door level of privacy here as they do anywhere in the developed world.

Do Words Hold Water?

Although by law and ethic your word is supposed to be your deed, in today's global climate a deal that is not confirmed in writing holds very little water. Verbal deals can be enforced by the courts, but the cost, time loss and responsibility to prove the deal was concluded is often not worth the effort. It really is worth putting it all in writing, even if the person you are making a deal with feels it unnecessary.

Exchange Control: The Bane Of Business Life

Rest assured that the government is committed to doing away with the whole system of exchange control in the not too distant future, but also take note of the fact that it will not happen in a big-bang way, but rather piecemeal as is happening all the time. Introduced in 1961 to stem the outflow of capital from the country and to ensure a measure of stability in currency markets, the process of exchange control limits or controls the amount of money you or a company can take out of the country.

Since 1994, various aspects of exchange control have been eased or simplified, some measures have been scrapped totally, and where it does still apply, the administration of the process has been streamlined to some degree. That is not to say it is not still a real hassle, but it is far less onerous than it used to be, and there is good reason to believe it will be scrapped totally one day. I highly recommend you get full details of how it will affect you from the nearest South African embassy at the time you are planning your trip to South Africa, and then also discuss the matter with an accountancy firm when you actually make those final decisions, to ensure you are aware of the processes you need to comply with to enable you to repatriate your funds when you want or need to.

The Vexations of Taxation

Most taxes are levied by the central government, but local authorities charge assessment rates based on the value of properties situated in their areas. These are commonly called 'rates and taxes'. In addition, the regional services councils charge levies to businesses in their regions, and then there are also skills training levies and a system of Value Added Tax (VAT). Capital gains tax is payable on equity investments and also on property should you sell it, but the level is not onerous.

As with any country in the world, particularly one you are not familiar with, it is sane advice to seek good tax advice at what ever level you need. Don't get on the wrong side of the receiver of revenue either by being ignorant of the tax structures or by just not getting round to it, as tax penalties are fairly tough here. Also remember that permanent residents in South Africa are taxed on their worldwide income, not just the income arising within the country.

Obviously once you are living and working in the country, you will be able to get a handle on the complexities of the taxes that affect you and your business. Those taxes that don't affect you, you can happily ignore. In general though,

The Kaapse Klopse is a minstrel festival held annually in January with thousands of brightly-dressed minstrels dancing and singing in what is Cape Town's longest-running street party. The festival originated in the 1800s when Malay slaves in the past celebrated their only day off in the year.

Street vendor in Greenmarket Square, Cape Town, with a selection of African-themed paintings for sale.

A Xhosa woman stitches glass or plastic beads onto a cowhide or goatskin backing. Despite the pressures of increasing Westernisation, African beadwork has been kept alive in rural communities.

Traditional glass beadwork on sale in Zululand District Municipality in KwaZulu-Natal, South Africa.

Johannesburg launched Rea Vaya, South Africa's first bus rapid transit (BRT) system in August 2009. The first 25 stations have become an important part of the daily commute for nearly 16,000 Johannesburg residents.

Houses in the Cape Malay Quarter, also known as the Bo-Kaap, which are inhabited by descendants of slaves from India and Southeast Asia. The first Muslim mosque in South Africa can be found here.

the tax regime has been structured to try to effect a fair balance between the needs of government—to upgrade the levels of services and infrastructure and the quality of life for all South Africans, not least those who were previously disadvantaged—and the need to drive the economy to new heights, sustain a good level of economic growth and also to attract new business. Most people feel it is doing pretty well in its juggling act.

OUTSIDE GOVERNMENT—ROLE OF NGOS

South Africa has a vibrant and active non-governmental organisation (NGO) sector, and it is mostly looked on fairly favourably by the government, as it is aware of the benefits these organisations can have not only in helping where help is needed, but also in helping the various groups or sectors develop their own structures, skills and self-sustainability.

Simultaneously, the government has been a bit touchy about them as it seems to feel embarrassed by the fact it is not doing some of the work the NGOs are. But in reality, no one takes much notice of this and the NGOs tend to go about getting their work done—or not—depending on their capabilities. There have been a few occasions when the presidency has commented less than favourably on some NGOs—it is reported to have questioned whether some South African NGOs were being manipulated by foreign donors and whether the civil society here was really independent. It appears there was some aversion to the NGOs taking a view on governance issues in the country.

A fair number of NGOs operate in or from the country: home-grown ones like the Nelson Mandela Children's Fund or the Treatment Action Campaign (TAC) which plays a big role in the HIV/AIDS problem; local NGOs that partner European or American ones; and of course many of the major international ones like Oxfam, United Nations' Children's Fund (UNICEF), World Wildlife Fund for Nature (WWF), Action Aid, World Vision and many more.

Since democracy, many of the larger international NGOs have made their African or regional headquarters in South Africa. I could be kind and say it is probably because we have one of the most developed infrastructures on the continent, thus making their work more effective. But I can't help notice that they also enjoy tremendously the easy, middle-class lifestyle that living in urban South Africa brings, especially when compared with some of the less fortunate developing countries on this continent.

Your first port of call should you want to do voluntary work for an NGO while you are in South Africa is to visit the website of SANGONeT (website: http://www.sangonet. org.za). Although an NGO itself, it has a lot of information about a great many other NGOs and the various issues that arise from the whole NGO sector—it's a good starting point. Of course you can also just call up any of the NGOs you know or become aware of through your friends and work colleagues. Your help will be welcomed by so many of them. For example, the high incident of HIV/AIDS-related deaths in this country is leaving ever more small children parentless, so care centres, orphanages and hospices for those who are ill are very worthwhile places to direct your energies.

THE POWER OF THE WORKERS

Labour relations and the power of organised labour are major factors in the South African business arena. Today the majority of the unions are well organised, generally well supported and tend to be skilled in their negotiations with management.

The first threshold of the labour movement in the 1920s and 1930s was slowly battered by waves of segregationist laws until much of the unions' influence was curtailed, if only temporarily. The racial divisions in the country were forcefully echoed in the unions as most unions had to be racially segregated. Today, of course, they are not.

The fight for recognition, and the fact that most of the population had no political rights, made it inevitable that the new surge of union activity, which burst upon the 1970s and continued into the 1980s, would be more militant and politically driven. As the only voice of the masses, trade unions used strikes, work stoppages and the like to not only gain a living wage, but also to flex political muscles.

One of the most successful union leaders of the time, Cyril Ramaphosa, who headed the massive National Union of Mineworkers (NUM), learned his negotiating skills thoroughly in this field. He later became the ANC's chief negotiator in the pre-independence mediations for majority rule with the then white government. Ramaphosa, having spent a stint in government after the first general elections, then entered the private sector and is now a very successful and high-powered businessman. He has also been called on to help facilitate other major international negotiated settlements, such as that in Northern Ireland, and is currently on the board of the International Commission on Intervention and State Sovereignty.

With more normalised channels for the nation's political energy, today's union leaders have focused their activities far more on the realities of the workplace. Demands are usually tempered by an understanding of the current economic conditions and the need for a joint management-union solution beneficial to all. There is also far more emphasis on the improvement of labour quality, with many of the negotiations centering around skills upgrading, rather than merely a cash package. However, never lose sight of the low quality of life experienced by many workers still, especially when compared to management staff.

The labour laws, including the minimum wage in South Africa, are considered very labour friendly, and in the views of some have priced some South African manufactured goods out of the international market. However, a balance has to be struck between the cost of labour and the fact that a large proportion of South Africans still live in relative poverty, and upgrading the standard of living is of primary importance.

The largest umbrella body for trade unions is the Congress of South African Trade Unions, COSATU, which is an extremely powerful organisation. When it lends its muscle to issues like wage negotiations or even various political issues, it can enlist the support of millions of workers.

THE OLD BOYS' NETWORK

There used to be a very specific old boys' network, also called the 'old school tie' syndrome, in South African business. Mostly links and friendships were established at high school, and very specific high schools too—the private, elite boys' schools of Michaelhouse, Hilton, Bishops, St Johns and a few others. In later life, these links were used in the business community to pass business and good career opportunities in the direction of friends. But today there is a lot less of this since our evolving new society has to a large extent broken free of these bounds, either by choice or because laws such as anti-discrimination legislation, active support for previously disadvantage communities such as women and other minority groups, or the implementation of Black Economic Empowerment has enforced it. Of course there are still cliques, networks and political affiliations that help some get into prominent positions, but far less than in the past.

SMALL IS BEAUTIFUL

Since South Africa is still faced with high levels of under-employment and unemployment, together estimated to be between 25 per cent and 35 per cent, every avenue to create employment is being explored. One of the most successful attempts seems to be the encouragement of small and medium size businesses. Current economic trends indicate that neither the conglomerates nor the public sector, in the longer term, are likely to be able to make much of a dent in the unemployment figures.

According to a report issued by the South Africa National Treasury, the small and medium businesses generate 50 per cent of the GDP and employ about 60 per cent of the work force and could (and should) become the major driving force of the economy in the near future. For this reason, the government believes that promoting these sectors is one of the most important ways of tackling the country's large-scale unemployment level. It is also seen as one of the better ways of redistributing wealth creation opportunities to a broader sector of the population, one of the best tools for real black economic empowerment!

To promote this sector of the business community the government has established the Small Enterprise Development Agency (SEDA) under the auspices of the Department of Trade and Industry. It offers would-be entrepreneurs and existing small businesses (called SMMEs or small, medium and micro enterprises) a vast array of help and information, including support for access to finance. It also creates a facilitative regulatory environment, expanding market opportunities for SMME's products, and opening up access to information through advice centres around the country.

FAST FACTS

CHAPTER 10

'I envision someday a great, peaceful South Africa
in which the world will take pride, a nation in
which each of many different groups will be
making its own creative contribution.'
—Alan Paton, South African writer, 1960

THE EASIEST WAY TO BEGIN TO FIT into a new society is to be able to hold your own in social conversation. Every nation has its pet subjects of conversation and, in South Africa, some of these are hung around the current volatile and changing political situation that is easiest gleaned from the daily press. But there are other facts that the locals grow up learning at school and at play which become part of their sub-conscious.

To help you get through some of those tricky moments when you simply don't understand the flow of the conversation, here are some names and numbers. This is not an exhaustive list as important facts covered in the previous chapters will be left out. But it should help you out until you get to know the ropes.

Where in The World Are You Living?

South Africa, more correctly called the Republic of South Africa, is the country at the southernmost tip of Africa.

However southern Africa (with a small 's') is the southern region of the continent and includes the countries of Angola, Zambia, Malawi, Mozambique, Namibia, Botswana, Zimbabwe, South Africa, Swaziland and Lesotho. Using the phrase 'sub-Saharan Africa' is slightly more complicated. Politically speaking, and this is also how the United Nation defines it, it is all of Africa excluding Algeria, Egypt, Libya, Morocco, Sudan, Tunisia and Western Sahara (which is a disputed territory). These countries make up North Africa. But if one is talking geographically, sub-Saharan Africa is all the countries south of the Sahara Desert. And by the way, there are 54 countries in Africa, which includes the nearby islands like Cape Verde, Comoros, or Sao Tome and Principe, but not the Indian Ocean Islands like Mauritius or Seychelles.

Population

Population estimates are never totally accurate in developing countries, but by South Africa's 2001 full population census, and extrapolated as an estimate by Statistics South Africa, in July 2010, there were approximately 49.9 million South Africans. The breakdown is as follows: about 79.6 per cent are Africans, 9.1 per cent are white, 8.9 per cent are Coloured and 2.5 per cent are Indian/Asian. Some 51 per cent are women, and life expectancy at birth is 49 years for men and 52 years for women.

Capital Cities

South Africa has three capitals: Pretoria, the administrative capital; Cape Town, the legislative capital; and Bloemfontein, the judicial capital. Johannesburg has no such official status, but is by far the largest city and the driving force of the economy.

Time Zones

Although the country is wide from east to west, there is only one time zone, South African Standard Time (SAST)—two hours ahead of Greenwich Mean Time or GMT (we use the term GMT here far more than UTC or Coordinated Universal Time). This means that life tends to start earlier in Durban than Cape Town, since many South Africans tend to rise with the sun, or just after it. Also, there are long enjoyable summer evenings in Cape Town when darkness falls way after 8 pm, while in Johannesburg there is not much summer twilight after 7 pm. There is no daylight saving in South Africa because the difference between the length of day in summer and winter is not substantial.

Currency

The South African Rand, which came into existence with the formation of the Republic in 1961, is a metric currency with 100 cents to the Rand. Coins range from the silver-coloured, or silver with a brass centre R 5, to plain silver coloured R 2 and R 1 then brass coloured 50- 20- and 10-cent pieces, the latter being not much larger than a tiny finger nail. There are also copper coloured 5-, 2- and 1-cent coins. The last being worth virtually nothing!

The bank notes, sometimes called the Big Five—because they have the heads of the big five wild animals found in the country, start with R 10 (green, rhino), R 20 (brown, elephant), R 50 (red, lion), R 100 (blue, buffalo) and R 200 (orange-brown, leopard).

National Symbols

Some of our national symbols, especially those that are more emotionally charged like the flag, coat of arms and the national anthem, have been changed to reflect our multicultural nation, while others that already reflect the land and its bounty have remained such as the national bird, flower or animal.

South African Flag

The new national flag, colourful, cheerful and symbolic of the newly emerging 'rainbow nation', was first used on 27 April 1994, the official independence day. Here is how the government has described its symbolism:

The design and colours are a summary of the country's flag history. Individual colours, or colour combinations mean different things to different people so no universal symbolism should be attached to any of the colours. The central design of the flag, beginning at the flag-pole in a 'V' form and flowing into a single horizontal band to the outer edge of the fly, can be interpreted as the convergence of diverse elements within South African society, taking the road ahead in unity.

Coat of Arms

The new coat of arms, launched on Freedom Day, 27 April 2000, is said to highlight the democratic change in South Africa and a new sense of patriotism. The motto in the Khoisan language of the Xam people, means 'diverse people unite'.

National Emblems

National tree is a Real Yellowwood
National bird is a Blue Crane
National fish is a Galjoen
National flower is a King Protea
National animal is a Springbok

The national flower, the protea, is used as the symbol for all sports people who represent their country. At the same time, the national rugby players have been allowed to keep the image of the springbok as part of their logo, as they were and are still internationally known as the Springboks.

National Anthem

I think one of our most successful newly-wrought images is our national anthem. It combines two verses of *Nkosi Sikelel' iAfrika* with an Afrikaans verse and then an English verse from the old apartheid national anthem. *Nkosi Sikelel' iAfrika* is a beautiful hymn of peace and blessing sung across southern Africa and was also the song of the African National Congress (ANC) before it came to power. The tune is fairly melodic, especially the first two verses, and there is barely a South African who does not at least try to sing it. The first verse is in Xhosa and Zulu, the second in Sesotho, the third in Afrikaans and the last in English. You don't get much more inclusive than that!

PUBLIC HOLIDAYS

Lucky for us! We have quite a few more public holidays than in some other countries! Some originate from the traditional international ones, such as Christmas Day or New Year's Day, and the rest are a blend of what is important to our rainbow nation—some are even open to interpretation by various sectors of the community as they see fit. In addition, various religions celebrate their special days even though they are not formal public holidays. To do this, followers of the various faiths just take a day or two's leave if they choose to celebrate a particular holy day. On major religious holidays, most shops and all businesses are closed, but on other public holidays many shops are open, although offices remain closed. If a public holiday falls on a Sunday, the following Monday becomes a holiday.

National Public Holidays

- 1 January New Year's Day
- 21 March Human Rights Day
- *March/April Good Friday (Friday before Easter Sunday)
- *March/April Family Day (Monday after Easter Sunday)
- 27 April Freedom Day
- 1 May Workers Day
- 16 June Youth Day
- 9 August National Women's Day
- 24 September Heritage Day
- 16 December Day of Reconciliation
- 25 December Christmas Day
- 26 December Day of Goodwill

* This date changes as Easter moves in the calendar

STEPS THROUGH HISTORY

Human existence in South Africa dates to Stone Age man who lived two to three million years ago. Then the San/Bushmen and Khoikhoi moved in too. And only much, much later did the Europeans arrive, after they got over their fear of falling off a flat earth!

2.5 billion years ago	Ancient forms of animals and plants existed in South Africa
3.3 million years ago	Hominins, our early ancestors, lived in parts of South Africa

15,000 BC   Rock paintings show that San/Bushmen were spread across South Africa and are deemed the earliest known people to live in South Africa—they were hunter gatherers.

7000 BC   Estimaged age of the man-made shelters discovered north of current-day Johannesburg

2200 BC   Khoikhoi (in the past, sometimes called Hottentots) joined the San/Bushmen. Khoikhoi were hunter-pastoralists who migrated down from Botswana into western South Africa.

AD 300   Around this time, ancestors of the Bantu-speaking majority of the population settled south of the Limpopo River, joining the Khoikhoi and San who had lived there for thousands of years.

AD 500   A group of Bantu speaking tribes migrating southwards reached present-day KwaZulu-Natal Province

1050–1270   Mapungubwe in Limpopo province was the centre of the largest kingdom in the subcontinent, where a highly sophisticated people traded gold and ivory with China, India and Egypt.

Up to 1488   Basing information on world maps thought to be drawn before 1488, there seems to be some evidence that the Chinese, Arabs and Indians may well have visited the Cape of Good Hope before the first European.

1488   Portuguese sailor Bartholomeu Dias is thought to be the first European to round the Cape and land on what is now South African soil. Inadvertently missing Cape Town due to storms, he first sighted land on the eastern seaboard, and put in at Algoa Bay.

1652	Dutchman Jan van Riebeeck set up a refreshment station at what is now Cape Town as the halfway mark between Europe and the Far East.
1688	French Huguenot refugees arrived and settled at the Cape.
late-1780s	Shaka, the great Zulu chief and warrior, was believed to be born in either 1785 or 1787.
1795	The first British occupation of the Cape.
1806	Second British occupation of the Cape.
1807	A year later, the British abolished slavery.
1820	The British settlers arrived.
1835	The Great Trek began.
1856	The famous Xhosa mass cattle slaughter that was predicted by the young orphan girl, Nongquasi, occurred.
1860	British colonists bring labourers from India to work in sugar plantations in KwaZulu-Natal.
1867	The Hope Town diamond was found and the diamond rush was on.
1886	Gold was discovered and Egoli, or Johannesburg, was born.
1893	Mohandas (Mahatma) Gandhi arrived in the country to defend an Indian client. The first ever South African world champion, cyclist Lourens Meintjies, is crowned.

1896	A highly contagious disease swept through cattle and game, killing thousands across the land. It was called the Rinderpest, and this word is sometimes used colloquially to mean someone of great age, as in "He is as old as the Rinderpest".
1897	The first motor car arrived in South Africa.
1899	The traditional liberation hymn of the masses, *Nkosi Sikeleli iAfrika* or *God Bless Africa*, was written. The Boer War started. The famous colonial hotel in Cape Town, the Mount Nelson, opened its doors for the first time.
1902	The Rand Daily Mail, was started, one of the first liberal newspapers in the country.
1905	The Cullinan diamond, one of the largest in the world was found. It is now part of the British crown jewels.
1906	The first Springbok rugby team went to play in England.
1908	South Africa went to the Olympics and sprinter Reggie Walker won a gold medal.
1910	The Union of South Africa was formed with General Louis Botha as the first Prime Minister. The South African Native National Congress, the forerunner of the ANC, was formed.
1913	Gandhi began the Passive Resistance Movement against racial discrimination. The Native Land Act was passed, preventing Africans from owning land where they chose.
1914	South African troops invaded German West Africa

—now Namibia. (My grandfather was one of them.)

1916   In the Battle of Delville Wood, thousands of South African troops were killed. Altogether, an estimated 12,000 South Africans were killed fighting in the First World War.

1918   A great flu epidemic killed many people.

1920   Van Ryneveld and Brand made the first air flight to England.

1922   The Rand Revolt occurred, and 214 people were killed when a major miners' strike was put down by the government of the day.

1924   Radio broadcasting began.

1927   The first tourists visited the now famous game reserve, the Kruger National Park.

1928   The South African flag was flown with the Union Jack for the first time.

1930   White women were given the vote.

1931   South Africa followed Britain in coming off the gold standard.

1932   *The Bantu World*, a daily newspaper aimed at blacks was started. It was the forerunner of today's Sowetan, the large Johannesburg black-oriented daily.

1938   Professor J L B Smith identified the coelacanth fish, presumed to be extinct until then, and considered one of the greatest ichthyological finds in the world.

1948	The National Party won the 'white's only' elections for the first time. This is seen as the beginning of formalised apartheid.
1953	Bertha Solomon steered the Matrimonial Affairs Act through Parliament.
1955	Dr Hendrik Verwoerd became Prime Minister and the harsh realities of apartheid were enforced.
1960	The Sharpville shootings occured, killing 67 people. Whites voted on a referendum for republican status for the country. Great African leader and member of the ANC, Albert Luthuli, won the Nobel Peace Prize.
1961	South Africa became a republic and adopted decimal coinage.
1964	The Rivonia Treason Trial of eight members, including Nelson Mandela, took place. They were sentenced to life imprisonment.
1967	Chris Barnard performed the first heart transplant in the world at the Grooteschuur Hospital in Cape Town.
1976	Soweto student riots began. Television came to South Africa!
1984	The last sitting of the Westminster-style parliament in South Africa. The new constitution came into force, allowing for three separate houses—whites, Coloureds and Indians. The National Union of Mine Workers, to become one of the most powerful unions, was formed.

1985-86   A state of emergency was declared in 36 magisterial districts around the country, particularly in the big urban areas.

The major trade union umbrella body, the Congress of South African Trade Unions (COSATU), was formed.

1987   The United States stepped up its sanctions campaign against South Africa.

The ultra-conservative Conservative Party became the official opposition in the whites-only government.

1990   Nelson Mandela and the other Treason Trialists were released from jail after being imprisoned for life for trying to end apartheid.

The ANC, the South African Communist Party and many other banned political organisations were legalised.

1991   President F W de Klerk made a watershed speech, declaring the removal of the major legal pillars of apartheid. The Convention for a Democratic South Africa (CODESA) was created and empowered to draw up a declaration of intent to move South Africa from apartheid to democracy.

1992   The whites voted 'Yes, for change' in a referendum seeking a mandate for the government of the day to continue toward democracy for all.

The wheels fell off CODESA and it came to a standstill. Along with it, the economy spiralled even further downward.

1993   Nelson Mandela and the then-president F W de Klerk jointly won the Nobel Peace prize for "their work for the peaceful termination of the apartheid regime, and for laying the foundations for a new democratic South Africa".

The new CODESA, called the Multi-party Negotiating Council, came into operation and an agreement is reached on the interim constitution.

1994   The first ever non-racial, democratic elections in the country took place from 26 to 27 April, but the overwhelming response saw voting extended another day to 28 April.
The ANC won in an alliance with COSATU and the South African Communist Party.
On 10 May, Nelson Mandela was sworn in as president, with ex-president F W de Klerk and the ANC stalwart Thabo Mbeki as deputy presidents in a government of national unity.
The country re-joined the Commonwealth, remaining sanctions were lifted and South Africa took its seat in the United Nations General Assembly after a 20-year ban.

1996–2003   The Truth and Reconciliation Commission, chaired by Archbishop Desmond Tutu, began hearings on human rights crimes committed by the former government and the liberation movements during the apartheid era.

1996   Parliament adopted a new constitution. The National Party withdrew from the coalition, saying it was being ignored.

1998   The Truth and Reconciliation Commission report branded apartheid a crime against humanity, and found the ANC accountable for human rights abuses as well.

1999   ANC won the second general elections and Thabo Mbeki took over as president.

2003   The Truth and Reconciliation Commission released its report.

2004   In the third-ever democratic elections, the ANC won a landslide victory, gaining nearly 70 per cent of the votes. Thabo Mbeki began a second term as president.

2006   South Africa became the first African country, and the fifth in the world, to legalise same-sex unions.

2007   South Africa chaired the UN Security Council for the first time, having been elected to one of 10 non-permanent seats.

2009   The ANC again won the general elections and President Jacob Zuma is sworn in as president, a speedy recovery from his fall from grace a few years earlier.

2010   South Africa hosted the first ever football world cup held on the African continent – the 2010 FIFA World Cup South Africa was a great success.

RECENT LEADERS
Heads of Government

Initially, the leaders of the government were prime ministers, but when the Westminster system of government was swapped for the tricameral parliament, the state president became the leader of the country. Then after the first multiracial elections, South Africa became a constitutional democracy with a three-tier system of government. Here follows a list of state leaders starting from the most recent:

- Jacob Gedleyihlekisa Zuma – President
- Kgalema Petrus Motlanthe – President
- Thabo Mvuyelwa Mbeki – President
- Nelson Rolihlahla Mandela – President
- Frederik Willem de Klerk – President
- Pieter Willem Botha – Prime Minister, then President

- Balthazar Johannes Vorster – Prime Minister
- Hendrik Frensch Verwoerd – Prime Minister
- Johannes Gerhardus Strydom – Prime Minister
- Daniel Francois Malan – Prime Minister
- Jan Christiaan Smuts – Prime Minister
- Louis Botha – Prime Minister

Liberation Leaders; Political High-Flyers; Important People

- **Albert Luthuli** One of the earliest members of the ANC and recipient of the Nobel Peace Prize in 1960.
- **Oliver Tambo** Leader of the ANC who was in exile for many years. He became its head in South Africa once it was legalised, but later retired due to ill health. Nelson Mandela then took over.
- **Walter and Albertina Sisulu** This husband and wife team were members of the ANC. Walter went to jail with Nelson Mandela and was released at the same time too. Albertina devoted her whole life to the fight against apartheid and was very prominent in the women's movements.
- **'Pik' Botha** South Africa's minister of foreign affairs in the apartheid era and was one of the world's longest-serving foreign minister. He served as a minister in the first ANC government and in 2000, applied for ANC membership.
- **Stephen Bantu Biko** He was a noted non-violent anti-apartheid activist and founder of the Black Consciousness Movement. He suffered major head injuries while in police custody, then was driven in this state some 1,000 km (621.4 miles) to a Pretoria prison where he died of his injuries. He became a major symbol of the struggle against apartheid.
- **Archbishop Desmond Tutu** The Anglican archbishop spoke out for the oppressed when most other leaders were in exile or in jail. Still the guardian of South African human rights morals, he won the 1984 Nobel Peace Prize.

- **Cyril Matamela Ramaphosa** Originally leader of the National Union of Mineworkers, he then became the leader of trade union umbrella COSATU. With superb negotiating skills, he was one of the chief negotiators for a government of national unity. He is now a highly successful businessman, having built up a major, listed corporation. He is on many company boards and is one of the hot favourites for president.
- **Mamphela Ramphele** An anti-apartheid activist who, with Steve Biko, founded the Black Consciousness Movement. She is also a notable academic, businesswoman and medical doctor. She has been vice-chancellor of University of Cape Town, one of the four managing directors of the World Bank, and is a current trustee on the board of the Rockefeller Foundation in New York.
- **Mark Richard Shuttleworth** An entrepreneur who was the second self-funded space tourist and first African national in space. He founded Thawte in 1995, which specialised in digital certificates and Internet security, and then sold it to VeriSign in December 1999, earning about US$ 575 million at the time. Now, he owns a business incubator and venture capital provider and also promotes and supports free software projects financially.
- **Shaka** The King of the Zulus. After assuming the Zulu throne, he became the military strategist responsible for transforming the Zulu tribe into a formidable fighting force and powerful nation in the early-1800s. Some felt he was a military genius.
- **Nkosi Johnson** He was an Aids activist, the longest-surviving child born with the virus, who became a symbol for sufferers after an emotional speech he made at the World Aids Conference in 2000. He died in 2001 aged 12.

CULTURE QUIZ

SITUATION 1

You and many other rugby/cricket/soccer fans have been in a pub or someone's home watching the last match in a rugby/cricket test series or finals of the African Cup of Nations on TV. The South Africans have just lost to the Australians/Nigerians. Do you:

Ⓐ Cheer loudly because you are really an Australia/Nigeria supporter, having just come from that part of the world?

Ⓑ Commiserate with your hosts or pub mates, but give reasons for why you feel the other side deserved to win?

Ⓒ Keep your feelings to yourself and just discuss the merits and demerits of the play?

Comments

Perhaps not the most honest approach, but certainly the most likely to keep your nose in its rightful place on your face and your friends as your friends, is **Ⓒ**. Besides, discussing the game can keep you drinking with the buddies for a number of hours.

Ⓐ is the worst response you could have. Sport is as close as you can get to a religion without a god to many South Africans. Insulting their national team is as bad as insulting them personally. Beware of even taking sides in the national league of the various sports until you know your ground a little better.

Ⓑ will most likely not get you into trouble, but it may exclude you from the general conversation, as the locals will think you are just not part of them.

SITUATION 2

You are negotiating a deal with a South African supplier of a material that you need in your newly established factory. You have set up the preliminary discussions via email and/or telephone. You then arrive at the supplier's head office to discuss the final deal with the national sales and marketing director. He puts forward an offer of a given price for the product. Do you:

Ⓐ Jump at the offer, sign on the dotted line and hope you can make enough mark-up on the product to keep in business?

Ⓑ Throw up your hands in horror and propose a 50 per cent reduction, expressing your disbelief at the outrageous price and mentioning that you could get it elsewhere at a better price?

Ⓒ Quietly and knowledgably discuss the offer, making it clear that the price is too high, but that for a better deal you could perhaps guarantee quicker payment, or a larger quantity of purchase among other alternatives.

Comments

If you follow option Ⓐ you will probably not get a good deal, as South Africans may do business 'European' style, but that does not preclude them from trying to get as much for their product as possible.

Ⓑ is most likely to antagonise and perhaps even intimidate your supplier—and sometimes a South African with their back against the wall can be quite unreasonable. There is a chance they will just say, "Well get it elsewhere, then." You may not be able to get the product cheaper anywhere else.

This leaves you with Ⓒ which is the most common way business is conducted here. Give a little, take a little. The most favoured catch phrase at present is to try for a win-win situation. It is probably the most appropriate way to go, unless you are VERY sure of your options.

SITUATION 3

You are invited to a dinner party by your boss at their home. Do you:

Ⓐ Accept quietly and verbally, ensuring you know the time, address and date, also asking what the dress code should be and if there is anything you could bring to add to the meal?

Ⓑ Say "yes" and whoop around the office telling everyone, including those who may well have not been invited, that you are off to eat with the boss?

Ⓒ Nonchalantly say you guess it would be fine, but you need to check to see that you are not otherwise engaged and will get back to him/her nearer the time?

Comments

Option **B** will ensure that you will not ever be invited again, and may well even get you a terse note that the dinner is off or postponed. It is not a done thing to discuss overtly with your colleagues matters such as a private dinner invitation from the boss.

A is the most usual way a South African employee would respond to the invitation. Express the pleasure at being invited without being obsequious about it, get the correct information about the nature of the function, so as not to be too casually or formally dressed. The offer of a little assistance will most likely be turned down in a boss-employee situation, although it would be wise to bring a small gift of chocolates or flowers to the function.

C is not a wise option as it is too casual an approach for a boss-employee invitation. It is more likely the approach you would use if a good friend made you a casual invitation to have supper with them.

SITUATION 4

You and your spouse are invited to a provincial level rugby/soccer/cricket match to be played in the big sports stadium in the city where you live. Mention is made of going out to dinner after the game. Do you:

A Dress for dinner in smart casuals: women in evening make-up and high-heel shoes, and men in tie and sports jacket?

B Wear jeans or shorts (depending on the weather and if you are in a covered stadium or not), T-shirt and sneakers, hats and sunglasses and a lot of sunscreen on your exposed skin?

C Do you decline because you know it will be shown on TV and you just don't know how to act at a South African sports match?

Comments

Option **C** is certainly not the way to make friends nor get to know the local way of life. South Africans will make an effort to encourage shrinking violets into the group, but only for a limited time. If you are invited to a game and it's the kind of recreation you like, go even if you do feel a little ill at ease. It is the best way to learn how it's done. And your friends will certainly help you understand anything about the game and the whole outing if you just ask!

B is the way to dress for sport matches, unless you are invited to a 'box', which is more smart-casual than described. In that case, it may be a bit more formal and it would then be quite in order to ask what dress code is best. Casual is the code word at sports matches, especially as behaviour and team support gets quite rowdy and boisterous. If you know where you going for the meal after the match, you could bring a change of clothes with you, but chances are that you will go somewhere casual or have sufficient time to go home to shower and change.

A would make you stand out like a sore thumb at the match, and perhaps make your hosts feel a little ill at ease for not explaining the causal nature of the event to you. You would not be ostracised, but you would feel a little left out.

SITUATION 5

You are at a cocktail or dinner party with a group of acquaintances and the subject of South African politics arises. The locals start a heated debate over a party-political issue or something the government has done that some disagree with and others think is perfectly fine. Do you:

A Join in, taking sides and expressing strong views on which you think is correct and why, adding for good measure just what is wrong with the way the country is, or was, run?

B Listen politely and keep mum. Or make as innocuous a comment as you can when asked for your view?

C Switch the conversation to the politics of your home country?

Comments

Option **C** may well work if the rest of the group know of your country's politics, and it could be a great way to diffuse what so often becomes an unpleasant slanging match with little logic and no point. But if your land is too distant for them to know much about, it will probably not draw their swords from each other's necks.

Ⓐ could be quite exhilarating as long as you are well-informed on matters, and as long as you are prepared for the severe knocks you may get for 'being a foreigner meddling in our affairs'. You may lose friends if they become too upset at your views.

Ⓑ is the easiest way out, rather boring but safe. Politics and religion tend to bring some of the most rational and sane people to irrational flash point in a matter of moments. Stay out of the fray until you are sure of the sensitivities of your friends.

SITUATION 6

You are with a group of people, all of one race/gender. You suddenly find the conversation has become belittling to another race or to and about women/gays. (And this can even happen in a mixed group with the silly phrase of 'present company excluded'.) Do you:

Ⓐ Join in, pretending that it is quite OK to talk about people in this way, despite the fact you feel uncomfortable and disloyal to other friends and colleagues?

Ⓑ Stand around listening, but not actually taking part in the conversation and hope it will just peter out, or try and change the subject without actually seeming to?

Ⓒ Tell the company politely but firmly that these are not your views or the way you like to talk and behave, and so would prefer it if people did not speak/behave like this at all, or at least not in your presence?

Comments

Frankly option **Ⓒ** is the only correct one! But I do realise that it can be VERY difficult to act in this way when you are still not at all familiar with the people and the country. If you are confident and/or very offended (and I would be), then perhaps try to let them know that you are very uncomfortable in this situation. Otherwise try **Ⓑ** (and resolve to have as little to do with them in the future as you can). Of course **Ⓐ** is not an option at all.

DO'S AND DON'TS

DO's

- Do stay a while to greet others. The norm is to exchange a few pleasantries rather than rush off with a quick "Good day!". This practice builds strong working relationships and friendships.
- Do make every effort to socialise and meet new people. It is not difficult to start a conversation with a South African. Listen and observe, and you will learn quite a bit about living and working in the country.
- Do use socially correct language. There is a growing awareness of the need to refer to the 'challenged', rather than the blind or deaf, and to steer clear of offensive terms and names.
- Do tip your waiter. Tipping constitutes the bulk of a waiter's income. Only a few places charge a service fee, and that usually applies to tables of more than 10. So leave a tip of about 10 per cent or more if you have been served reasonably well.
- Do tip the parking attendant. It's a lot cheaper than a parking meter in London, and he will look after your car, wash it (for an additional fee) and help you in and out of the parking space.
- Do ask those seated around you if they would mind you smoking, before you light your cigarette.
- Do drive very carefully and slowly (and on the correct side of the road) on city roads, being particularly wary of mini-bus taxis which stop without much warning.
- Do wear your seatbelt and don't talk on your mobile phone while driving unless you have a hands free device.
- Do try to see as much of the country as possible early in your stay. Suddenly your posting will be over and you will realise you have not experienced nearly as much as you could have.
- Do be respectful of all people, especially people older than you.

DON'Ts

- Don't be part of things racist, be it conversation, language, opinions. Just change the subject if you can, and move away if you cannot. I believe you should also tell people politely that you don't tolerate that sort of behaviour, although it could be a bit too overwhelming if you are a very new arrival.

- Don't smoke in public places. Stringent anti-smoking laws allow smoking only in designated areas or outdoors. All restaurants, bars and offices are non-smoking environments. There are usually signs at the entrances indicating the policy that prevails in a particular place.

- Don't give your Muslim host alcohol as a gift. A box of chocolates would make an appropriate gift.

- Don't eat with your left hand in a traditional Indian home if people are eating with their hands as this could be seen as an insult to the host. Eat with your right hand only.

- Don't serve your Muslim or Jewish guests pork. Muslims, Jews and a majority of the black cultures do not eat pork (or any of its derivatives). Some Jews do eat bacon and shellfish, depending on how strictly they follow their religious practices.

- Don't swear. Swearing is generally unacceptable. Although this is changing as the country continues to modernise and open up to the international community, it is still not worth the risk of offending people for something that is so avoidable.

- Don't touch a wild animal, or pick plants and flowers, or even pick up dried wood in a nature reserve. The penalties for this are huge. It is also an offence to capture or keep certain wild animals.

- Don't let your estate agent push you into making a hasty decision. Clarify from the start what you are looking for, and consider carefully before deciding to purchase or rent a property. Remember contracts are binding. You are not required to pay the estate agent a cent.

- Don't engage with road rage fiends, or become one yourself. Some people could be more violent in this type of situation, even using a weapon, than you would expect.

GLOSSARY

A couple of	a few not necessarily only two
Ag shame	expression of sympathy
Atchars	chutney
Babelas	hangover
Bakkie	small truck or van
Biscuit	a cookie
Bobotie	special Cape Malay meat dish
Boerewors	local sausage
Braai/braaivleis	barbeque
Bredies	stew, casserole
Bru or bro	buddy, mate, friend
Biltong	dried meat snack, jerky
Eina	ouch!
Flick	film, movies.
Ja	yes
Ja well, no fine	an opener or even a conversation closer, doesn't mean anything.
Joll	a good time
Kabbeljou	type of local sea fish
Lekker	nice, good, tasty
Mealie, Mealie meal	maize (or corn), maize meal
My China	my friend, good buddy
Piri-piri	very hot chilli condiment
Putu	stiff porridge made from maize meal
Robot	traffic light
Rondawel	circular, thatched room or cottage
Rooibos	local herb tea

Sharp or sharp-sharp	cool, ok
Shebeen	township pub
Skollie	scoundrel
Snoek	type of local sea fish
So long	goodbye, cheers
Sosatie	kebab
Spoor	track of a person, animal or vehicle.
Sis	expression of disgust or dislike
Takkies	sneakers, trainers, or sports shoes.

RESOURCE GUIDE

EMERGENCIES AND HEALTH
Emergency Numbers

- Emergency police 10111
- Ambulance 10177

City telephone directories list all emergency numbers at the very front of the book (fire brigade, electricity and water supply, rescue, weather, etc.). Also look in any telephone directory for a list of police stations and keep the number of the one nearest you at the phone.

If you have trouble with an emergency number—to call for an ambulance, fire brigade or police—dial **1022**. Mobile phone users can call **112** (same number for all mobile phone networks). The operator will contact the police or ambulance, depending on the emergency.

Hospitals

South Africa has a number of state hospitals, but most people who can afford either private medical insurance or private hospital care do make use of it. I suggest that as soon as you have found a home, you research the best and closest hospitals to you and keep the numbers handy. I have listed below the head office contacts for the major hospital groups. Call them or look up their hospital and outpatient facility lists on the Internet to find one close to you that suits your needs.

- **Netcare Group**
  Tel: (011) 301-0000; website: http://www.netcare.co.za/live/index.php
- **Life Healthcare**
  Tel: (011) 219-9000; website: http://www.lifehealthcare.co.za
- **Medi-Clinic**
  Tel: (021) 809-6500; website: http://www.mediclinic.co.za

Note: these are not emergency numbers

For quick access, before you have settled in and had time to find a hospital of your choice, here is a list of some of the larger ones in the big cities—both state and private.

Johannesburg

- Johannesburg Hospital (state)
  Jubilee Road, Parktown
  Tel: (011) 488-4911; emergency tel: (011) 488-3165
- Sandton Hospital Medi-Clinic (private)
  HF Verwoerd Drive, Bryanston
  Tel: (011) 709-2000; emergency tel: (011) 706-7710/11
  Website: http://www.sandtonmc.co.za/
- Morningside Hospital Medi-Clinic (private)
  Rivonia Road, Morningside
  Tel: (011) 282-5000; emergency tel: (011) 282-5127
  Website: http://www.morningsidemc.co.za
- Milpark Hospital (private)
  Guild Road, Parktown
  Tel: (011) 480-5600 (this is also the emergency number)
- Linksfield Park Clinic (private)
  12th Avenue, Linksfield West
  Tel: (011) 647-3400; emergency tel: (011) 637-3463

Cape Town

- Groote Schuur Hospital (state)
  Observatory tel: (021) 404 9111 (also for emergencies)
  Website: http://capegateway.gov.za/gsh
- Red Cross War Memorial Children's Hospital (state; also
  known simply as Red Cross Children's Hospital)
  Klipfontein Road, Rondebosch
  Tel: (021) 658-5111 (also the emergency number)
  Website: http://capegateway.gov.za/redcrosshospital
- Tygerberg Hospital (state)
  Franzie Zyl Avenue, Tygerberg
  Tel: (021) 938-4911 or (021) 938-6911
- Cape Town Medi-Clinic (private)
  21 Hof Street, Oranjezicht
  Tel: (021) 464-5500; emergency tel: (021) 464-5555
  Website: http://www.capetwonmc.co.za
- Durbanville Medi-Clinic (private)
  45 Wellington Road, Durbanville
  Tel: (021) 980-2100; emergecny tel: (021) 980-2126
  Website: http://www.durbanvillemc.co.za

Durban

- Addington Hospital (state)
  Erskine Terrace, South Beach
  Tel: (031) 327-2000; emergency tel: (031) 327-2311
  Website: http://www.kznhealth.gov.za/addingtonhospital.htm
- Crompton Hospital (private)
  102 Crompton Street, Pinetown
  Tel: (031) 702-0777 (also for emergency)
- Life Entabeni Hospital (private)
  148 South Ridge Road, Berea
  Tel: (031) 204-1300 (also for emergency)

Sports and Fitness Facilities

Besides the major health club groups Virgin Active and Planet Fitness, which run chains of fitness centres, there are individual gyms and health centres, tennis clubs, running clubs, cycling clubs, golf courses, shooting ranges and bowling clubs in the major metropolitan areas. Clubs are advertised in the local knock-and-drop newspapers and the *Yellow Pages* telephone directory for each city.

Facilities for the Disabled

Overall, facilities for the disabled are not up to the standard one tends to find in the developed world, but they are being improved, upgraded and/or built into restaurants, hotels, shopping malls, government buildings and on the streets. But standards vary widely from place to place. Anyone with a disability should call in advance to check the accessibility of the hotel or restaurant.

HOME & FAMILY
Estate Agents

Those listed below operate in all the major cities, but also look out for local operations that are town and city specific.

- **Estate Agency Affairs Board**
  They can help you with any matters regarding estate agents and home renting or buying.
  Tel: (011) 731-5600
  Website: http://www.eaab.org.za

- **Acutts**
  Tel: (031) 209-8111 (Durban)
  Website: http://www.acutts.co.za
- **Pam Golding**
  Tel: (021) 851-2633 (Cape Town), (031) 312-8300 (Durban),
  (011) 380-0000 (Johannesburg)
  Website: http://www.pamgolding.co.za
- **Realty 1**
  Tel: (012) 682-9599 (head office Pretoria), (021) 465-8736
  (Cape Town), (031) 561-1391 (Durban), (011) 882-2800
  (Johannesburg)
  Website: http://www.realty1.co.za
- **Seeff**
  Tel: (021) 557-1115 (Cape Town), (011) 784-222
  (Johannesburg). Website: http://www.seeff.com
- **Remax**
  Tel: (021) 761-1110 (Cape Town head office)
  Website: http://www.remax.co.za

Childcare and Education

For a list of state schools in your area, contact the provincial department of education (tel: (012) 357-3000; website: http://www.education.gov.za). Most private school details can be found at http://www.isasa.org. Estate agents in the areas in which you are considering living can tell you about the local schools and facilities.

Housekeeping Services

Organised maid services are limited and not highly competent. Domestic workers and full- or part-time gardeners are usually employed through word-of-mouth. It is not wise to employ someone who just turns up on your doorstep, unless they have good references which you check out first.

MANAGING YOUR MONEY
Tax and Legal Advice

Listed below are the major organisations which have offices in all major centres. You will of course also find independent companies in each city and town.

- **Deloitte & Touche**
  20 Woodlands Drive, Woodmead, Johannesburg
  Tel: (011) 806-5000. Website: http://www.deloitte.com
- **Ernst & Young**
  4 Pritchard Street, Johannesburg
  Tel: (011) 498-1000. Website: http://www.ey.com
- **Grant Thornton Kessel Feinstein**
  137 Daisy Street corner, Grayston Drive, Sandton
  Tel: (011) 322-4500. Website: http://www.gt.co.za
- **KPMG**
  85 Empire Road, Parktown, Johannesburg
  Tel: (011) 647-7111. Website: http://www. kpmg.co/ZA
- **PriceWaterhouseCoopers**
  2 Eglin Road Sunninghill, Johannesburg
  Tel: (011) 498-4000. Website: http://www.pwc.com/za/

Banks

- **Standard Bank**
  Website: http://www.standard.co.za
- **First National Bank (FNB)**
  Website: http://www.fnb.co.za
- **Nedbank**
  Website: http://www.nedbank.co.za
- **Absa**
  Website: http://www.absa.co.za

Insurance Companies

- **Old Mutual**
  Tel: (0860) 50-6070. Website: http://www.oldmutual.co.za
- **Auto & General**
  Tel: (0860) 25-2571
  Website: http://www.autoandgeneral.co.za
- **Fedsure Life Assurance**
  Tel: (0860) 086-0086. Website: http://www.fedsurelife.co.za
- **Sanlam**
  Tel: (021) 916 5000. Website: http://www.sanlam.co.za
- **Liberty Life**
  Tel: (0860) 45-6789. Website: http://www.libertylife.co.za

ENTERTAINMENT AND LEISURE
Restaurants and Cafés

Look for the *Top 100 Restaurants in South Africa* in bookstores across the country, as well as the *Wine* magazine. John Platter's *South African Wine Guide,* also found in bookstores and updated annually, walks you through the many, often very good, South African wines. In South Africa's bigger cities the bistros and pavement cafés line favoured streets, particularly in mixed-zone business/residential areas, while the more formal restaurants tend to be ensconced in shopping malls with secure parking. A useful online restaurant guide is found at http://www.eatout.co.za.

Some Restaurants in Johannesburg

- **Osteria Tre Nonni.** 9 Grafton Avenue, Craighall Park. Tel: (011) 327-0095. Website: http://www.osteriatrenonni.co.za/
- **La Cucina di Ciro**, 43, 7th Avenue, Parktown North Tel: (011) 442-5187. Website: http://www.lacucinadiciro.co.za/
- **Lucky Bean**, 16, 7th Street, Melville Tel: (011) 482-5572. Website: http://www.luckybeantree.co.za

Restaurants in Cape Town

- **Aubergine.** 39 Barnet Street Gardens. Tel: (021) 465-4909. Website: http://www.aubergine.co.za
- **Savoy Cabbage**. 101 Hout Street. Tel: (021) 424-2626 Website: http://www.savoycabbage.co.za
- **Caveau Wine Bar and Deli.** Heritage Square, 92 Bree Street, City Bowl. Tel: (021) 422 1367
- **Olympia Café and Deli**. 134 Main Road, Kalk Bay Tel: (021) 788-6396

Restaurants in Durban

- **Jaipur Palace.** Riverside Hotel, 10 Northway, Durban North. Tel: (031) 563-0287
- **Le Troquet.** The Village Market Centre, Jan Hofmeyer Road, Westville. Tel: (031) 266-5388
- **Wodka**. 40 Mahatma Gandhi Drive, Beachfront Tel: (031)332-8190.
- **Nourish.** 191 Musgrave Road, Berea, Durban Tel: (031) 202-2511

- **JAM Restaurant at Quarters**, c/r Sindile Thusi and Avondale, Morningside. Tel:(031) 303-8200. Website: http://www. quarters.co.za/quarters-on-avondale/dining.html

Major shopping areas:
Cape Town
Victoria & Alfred Waterfront; Century City shopping centre; Green Market Square (open-air market)
Durban
Pavilion shopping centre; Musgrave shopping centre; the Mall La Lucia shopping centre; the Stables craft market and the beach front craft; artefact and hawker stalls
Johannesburg
Sandton City shopping centre; Rosebank Mall shopping centre and its rooftop flea market open every Sunday; the African Craft Market is adjacent to the Rosebank Mall; Eastgate shopping centre

Nightspots
In Johannesburg, nightlife is spread across this large city, but there is always a buzz in Melville which has a plethora of restaurants, bars and clubs. The Newtown Precinct, around the Market Theatre and west of it too, is the new hip place with many great music venues, bars and clubs as well as theatres and galleries. This area is my top choice for the best multicultural vibe in town. If you really need to be where the highest rollers are, try Melrose Arch in Illovo, but be prepared to pay for the pleasure.

Aside from the Waterfront in Cape Town, the area around the streets Loop and Long, between Strand and Riebeeck in the city centre, is the best place to get a feel for what is happening on the dance scene. Greenpoint and Camps Bay, both overlooking the sea, are great for a sundowner too. Many of the mainstream jazz clubs double as restaurants, and the Captour *Jazz in the Cape* brochure highlights current venues.

The Durban beachfront is a favourite place for a lot of nightlife as the ambient climate and the ocean make open air nightlife a delight. The new Point Road development is fast becoming a cool area to take in, as is the nearby

Embankment which has a variety of nightspots. And if you want to head out to Pinetown, don't miss the Rainbow Restaurant and Jazz Club—an institution of note.

Cinemas and Theatres

The dominant film distributors, and hence owners of the movie theatres, are Ster-Kinekor and Nu Metro, which show most of the global mainstream films, but they also have specific venues devoted to arthouse and alternative films that show a good selection. Tourist information bureaus for each city publish guides on what is happening every month. Tickets for shows, movies, concerts and other events can be purchased at the door or booked through Computicket outlets across the country, on their Internet site (http://www.computicket.com), or call 083-909-0909/083-915-8000. Movies can also be booked directly online at http://www.sterkinekor.com or http://www.numetro.co.za

Bookstores and Libraries

There are public libraries in most municipalities, and membership is free to people living or working in the neighbourhood. Many libraries have interconnected computer systems allowing borrowers to utilise the facilities across a broad spectrum of libraries. Not all areas are equally well-served by our public libraries, but generally the service is fair. National bookstore chains include Exclusive Books, CNA and Adams. They have outlets in shopping centres and central business districts across the country. They carry a good selection of local books and a fair array of international books too and you can always order books not immediately available. There are a few independent and/or used bookstores around where frequently you will find gems.

Books On-line

Exclusive Books has an excellent website that is also good for locating old editions or hard-to-find books on South Africa, which cannot be found on international websites like Amazon.com.
http://www.exclusivebooks.com Also try: http://www.kalahari.net

Museums and Art Galleries
Johannesburg
A quick guide to the museums in Johannesburg is through the website: http://www.joburg.org.za/whatson/museums. stm. The list below is a brief selection of the wide variety of museums found in the city.

- The Apartheid Museum.
  Northern Parkway and Gold Reef Road
  Tel: (011) 309-4700
  Website: http://www.apartheidmuseum.org
- Hector Pieterson Museum
  8288 Khumalo Street, Orlando West, Soweto
  Tel: (011) 536-0611
- The Origins Centre
  The Wedge Complex, University of Witwatersrand,
  Corner Yale Road and Jorissen Street, Braamfontein
  Tel: (011) 717-4700/4703
  Website: http://www.origins.org.za
- Mandela Family Museum
  8115 Ngakane Str, Orlando West, Soweto
  Tel: (011) 936-7754
- Constitution Hill Museum
  Corner Kotze and Hospital Streets, Braamfontein
  Tel: (011) 381-3100
  Website: http://www.constitutionhill.org.za
- South African Museum of Military History
  22 Erlswold Way, Saxonwold
  Tel: (011) 646-5513
  Website: http://www.militarymuseum.co.za
- Bensusan Museum of Photography and Library
  (In MuseuMAfricA)
  121 Bree Street, Newtown.
  Tel: (011) 833-5624
- Gold Reef City
  Northern Parkway off N1 Ormonde.
  Tel: (011) 496-1600
  Website: http//www.goldreefcity.co.za/home/index.asp

Cape Town

A good place to find museums in Cape Town is through the Iziko Museums of Cape Town website at http://www.iziko. org.za, some of which are listed below:

- South African National Gallery
  Government Avenue, Companies Garden
  Tel: (021) 467-4660
- Rust en Vreugd (art museum)
  78 Buitenkant Street. Tel: (021) 464-3280
- Castle of Good Hope
  Buitenkant Street, opposite the Grand Parade
  Tel: (021) 464-1260/1264
- South African Museum
  25 Queen Victoria Street, Gardens.
  Tel: (021) 481-3800
- Groot Constantia
  Groot Constantia Estate, Constantia.
  Tel: (021) 795-5140

The following museums are not part of the Iziko group, but are just as interesting to explore:

- District Six Museum
  25a Buitenkant Street. Tel: (021) 466-7200
  Website: http://www.districtsix.co.za
- South African Cultural Museum
  Corner of Adderley and Wale streets. Tel: (021) 461-8280
- Rhodes Memorial
  Off Rhodes Drive, Rondebosch. Tel: (021) 689-9151

Durban

Durban has several exciting art and cultural museums, as well as marine and animal parks that will engage both children and adults. A good online site for more information is at http://www.warthog.co.za/dedt/tourism/durban/culture/museums.htm. Below is just a small selection of what's available:

- Durban Art Gallery
  Second Floor, City Hall, Smith Street.
  Tel: (031) 300-6238
  Website: http://www.durbanet.co.za/exhib/dag/dagmain.htm

- African Art Centre
  94 Florida. Tel: (031) 312-3804/3805
  Website: http://www.afriart.org.za
- Local History Museum
  Old Court House, Aliwal Street. Tel: (031) 300-6241
- uShaka Marine World
  1 King Shaka Avenue, South Beach. Tel: (031) 328-8000
  Website: http://ushakamarineworld.co.za/home.htm/
- Natal Museum of Military History
  Corner of Snell Parade and Old Fort Road
  Tel: (031) 332-6302
- Natal Sharks Board
  1a Herrwood Drive, Umhlanga.
  Tel: (031) 566-0400
  Website: http://www.shark.co.za
- Fitz Simons Snake Park
  240 Lower Marine Parade. Tel: (031) 337-6456

Please see also each city's *What's On* guide, books like the *Readers' Digest Illustrated Guide to Southern Africa*, or visit the local tourist offices.

Gay Life

The South African constitution specifically includes a sexual orientation clause that guarantees full and equal rights for gays, lesbians, bisexuals and transgender people. The website: http://www.q.co.za is a comprehensive introduction to gay and lesbian activities and lifestyles in this country, offering information on news, entertainment, equality and travel.

TRANSPORT & COMMUNICATIONS
Telephone Codes

The international dialling code for South Africa is **27**, followed by the area code (minus the zero) and the subscriber's number. Area dialling codes are: Cape Town **021**; Durban **031**; Johannesburg **011**. Area codes for the rest of the country can be found in the introductory pages of the telephone directories. It is now essential to use the local area code even to dial numbers within that area. To dial an international call use 00 before your full number.

Telephone Service Numbers

- Local enquiries 1023
- International enquiries, including collect calls dial 10903
- National collect calls 1025

The dial tone here is a constant purr, the engaged signal is repeated beep tone, and a long repeated beep tone means the number is no longer in operation. Mobile phones work in all built-up areas and in most other parts of the country. Deep in the rural areas you may find fairly large 'dead patches' where there is no coverage.

Post Offices

The Post Office operates in most suburbs and central business districts across the country. There is also a private postal agency, Postnet, which is usually very efficient. In the urban areas, South Africans can choose street deliveries for their mail or post box numbers at the local post office. Street deliveries are free-of-charge. Post boxes carry an annual rental charge, when there is a street delivery option. Otherwise the post box address is free. Postage stamps are bought at the post offices.

Buses, Taxis and Trains

The public transport system in South Africa is not as developed as in other parts of the world. Besides the ubiquitous mini-bus taxis, each city has more subdued, Western-style taxis. But these do not always cater sufficiently to individual needs, and most business people and visitors prefer to hire cars or purchase their own vehicle. Bus and train routes and schedules can be obtained from tourist information outlets.

South Africans drive on the left side of the road. The country has a superb network of multi-lane roads and highways, some of which charge a toll. The speed limit is 120 kmph (75mph) on major highways and 60kmph (37mph) on city streets, but drivers are notorious for breaking these. Seat belts are compulsory.

MEDIA
Newspapers and Magazines

There are about 30 major publications, the best know of which are owned by a handful of commercial groups, namely Independent Group, Times Media Newspapers and Caxton Group. The *Mail & Guardian* is one of very few fully independent newspapers in the country.

A wide selection of local magazines covers interests from health, sport and cooking to cars and travel. The satirical *Noseweek*, one of few investigative magazines, has developed a reputation for uncovering corruption in high places.

Television and Radio Channels

The state-owned South African Broadcasting Corporation currently runs three channels broadcasting news, entertainment and sport in all major languages, but with a fairly large amount of English language programming. SABC competes directly with the powerful and lucrative pay-TV, Multichoice, and the private free-to-air e-TV station.

Once a state monopoly, South African airwaves have been opened up to hundreds of radio stations licensed by the **Independent Communications Authority of South Africa** (Tel: (011) 321-8200). Most are local community radio stations, but there are commercial stations broadcasting talk shows, sports programmes and music on both AM and FM channels.

LANGUAGE

Although English is widely spoken, South Africa actually has 11 official languages: Afrikaans, English, isiNdebele, isiXhosa, isiZulu, Sepedi, Sesotho, Setswana, siSwati, Tshivenda and Xitsonga. Language classes for a range of our national languages as well as some foreign languages are listed in the *Yellow Pages* telephone directory of services for each city under 'language tuition', on the Internet or in the local newspapers.

RELIGION AND SOCIAL WORK
Religious and Volunteer Organisations
Based on the 2001 census, religious South Africans are made up of the following: Protestants (25.5 per cent); Pentecostals (7.6 per cent); Roman Catholics (7.1 per cent); the Christian-based African Independent Churches (31.8 per cent); and a small percentage each of Hindus, Muslims and Jews. At least 15 per cent of the population have no religious affiliations. Each religion has a presence and meeting groups and times and places of worship are advertised in local newspapers. The Constitution guarantees total freedom of religion.

Contact Information for NGOs
- **SANGONeT**
  Equally useful if you are interested in getting involved with an NGO is the web portal for development information in South Africa:
  Website: http://www.sangonet.org.za/portal/

GENERAL COUNTRY INFORMATION
Weights and Measures
South Africa uses the metric system.

Appliances and Utilities
Appliances must be 220V or adaptable to this voltage. Water and electricity supply come under one account, opened through the local municipality. Take identification documents, a copy of your property lease or purchase agreement and a cash deposit to the municipality's customer centre to open the account. The connection can be made in 24 hours, but you could have to wait a little longer. For information and help, try the city website as phone numbers differ depending on the area you live in. Of course local phone directories will also list the relevant numbers. City websites: http://www.joburg.org.za/ (Johannesburg); http://www.capetown.gov.za (Cape Town); http://www.durban.gov.za (Durban)

Telkom landline applications can be made by phone at **10219** (the same number anywhere in the country) or in person at branches in the city of residence. Applications should not take longer 10 to 14 working days to process. Mobile telephones, contracts and prepaid user packages can be acquired through a host of service providers.

Necessities and Documents to Bring

South Africa has a sound infrastructure, and almost all goods and medications can be acquired in the country. Bring your birth and marriage certificates (including birth certificates for accompanying children), qualifications, medical certificates, police clearance certificate, passport and identity documents. Full details on what is required to apply for a work permit should be acquired from South African embassies and consulates. The requirements differ according to the terms under which you will be staying in the country. Also bring your driver's licence.

Pre-Entry Vaccinations

Pre-entry vaccinations are not required, except for people travelling from areas affected by yellow fever. Although some travel clinics recommend people be vaccinated against Hepatitis A and B, typhoid, tetanus, polio and rabies, I would consider asking a South African doctor for advice on this too. Certain parts of South Africa are malaria high-risk areas, and travellers should seek medical advice on which anti-malaria prophylactic to use from a local doctor or pharmacy before visiting these areas.

Government Internet Sites

Most South African government websites are fairly good and usually end in org.za or gov.za.

- http://www.gov.za
  The official website for the government where you can find your way to almost any other government ministry of department.
- http://www.gcis.org.za
  The government's communication and information services website.
- http://www.sars.gov.za
  For information on the South African Revenue Services.

- http://www.dfa.gov.za
  The Department of Foreign Affairs website, which is a good
  place to find the nearest embassy or consulate to you.

There are local search engines like Ananzi, but the calibre
and scale of the international giants like Google tend to get
my vote for quick and easy information gathering.

General and Tourist Advice Bureaus and Websites

- http://www.southafrica.net
  The South African government tourism website.

Gauteng/Johannesburg

- Gauteng Tourism Authority (head office)
  1 Central Place, c/r Jeppe and Henry Nxumalo street,
  Newton, Johannesburg. Tel: (011) 639-1600
  Website: http://www.visitgauteng.net or
  http://www.gauteng.net
  There are regional offices in Rosebank, Sandton and at
  OR Thambo International Airport.

Cape Town

- Cape Town and Western Cape (Official tourism website)
  Tel: (021) 487-6800 (Head Office); (021) 405-4500
  (Waterfront office)
  Website: http://www.tourismcapetown.co.za
  The Waterfront office is opened on weekends too.

Durban

- KZN Tourism Authority/Tourism KwaZulu-Natal
  Tel: (031) 366-7500 (Head Office, working hours only)
  Website: http://www.kzn.org.za
- Durban
  Tel: (031) 304-4934
  Website: http://www.durban.kzn.org.za

Immigration, Residency and Nationality Issues

Contact the nearest South African embassy or consulate in
your country before leaving. They will be able to give you
full information on matters such as documentation, permits
and visas you will need (embassy and consulate details can
be found at http://www.dfa.gov.za).

Business Organisations (listed alphabetically)

- **Afrikaanse Handelsinstituut (AHI).** Tel: (012) 348-5440.
  Website: http://www.ahi.co.za
- **Business Unity South Africa.** Tel: (011) 784-8000.
  Website: http://www.busa.org.za
- **Chamber of Mines of South Africa.** Tel: (011) 498-7100.
  Website: http://www.bullion.org.za
- **Johannesburg Chamber of Commerce and Industry
  (JCCI).** Tel: (011) 726-5300. Website: http://www.jcci.co.za
- **National Economic Development and Labour Council
  (Nedlac).** Tel: (011) 328-4200.
  Website: http://www.nedlac.org.za
- **South Afrian Chamber of Commerce & Industry (SACCI).**
  (formerly South Afrian Chamber of Business (SACOB).
  Tel: (011) 446-3800. Website: http://www.sacci.org.za

Legal Aid Agencies

- **The Legal Aid Board**
  Tel: (011) 877-2000 (Head Office)
  Website: http://www.legal-aid.co.za

FURTHER READING

HISTORY, CULTURAL HISTORY AND CURRENT AFFAIRS

- *A Prisoner in the Garden: Photos, Notes and Letters From Nelson Mandela's 27 Years in Prison.* Nelson Mandela Foundation. New York, NY: Studio, 2006.
- *NUMBER 4: The Making of Constitution Hill.* Constitution Hill Foundation. Johannesburg, South Africa: Penguin, 2006.
- *10 Years 100 Artists: Art in a Democratic South Africa.* Ed. Sophie Perryer. Cape Town, South Africa: Struik Publishers, 2005.
- *Long Walk to Freedom: The Autobiography of Nelson Mandela.* Nelson Mandela. London, UK: Little, Brown and Company, 2000.
- *Mandela: The Authorised Biography.* Anthony Sampson. London, UK: Harper Collins, 2005.
- *Country of My Skull: Guilt, Sorrow, and the Limits of Forgiveness in the New South Africa.* Antjie Krog. Johannesburg, South Africa: Random House, 2002.
- *Into Africa: A Journey through the Ancient Empires.* Marq De Villiers and Sheila Hirtle. Toronto, Canada: Key Porter Books, 1999.
- *White Tribe Dreaming: Apartheid's Bitter Roots as Witnessed by 8 Generations of Afrikaner Family.* Marq de Villiers. London, UK: Penguin, 1990.
- *Hot Type: Icons, Artists and God Figurines.* Bongani Madondo. Johannesburg, South Africa: Picador Africa, 2007.
- *The Scramble for Africa.* Thomas Pakenham. Johannesburg, South Africa: Jonathan Ball Publishers, 2004.
- *Beyond the Miracle: Inside the New South Africa.* Allister Sparks. Chicago, IL: University of Chicago Press, 2007.
- *The Mind of South Africa: The Story of the Rise and Fall of Apartheid.* Allister Sparks. Johannesburg, South Africa: Jonathan Ball Publishers, 2003.
- *Uprooting Poverty: The South African Challenge: Report for the Second Carnegie Inquiry into Povery and Development in South Africa.* Francis Wilson and Mamphela Ramphele.

New York, NY: W W Norton & Company, 1989; Cape Town, South Africa: David Phillips Publishers, 1989.

- *Washing of the Spears.* Donald R Morris. Cambridge, MA: Da Capo Press, 1998.
- *Indaba My Children.* Vusamazulu Credo Mutwa. Emeryville, CA: Avalon Travel Publishing, 2000.
- *Memory is the Weapon.* Don Mattera. Johannesburg, South Africa: Ravan Press, 1987.
- *Culture in Another South Africa.* Ed. W Campschreur and J Divendal. London, UK: Zed Books Ltd, 2002.
- *The Story of Earth & Life: A Southern African Perspective on a 4.6 billion-year Journey.* Terence McCarthy and Bruce Rubidge. Cape Town, South Africa: Struik Publishers, 2006.
- *2010 When the World Cup Came to South Africa.* Produced and published by the 2010 FIFA World Cup Organising Committee South Africa. Johannesburg, South Africa. 2010.

WOMEN IN SOUTH AFRICA

- *Unconfessed: A Novel.* Yvette Christianse. Capetown, South Africa: Kwela Books, 2007.
- *The Story of An African Farm: A Novel.* Olive Schreiner. London, UK: Penguin Classics, 2006.
  First published in 1883 under a male pseudonym, this is a South African classic by a dedicated feminist who was many decades ahead of her time.
- *Call Me Woman.* Ellen Kuzway. San Francisco, CA: Aunt Lute Books, 1992.
- *Women and Resistance in South Africa.* Cherryl Walker and Jane Alan Walker. New York, NY: Monthly Review Press, 2001.
- *Putting Women on the Agenda.* Ed. Susan Bazilli. Johannesburg, South Africa: Ravan Press, 1992.

DICTIONARIES AND THE LIKES

- *South African Concise Oxford Dictionary.* Cape Town, South Africa: Oxford University Press, 2002.
- *Township Talk: The Language, the Culture, the People.* Lebo Motshegoa. Cape Town, South Africa: Double Storey Books (Juta), 2005.

NOVELS BY SOUTH AFRICANS ABOUT SOUTH AFRICA

Do read any works, especially the early ones, by **J M Coetzee**, who won the Nobel Prize in Literature and also the Booker/ Mann Booker prize twice. (He now lives in Australia and recent works tend to be about that country.) Here is a short list of his books set in South Africa:

- *Dusklands.* Chicago, IL: Vintage (Rand), 1998.
- *In The Heart of the Country.* London, UK: Vintage, 2004.
- *Waiting for the Barbarians.* Chicago, IL: Vintage (Rand), 2004.
- *Life and Times of Michael K.* London, UK: Vintage, 2005.
- *Boyhood: Scenes From a Provincial Life.* Chicago, IL: Vintage (Rand), 1998.
- *Disgrace.* New York, NY: Penguin, 2005.

At the same time, do check out the many novels and collections of short stories written by **Nadine Gordimer**, also a Nobel Prize Winner in Literature.

Novels:

- *Burger's Daughter.* London, UK: Bloomsbury Publishing, 2000.
- *July's People.* London, UK: Bloomsbury Publishing, 2005.
- *The Conservationist.* London, UK: Bloomsbury Publishing, 2005.
- *The House Gun.* London, UK: Bloomsbury Publishing, 1999; New York, NY: Penguin, 1999; London, UK: Trafalgar Square, 1999.
- *My Son's Story.* London, UK: Bloomsbury Publishing, 2003.

Collections of short stories :

- *Jump and Other Stories.* London, UK: Bloomsbury Publishing, 2003.
- *Loot and Other Stories.* London, UK: Penguin, 2004.
- *Beethoven Was One Sixteenth Black.* London, UK: Bloomsbury Publishing, 2007 (September).

Other South African Authors

- *Bitches Brew.* Fred Khumalo. Johannesburg, South Africa: Jacana Media, 2006.
- *Mandela's Ego.* Lewis Nkosi. Johannesburg, South Africa: Umuzi, 2006.

- *The Whale Caller.* Zakes Mda. London, UK: Penguin, 2006.
- *The Heart of Redness.* Zakes Mda. New York, NY: Picador, 2003.
- *Frankie and Stankie.* Barbara Trapido. London, UK: 2007.
- *Gem Squash Tokoloshe.* Rachel Zadok. London, UK: Pan Books, 2005; Johannesburg, South Africa: Pan Macmillan, 2005.
- *Jock of the Bushveld.* Sir Percy Fitzpatrick. Johannesburg, South Africa: Donker, 2002. This classic was first published in 1907.
- *Confession of an Albino Terrorist.* Breyten Breytenbach. London, UK: Thomson Learning, 1994.
- *A Good Looking Corpse: World of Drum: Jazz and Gangsters, Hope and Defiance in the Townships of South Africa.* Mike Nicol. London, UK: Minerva, 1995.
- *Circles in the Forest.* Dalene Matthee. Johannesburg, South Africa: Penguin, 2005.
- *Cry the Beloved Country: A Story of Comfort in Desolation.* Alan Paton. London, UK: Vintage, 2002.

Anything by Alan Paton is good, including his excellent nonfiction titles.

Anything written by Herman Charles Bosman, such as:
- *Jurie Steyn's Post Office.* Cape Town, South Africa: Human & Rousseau, 1991.
- *A Bekkersdal Marathon.* Cape Town, South Africa: Human & Rousseau, 1995.
- *Bosman at His Best.* Cape Town, South Africa: Human & Rousseau, 2004.

Anything by Andre Brink, including:
- *A Dry White Season.* New York, NY: Harper Perennial, 2006.
- *Looking on Darkness.* London, UK: Vintage, 1993.

POETRY

- *Azanian Love Song.* Don Mattera. Johannesburg, South Africa: Justified Press, 1994.
- *Halala Madiba: Nelson Mandela in Poetry.* Ed. Richard Bartlett and Morakabe Raks Seakhoa. Wiltshire, UK: Aflame Books, 2006.

- *Night Rider: Selected Poems*. Tatamkhulu Afrika. Roggebaai, South Africa: Kwela Books, 2003.
- *History is the Home Address*. Mongane Wally Serote. Roggebaai, South Africa: Kwela Books, 2004.

THE GREAT OUTDOORS AND CONSERVATION ISSUES

- *The Wildlife of Southern Africa: A Field Guide to the Animals and Plants of the Region*. Ed. Vincent Carruthers. Cape Town, South Africa: Struik Publishers, 2000.
- *Guide to South African Game and Nature Reserves*. Chris and Tilde Stuart. Cape Town, South Africa: Struik Publishers, 1997.
- *Sasol Birds of Southern Africa*. Ian R. Sinclair, Phil Hockey and WR Tarboton. Cape Town, South Africa: Struik Publishers, 2006.
- *Hiking Trails of South Africa*. Willie and Sandra Olivier. Cape Town, South Africa: Struik Publishers, 2007.

ON THE HUMOROUS FRONT

Two series of cartoon books (they both also run cartoons in a variety of local newspapers) that are really very funny and worthwhile reading, but only once you are here as, like all good cartoonists, they make huge fun of very local and often very poignant matters: The *Madam & Eve* series such as *Madams of the Caribbean*, *All Aboard the Gravy Train* or *Madams are from Mars, Maids are from Venus*, and the Zapiro series like *Zapiro Da Zuma Code, Zapiro: The Long Walk to Free Time, Zapiro: Bushwacked* and *Zapiro—the Devil Made Me Do It!*. Both series put out an annual bumper book for the year-end holiday.

ABOUT THE AUTHOR

Dee Rissik is of a typically mixed background common to many in South Africa. Her father's family is from generations-old Cape Dutch origins, while her mother's side is of British ancestry. A journalist by profession, she finds it an ideal career as it coexists with her penchant for travelling. Her home base is Johannesburg, with a bit of London thrown in too, but she believes she can live anywhere in the world for a period of time to gain cultural experience on a multi-dimensional level. Having lived and/or worked in many parts of Africa, South-east Asia, Europe including London, as well as Canada and New York, she has first-hand experiences of being a newcomer to a number of countries and cities.

A published writer many times over, she has written for a wide range of newspapers and magazines on topics ranging from business and socio-economic issues to travel, well-being and fitness. Dee is also the author of the book, *Women In Society, South Africa* published by Times Books International (now Marshall Cavendish International) and is currently working on a biography of a controversial African leader.

INDEX

Titles in the CultureShock! series:

Argentina	France	Portugal
Australia	Germany	Russia
Austria	Great Britain	San Francisco
Bahrain	Hawaii	Saudi Arabia
Beijing	Hong Kong	Scotland
Belgium	India	Shanghai
Berlin	Ireland	Singapore
Bolivia	Italy	South Africa
Borneo	Jakarta	Spain
Brazil	Japan	Sri Lanka
Bulgaria	Korea	Sweden
Cambodia	Laos	Switzerland
Canada	London	Syria
Chicago	Malaysia	Taiwan
Chile	Mauritius	Thailand
China	Morocco	Tokyo
Costa Rica	Munich	Travel Safe
Cuba	Myanmar	Turkey
Czech Republic	Netherlands	United Arab
Denmark	New Zealand	Emirates
Ecuador	Pakistan	USA
Egypt	Paris	Vancouver
Finland	Philippines	Venezuela

For more information about any of these titles, please contact any of our Marshall Cavendish offices around the world (listed on page ii) or visit our website at:

www.marshallcavendish.com/genref